THIRD EDITION

*the
designer's
guide to
professional
typography*

W9-BUC-201

type rules

*Ilene
Strizver*

WILEY

John Wiley & Sons, Inc.

Published by John Wiley & Sons, Inc., Hoboken, New Jersey
Published simultaneously in Canada
No part of this publication may be reproduced, stored in a retrieval system, or transmitted in any form or by
any means, electronic, mechanical, photocopying, recording, scanning, or otherwise, except as permitted under
Section 107 or 108 of the 1976 United States Copyright Act, without either the prior written permission of
the Publisher, or authorization through payment of the appropriate per-copy fee to the Copyright Clearance
Center, 222 Rosewood Drive, Danvers, MA 01923, (978) 750-8400, fax (978) 646-8600, or on the web at
www.copyright.com. Requests to the Publisher for permission should be addressed to the Permissions
Department, John Wiley & Sons, Inc., 111 River Street, Hoboken, NJ 07030, (201) 748-6011, fax (201) 748-6008,
or online at www.wiley.com/go/permissions.

Limit of Liability/Disclaimer of Warranty: While the publisher and the author have used their best efforts in
preparing this book, they make no representations or warranties with respect to the accuracy or completeness
of the contents of this book and specifically disclaim any implied warranties of merchantability or fitness for a
particular purpose. No warranty may be created or extended by sales representatives or written sales materials.
The advice and strategies contained herein may not be suitable for your situation. You should consult with a
professional where appropriate. Neither the publisher nor the author shall be liable for any loss of profit or any
other commercial damages, including but not limited to special, incidental, consequential, or other damages.

For general information about our other products and services, please contact our Customer Care Department
within the United States at (800) 762-2974, outside the United States at (317) 572-3993 or fax (317) 572-4002.

Wiley also publishes its books in a variety of electronic formats. Some content that appears in print may not be
available in electronic books. For more information about Wiley products, visit our web site at www.wiley.com.

Library of Congress Cataloging-in-Publication Data:
Strizver, Ilene, 1953-
    Type rules : the designer's guide to professional typography /
    by Ilene Strizver. – 3rd ed.
    p. cm.
  ISBN 978-0-470-54251-4 (pbk.)
  1. Type and type-founding. 2. Graphic design (Typography) I. Title.
  Z250.S92 2010
  686.2'21--dc22
                    2010004725

Printed in the United States of America

10 9 8 7 6 5 4 3 2 1

TABLE OF CONTENTS

DEDICATION

This book is dedicated to my father, Leonard Strizver, who taught me to believe in myself and that the sky was the limit to what I could accomplish. Unfortunately he did not live long enough to see his words take shape in my life.

I hope I have made you proud, Dad.

This third edition of *Type Rules!* has been revised and expanded in a number of ways. The content has not only been updated to reflect current standards and practices in typography, design, and technology, but also significantly expanded to include a chapter on nonprint typography, which covers type on the Web as well as type in motion. All chapters have updated TECHTIPS and TYPETIPS, as well as several new exercises with examples of some very exciting student work.

■ TECHTIPS are instructional sidebars on how to achieve some of the typographic principles and techniques mentioned within, using the two most popular and widely used design applications: Adobe InDesign CS4 and QuarkXPress 8.0.

■ TYPETIPS are sidebars containing helpful hints and tasty tidbits explaining some of the information in more detail.

■ And last, but definitely not least, the Exercises are tasks and assignments intended to assist in learning and understanding the typographic principles contained within, as well as applying them in actual design projects. These supplements, which follow each chapter, are intended for educators and students, but they can be used by anyone who wants to reinforce and apply the material within (and possibly wind up with some great portfolio pieces as well!).

* * * * *

This edition of *Type Rules!* has been written from the perspective of a Mac user using OS 10. Why? Although the PC still holds the lion's share of the personal computer market, the majority of graphic designers (excluding Web designers) use Macs. In addition, I wanted to maintain the integrity of the information presented here, and since I use a Mac, I write from that point of view.

ACKNOWLEDGMENTS

As someone whose academic beginnings focused on music and fine art, I was extremely lucky to have crossed paths with some of the most open-hearted and talented individuals in the world of typography and graphic design, almost in spite of myself. Aaron Burns, Ed Benguiat, Herb Lubalin, Bob Farber, and Allan Haley permanently altered my life's path, and I will be forever indebted to them. Their creative brilliance coupled with their incredible generosity of spirit ignited within me a passion for type that will never be satiated.

Through the years, there have been countless graphic designers, type designers, typographers, and other creative professionals who have unselfishly shared their knowledge and passion for type and design with me. To all of them I offer my deepest thanks, for without them, this book never would have come to be.

I want to extend a heartfelt thanks to my typographic "partners in crime," James Montalbano, Mark Jamra, Ken Barber, Otmar Hoefer, Thomas Phinney, and David Lemon, who have generously and willingly shared their expertise and resources.

A very warm thanks to my special friends Maxim Zhukov, Christopher Slye, Fred Brady, and Nat Brockman, who have so very graciously offered their time and professional assistance to help make this a better book.

In addition, a very special thanks goes out to Scott Fisk, Brian Lucid, Heather Shaw, and Jakob Trollbäck, whose knowledge and guidance helped make this edition a more useful, up-to-date tool for today's graphics designers and students of design. I would like to extend my deepest gratitude to all the instructors who willingly shared their teaching methods and assignments with me and, as well, to the students who allowed the use of their assignment solutions for publication.

I could never express enough appreciation to all my students and workshop attendees; they continue to keep me on my toes, push me to learn newer and better methods, technique, and software, challenge me to offer a better explanation, and their talent, enthusiasm, and passion for learning inspire me to be the best I can be.

And last but not least, a very special thanks to my editor, Margaret Cummins, whose belief in me and in this book, combined with her own vision of what it could be, inspired me to new heights.

INTRODUCTION

Type is all around us, in everything we read, from product packaging in the grocery store to television commercials, from greeting cards, books, and magazines to movie credits and storefront signs. Learning to read and write the alphabet is one of the first things we are taught in school, and that process often begins before nursery school with television shows and videos intended for the hungry and curious minds of two- and three-year-olds.

Type and printed matter communicate not only information to us but also influence decisions we make on a daily basis. Whether we realize it or not, type and the way it appears affects which CD or book cover catches our eye, which detergent might make the whites whiter, and which movie might be the scariest or most romantic. Much of this process goes on unconsciously, which is why the art and craft of typography is so invisible to the average person. But its unseen nature by no means diminishes the importance and influence type has on the quality and substance of our daily lives.

Type Rules! is intended for anyone interested in typography, be they a novice computer user or a professional graphic designer. There is something here for everyone, whether you know a little or a lot about type. This book does not have to be read front to back; you may thumb through the chapters and stop wherever something sparks your interest, or you may read it chapter to chapter, cover to cover. This book will stimulate and satisfy the neophyte's interest in type as well as offer advanced information and techniques to professional graphic designers who want to improve their work.

Typography is not taught (or taught effectively, in my experience) in every design school, as it should be. When it is, the focus is often on typographic design in its broadest sense, not the nuts and bolts of how to set type tastefully and effectively; addressing this void is my primary objective. This book is intended to help you learn how to communicate effectively and professionally with type, using features available in most page-layout programs.

* * * * *

I can trace my interest in type and letterforms back to the posters I drew for my junior high school elections. I remember spending hours on the lettering, measuring out the strokes of each character, the spaces between each letter, as well as the spaces between the lines. Those posters would appear extremely crude by professional standards, but my interest in the geometry of letters and the relationships between their positive and negative spaces was evident, even then.

After studying music and then fine art in college, I was lucky enough to have landed a seat in Ed Benguiat's lettering class at the School of Visual Arts in New York City; my life was never to be the same again. Ed instilled in me the passion for type that I have today and with which I will attempt to infect you. The bad news is if I succeed, there is really no cure for it; the good news is "catching it" will open your eyes to so many exciting things you have never seen before, and it allows you to enjoy and appreciate the world around you in a completely new way.

"The story of type doesn't begin with type per se, but with the beginning of mankind and civilisation. Type has only existed for about 55 years,

CHAPTER ONE

A BRIEF HISTORY OF TYPE

The story of type doesn't begin with type per se, rather it starts with the beginning of mankind and civilization. Type has only existed for about 560 years, but its beginnings are rooted in the life of the caveman himself, as it was his developing needs and habits that led civilization on a path toward the evolution of the alphabet and subsequently the invention of type and printing. It is certainly possible to learn to use type effectively and tastefully without knowing its roots, but to fully understand and appreciate type today, it is important to know something of the past.

Milestones in the history of type are highlighted throughout this chapter. Some of the dates, chronology, and details vary from source to source, but the spirit of the events remains the same. These events have taken mankind on a glorious ride from the crudest cave drawings to the bits and bytes of type in the digital age.

SOUNDS TO SYMBOLS

For many years, early humans communicated purely with sound. Verbal language–which is heard and not seen as opposed to visual language (or visible language, as it is often called)–has many limitations: it is gone the instant it is spoken and heard, and it is therefore temporary. Stories, history, and other information could not be passed on from generation to generation in a permanent way, only by direct word of mouth.

The earliest attempts to record stories and ideas were through cave drawings; the first known is dated around 25,000 BC. These drawings, or pictographs, were very simple representations of people, places, and things, and for this reason, they were relatively easy to learn and understand. Although this was a very simple form of written communication, it was certainly more permanent than sound, and much of it has survived the ravages of time and still exists today.

This aboriginal rock painting (c. 13,000 BC), located in a cave in Queensland, Australia, is a distinctive example of the earliest form of written communication. Photograph courtesy of Axel Poignant Archive.

Around 3000 BC the Sumerians developed cuneiforms, a writing system that consisted of wedge-shaped forms carved into clay tablets and other hard surfaces. Cuneiforms evolved from the pictographs that the Sumerians had adapted earlier and were one of the first writing systems to read left to right. Its wedge-shaped forms were the result of the increasing use of a stylus, a writing tool whose straight edges and triangular corners produced these geometric forms.

As time passed, there was a need for more symbols to represent ideas and other concepts in addition to just "things." This led to the development of ideograms, or symbols, to represent ideas and actions. This new, expanded system was more difficult for the masses to understand, as it was not purely representational but more symbolic in nature. This separated society into two groups: those who could understand this system and those who could not. The spoken and written language had become very different from each other, requiring the learning of two unrelated systems of communication.

As society became more complex, the existing writing system did not meet its increasing needs and was no longer satisfactory; something more was needed. This need subsequently led to the development of letter symbols that, when put together, represented words.

The Phoenicians, a society of traders and skilled craftsmen on the eastern coast of the Mediterranean Sea, took written language a giant step forward from the pictograms and ideograms of the Sumerians.

PHOENICIAN	NAME	PHONETIC NAME	EARLY GREEK	CLASSICAL GREEK	NAME	GREEK	ENGLISH
	aleph			A	alpha	A α	a
	beth	b		B	beta	B β	b
	gimel	g		Γ	gamma	Γ γ	g
	daleth	d		Δ	delta	Δ δ	d
	he	h		E	epsilon	E ε	e
	waw	w			digamma		
	zayin	z		Z	zeta	Z ζ	z
	heth	ḥ		H	eta	H η	ê
	teth	ṭ		θ	theta	Θ θ	th
	yod	y		I	iota	I ι	i
	kaph	k		K	kappa	K ϰ	k
	lamed	l		Λ	lambda	Λ λ	l
	mem	m		M	mu	M μ	m
	nun	n		N	nu	N ν	n
	samekh	s			xi	Ξ ξ	x
	ayin			O	omicron	O o	o
	pe	p		Π	pi	Π π	p
	sade	s			san		
	qoph	q			qoppa		
	reš	r		P	rho	P ρ	r
	šin	sh/s		Σ	sigma	Σ σς	s
	taw	t			tau	T τ	t
				Y	upsilon	Y υ	u, y
					phi	Φ φ	ph
				X	chi	X χ	kh
					psi	Ψ ψ	ps
				Ω	omega	Ω ω	ô

This chart shows the evolution of the Greek alphabet, which was originally adapted from the twenty-two-character, all-consonant Phoenician alphabet. The Greeks added several new characters as well as vowels.

Around 1000 BC the Phoenicians developed twenty-two symbols that corresponded to the twenty-two key sounds of their language. Their idea was to connect the twenty-two symbols (representing sounds) to imitate spoken words, eliminating the memorization of hundreds of unrelated symbols. This unique concept was the first attempt to connect the written language with the spoken word; we now call this phonetics.

Around 800 BC, the Greeks embraced the Phoenician invention and took it a step further by adding vowels and naming the symbols. They also employed boustrophedon (meaning "as the ox plows"), a system in which one reads from left to right on one line and right to left on the next.

Much later, the Romans, a highly developed society, made further changes by adding more letters, bringing this writing system even closer to our modern-day alphabet. They made other advances as well.

The Greek writing system employed boustrophedon ("as the ox plows"), a system in which one reads alternately from left to right on one line and right to left on the next. Notice how the letters are reversed from one line to another.

The Roman scribes, in their attempt to write more quickly and efficiently, began joining and slanting letters in harmony with the natural motion of the hand. In addition, they added ascenders and descenders, as well as condensed forms of the alphabet in order to conserve space.

One of the most important contributions to early writing by the Romans was Trajan's Column, dated 114 AD. It showcases one of the most beautiful and best-known examples of Roman letterforms. The lettering, which is incised at the base of the column, is a classical, elegant, and exquisitely balanced combination of form, proportion, and simplicity. It has been, and continues to be, a powerful inspiration to type designers throughout the world.

Upper: The lettering at the base of Trajan's Column, dated 114 AD. Lower: Close-up of the inscription on the base of Trajan's Column, considered to be one of the most beautiful and best-known examples of Roman letterforms. Photographs courtesy of Bill Thayer & Graphion.

Special mention should be made here of the tremendous contributions to the art of writing by the Chinese and by other Asian cultures. Although their writing systems are not alphabetic but rather consist of thousands of symbols, their extreme artistry, subtlety of form, and mastery of the art of calligraphy have been a continuous source of beauty, poetic elegance, and inspiration to all who come in contact with them.

Engraved portrait of Johannes Gutenberg from Andre Thevet's Les Vrais Portraits et Vie des Hommes, *Paris, 1584. Courtesy of Huntington Library.*

GUTENBERG AND MOVABLE TYPE

Until the fifteenth century, all books were hand copied by scribes, as exemplified by the many breathtakingly beautiful and exquisitely written and illustrated manuscripts created for religious purposes in monasteries.

In 1448 that all changed with the birth of printing, after which the world would never be quite the same. Johannes Gutenberg, a goldsmith from Mainz, Germany, is credited with the invention of movable type. (There is some controversy about that, as some credit Laurens Coster of Haarlem in the Netherlands with its invention; others credit Pi Sheng of China with inventing movable type in 1045, more than four-hundred years earlier.) Gutenberg accomplished his invention of movable type by carving the characters of the alphabet in relief onto metal punches, which were then driven into other pieces of metal called matrices.

Molten metal was then poured into these matrices, making the actual type, which was identical to the original relief punches. The type was then fit into printing presses that were capable of printing multiple images in a very short time. This was referred to as letterpress printing, and its distinct characteristic is that each character makes a slight impression on the paper, giving it a rich, tactile quality.

Early type design imitated the pen-drawn styles of the scribes. Gutenberg's first typeface was in the style of the heavy blackletter popular in Germany at that time. It contained over three hundred characters, including ligatures and abbreviations. As the popularity of printing became more widespread, a variety of typestyles emerged based on popular handwriting styles of that time, including those favored by Italian humanist scholars. Nicolas Jenson and Aldus Manutius were two printers of the time who designed typestyles that were influential and inspirational, even to this day.

Gutenberg went on to print the Bible, the first book printed from movable type. His invention truly changed the world, as it no longer was necessary for scribes to spend months and years (and lifetimes, actually) hand-copying books.

Close-up of the blackletter typeface used to set the Gutenberg Bible.

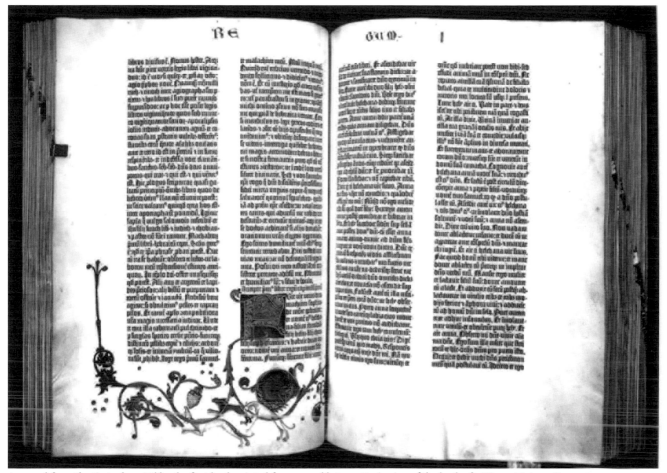

A spread from the Gutenberg Bible, the first book printed from movable type. Beginning of the book of 1 Kings, Mainz, Germany, 1450–5. Courtesy of Huntington Library.

This historical milestone–which enabled history, news, religious writings, and other kinds of information to be circulated more easily and freely– brought forth many other changes, such as improvements in printing presses, papers, and inks. It also inspired many others to design typefaces to make use of this transformational invention.

At this point in history, it is important to note the influence that the technology had on the look of type. The new printing technology with all its exciting advances, as well as the many beautiful and functional typefaces that were inspired by it, had its limitations, particularly when we look back from where we are now. Because each character was on a separate piece of metal, the space between the particular characters could not easily be adjusted to create a more even type color unless the letter combination was designed as a ligature and was combined on one piece of type. Additionally, line spacing could not be reduced beyond "setting solid," which allowed space for the ascenders and descenders. This meant that an all-cap setting had to have a lot of line spacing even if there were no ascenders and descenders. This created a very open, *letterspaced* look that was characteristic of that time and that is still desired by some for its historical accuracy and its readability.

DIT
ILES
GARES

Sample of Firmin Didot types cut around 1800.

De diſſectione partium corporis humani, Liber ſecundus.

Proœmium.

Væ partes in humano corpore ſolidiores & exteriores erant,quæ´q; ipſam machinam potiſſimum conſtituebant,ſatis iam explicatæ nobis videntur libro ſuperiore.Sequitur,vt internas percurramus quæ maximè pertinent ad vitam, & ad earum facultatum quibus incolumes viuimus conſeruatio-nem.In quo(quemadmodú inſtituimus) ſubſtan-tia,ſitus,forma,numerus,cônexio,earum partium de quibus ſermo futurus eſt,breuiter exponenda. Ad quod munus ſtatim aggrediemur,ſi pauca prius de inſtituto ac de iudi-cio noſtro ſubiunxerimus.Quanq̃ enim hic noſter in ſcribendo ac diſſecan-do labor,complures non modo in anatomes cognitione,ſed etiam in Gale-ni ſententiæ interpretatione iuuare poterit:tamen interdú veremur,ne qui-buſdam nomen hoc anatomicum ſit inuiſum : mirentúrq; in ea diſſectione tantum nos operæ & temporis ponere: cum alioqui ab ijs qui nummorum potius quàm artis aucupio dant operam facile negligatur.Atq; ita nobis oc curritur,dum quærunt:ſatiſne conſtanter facere videamur,qui cum corpo-ris humani partiú longiori indagationi ſtudemus , quæ magis ſunt vtilia, imprimíſq; neceſſaria prætermittimus:ſatius eſſe affirmantes,eius rei cogni tionem ſicco (vt aiút)pede percurrere,in qua alia certa,alia incerta eſſe di-

Quid dictum libro ſuperio-re.

Quid ſecun-do libro dice-tur.

Purgatio ad-uerſus eos, qui longiorem anatomes in-dagationem minus probat

Roman type by Claude Garamond, from the print shop of Simon de Colines, Paris, 1545.

Actual Bodoni punches. Carved punches were driven into other pieces of metal called matrices. Molten metal was then poured into these matrices, making the actual type. Courtesy of Sumner Stone.

The grace and elegance of the type of Giambattista Bodoni is evident in this page from the second edition of Manuale Tipografico (1818), which is considered one of the greatest type specimen books ever printed.

REALE

Quousque tandem a-butêre,Ca-
tilina , pa-tientiâ no-

AQUINO

abcdefghi
jklmnopqr
stuvwxyz

Typeface design by Herbert Bayer, 1925. This Bauhaus design is a minimalist, sans serif "unicase" typeface.

STAATLICHES BAUHAUS IN WEIMAR 1919-1923

This cover design by Herbert Bayer illustrates the influence of the Bauhaus, c. 1923. (Original: red and blue letters on a black background.)

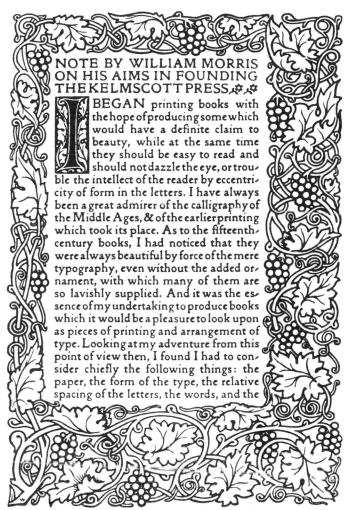

NOTE BY WILLIAM MORRIS ON HIS AIMS IN FOUNDING THE KELMSCOTT PRESS.

I BEGAN printing books with the hope of producing some which would have a definite claim to beauty, while at the same time they should be easy to read and should not dazzle the eye, or trouble the intellect of the reader by eccentricity of form in the letters. I have always been a great admirer of the calligraphy of the Middle Ages, & of the earlier printing which took its place. As to the fifteenth-century books, I had noticed that they were always beautiful by force of the mere typography, even without the added ornament, with which many of them are so lavishly supplied. And it was the essence of my undertaking to produce books which it would be a pleasure to look upon as pieces of printing and arrangement of type. Looking at my adventure from this point of view then, I found I had to consider chiefly the following things: the paper, the form of the type, the relative spacing of the letters, the words, and the

Golden Type and page border by William Morris. From a note by William Morris on his aims in founding the Kelmscott Press. Source: Kelmscott Press, 1898.

THE INDUSTRIAL REVOLUTION AND THE MECHANIZATION OF TYPE

The development of new and improved presses continued through the centuries, albeit slowly. But it wasn't until the Industrial Revolution in the late nineteenth and early twentieth centuries that groundbreaking improvements in typesetting equipment were achieved. In addition to the lack of speed and reliability of hand-set metal type composition (remember every letter of every word had to be set by hand), another of its significant limitations was the inability to justify type automatically, that is, without the manual insertion of metal spaces between the letters. The Linotype machine, invented by Ottmar Mergenthaler in the 1880s, as well as other typesetting machines that followed, including one from Monotype, sped up the printing process immensely (and included the ability to justify text) and finally eliminated the need to set type by hand one letter at a time. The greatly increased speed that resulted from the replacement of hand composition by machine composition had a major effect on newspapers, allowing them to extend their deadlines to print late-breaking news.

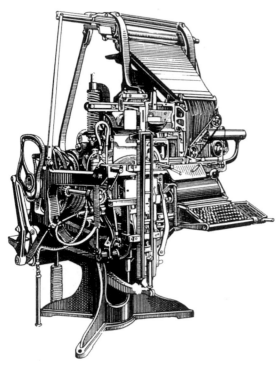

Linotype machine invented by Ottmar Mergenthaler.

Along with these groundbreaking developments in printing presses came the invention of a pantographic punch cutter in 1885 by Linn Boyd Benton. This device automated the process of creating punches with its ability to scale to any size a single master drawing, which could then be used to make the matrices. This eliminated the need to draw each and every size of type by hand, considerably speeding up the process of making type.

These typesetting innovations went hand-in-hand with other advancements taking place in the printing industry, such as offset lithography, a photographic process that gradually replaced letterpress printing.

PHOTOCOMPOSITION

Technology took a huge leap ahead in the mid-1950s with the development of phototypesetting. Several companies, the most prominent one being Mergenthaler and Intertype, developed and improved a photographic process of setting type whereby typefaces were made into negatives through which light was focused onto photosensitive paper, producing an image of the type. The improvements over hot metal typesetting were qualitative as well as quantitative. Typesetting could now be done electronically rather than mechanically, setting over five hundred characters per second compared to perhaps five or six previously, and the equipment took up much less space. Images became sharp and crisp, corrections could be made electronically, and most importantly, there was now complete flexibility with regard to intermixing styles, weights, and sizes; letter spacing and kerning; line spacing and word spacing; hyphenation and justification; overlapping; and other photographic special effects as well. The elimination of so many restrictions in the typesetting process had a major effect on typography and typographic design.

INTO THE DIGITAL AGE

The twentieth century continued to bring advances in typesetting technology at breakneck speed. Phototypesetting had been in use little more than two decades when digital typesetting methods took hold in the 1980s. Because it was so expensive and new, only professional typographers in type shops adopted this electronic technology. The new digital typesetters were capable of composing type and integrating photos and artwork and layout at one workstation. Digital color separation and retouching, stripping, and platemaking were to follow shortly. At this point, typesetting was still in the capable hands of professionals who spent many years learning the craft and trade of typography. This was all to change in the next few years.

Herb Lubalin and Expressive Typography

One of the most prominent figures in typography and typographic design in the 1960s and 1970s was Herb Lubalin (1918–1981), a hot, innovative, and fearless New York designer. His groundbreaking and adventurous use of type, particularly in the publication *U&lc* (designed and edited by Lubalin and published by the International Typeface Corporation) influenced designers around the globe. His work incorporated tight letter-and-line spacing, extreme kerning with acute attention to every typographic detail, and the overall use of type and innovative new typefaces in ways never before seen. In addition, he handled type in an illustrative way seldom done before, either by employing typographic forms as graphic elements of the design or by creating typographic puns.

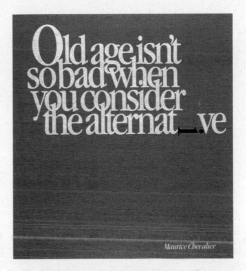

The work of Herb Lubalin broke with tradition in every possible way. He created these three pieces for U&lc, the typographic journal published by International Typeface Corporation. As the editor and designer of U&lc, he was able to present his innovative typographic ideas in the perfect vehicle. Courtesy of International Typeface Corporation.

Above: This piece combines a bold typeface set with tight letter and line spacing with a very elegant hand-lettered script to illustrate a point typographically.
Upper right: The overlapping ascenders and descenders of this piece take a back seat to the dramatic effect of the "i" lying on its side. The message is visual as well as editorial.
Lower right: The message expressed here with the use of very tightly set caps is made even stronger by the placement of black-and-white color breaks, especially the word "equal."

Why did he do this? Because he could—these were typographic capabilities never before possible prior to the arrival of phototypesetting. The typographic trends initiated by Herb Lubalin and imitated by countless others, particularly the emphasis on tight type at the occasional expense of readability, were a reaction to the restrictions of the hot metal typesetting that preceded them. This style has its critics (as well as its admirers) today, but it is important to understand how and why it came about to appreciate its tremendous importance and influence on the evolution of type and typographic design.

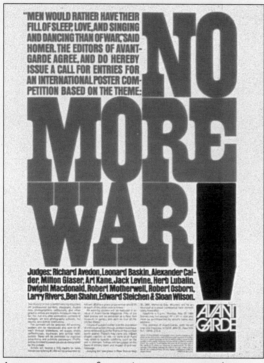

An announcement of an antiwar poster contest by Avant Garde *magazine. Herb Lubalin's use of color, tight type, and a very deliberate type alignment (including hung punctuation) creates a jigsaw puzzle effect in this powerful piece. Courtesy of Rhoda S. Lubalin (estate of Herb Lubalin).*

This award-winning logo designed for a never-published magazine not only states the name but illustrates it as well. Herb Lubalin considered the suggestion of a fetus inside the logo one of his finest typographic designs. Courtesy of Rhoda S. Lubalin (estate of Herb Lubalin).

In 1985, the world was irreversibly altered with the introduction of the Macintosh (Mac) computer, the first affordable "desktop computer" developed by Apple under the leadership of Steve Jobs. Other manufacturers, led by IBM, were developing versions of their own, which came to be known as personal computers (PCs). These PCs had different operating systems than Macs but the same affordability and focus. Now it was possible for virtually anyone to set type on the computer as desktop publishing blazed the path toward desktop typography.

This new, exciting, and increasingly more affordable technology was improving at every turn. At the same time, page-layout applications, such as PageMaker and QuarkXPress, as well as the more illustration-oriented programs, such as Adobe Illustrator and Aldus Freehand, were being developed. As the memory and speed of desktop computers increased, so did the features and capabilities of these programs, eventually including the ability to set and fine-tune type. Simultaneously, companies and foundries–such as International Typeface Corporation (ITC), Adobe, Linotype, Compugraphics, and Berthold–shifted their focus to developing digital versions of their existing typeface libraries as well as releasing new and different designs. Smaller, more specialized foundries–such as FontBureau, Emigre, T-22, and FontShop–began to emerge and introduced some very innovative and cutting-edge type designs. The introduction of type design programs–such as Letraset FontStudio, Macromedia Fontographer, and Ikarus-M–gave anyone the tools to create fonts. These developments led to the democratization of type design and contributed to the many thousands of fonts commercially available today. The quality of these typefaces ranged from very high end to extremely poor, leaving the daunting task of deciphering which was which to the end user.

Graphic design production methods were changing in dramatic ways as well. Pasteups and mechanicals (the manual creation of camera-ready artwork, using paper proofs and wax or rubber cement) were being replaced by digital page makeup, which was cheaper, faster, and more flexible. Type no longer needed to be sent out to expensive type shops–instead, it was set by graphic designers and production artists, as well as administrative assistants.

The problem with this new way of setting type is why a book like this exists. Setting good typography is an art and craft that in the past took many years to master and required highly skilled professionals who devoted their careers to developing such mastery. Today, however, most of those working with typography have little education in type, including many graphic designers (although more and more schools are beginning to address this important subject). The unfortunate result of this situation has been the proliferation of poor typography.

Another contributing factor to this problem was the fact that the earliest versions of page-layout programs did not have the capability to fine-tune type. Thankfully today's updated software programs are much more sophisticated and robust and are quite capable of creating excellent typography, but it still requires a skilled and knowledgeable person to achieve this. The computer is just a tool; it is a means to an end, not an end in itself. Many designers and production artists are not versed in the factors that contribute to the creation of fine typography, and they are not aware of and familiar with the features in their design software that can achieve this. With practice, however, you will acquire the eye necessary to see type as a professional does, as well as the ability and motivation to create it.

Notable Type Designers

Over the centuries, type designers were extremely influential in shaping the printed word. The sixteenth century brought us the beautiful proportions of the work of Claude Garamond and Robert Granjon. In the next hundred years, the balanced designs and readable typestyles of William Caslon emerged. With their elegant and graceful designs, Giambattista Bodoni and Firmin Didot were tremendously influential in the eighteenth century. The nineteenth century gave way to the oldstyle characteristics of William Morris's work, and the twentieth century brought us many designs inspired by the geometric style of Bauhaus. Many thousands of typeface styles available to us today are in large part due to the originality, artistry, and craftsmanship of five centuries of talented printers and designers, only a handful of which are highlighted in the following group of some of the most influential and important type designers of all time.

Claude Garamond (1480–1561) was a highly regarded French typefounder specializing in type for the publishing industry. He was unsurpassed as a classical designer and craftsman, and he was considered one of the best punch cutters of his day.

Garamond types are considered the highlight of the sixteenth century. His roman and italic types were considered groundbreaking designs and a primary factor in establishing the roman letter as standard, taking the place of gothic or blackletter, which were the standards of the time.

Garamond, the typeface (or some of the many versions thereof), remains one of today's most popular typefaces due to its elegance, warmth, and legibility. It is important to note that some of the Garamonds available today are interpretations of varying degrees of the original types.

abcdefghijklmnopqrstuvxyz1234567890
ABCDEFGHIJKLMNOPQRSTUVXYZ

Garamond

William Caslon (1692–1766) was a successful British engraver, punch cutter, typefounder, and typeface designer. He began as an engraver of gunlocks in London, then set up his own foundry. His types were instantly popular with printers and clients alike, due to their distinctiveness, grace, and beauty. They quickly became the new standard in British newspapers and were used for the Declaration of Independence and the Constitution of the United States.

The popularity of Caslon typestyles has waxed and waned over the years, but today they are considered some of the most beautiful and functional of typefaces, and they have probably been imitated, copied, revived, and reissued more than any other typeface.

abcdefghijklmnopqrstuvxyz1234567890
ABCDEFGHIJKLMNOPQRSTUVXYZ

ITC Founder's Caslon

John Baskerville (1706–75) was an unconventional British printer, calligrapher, typefounder, stonecutter, and writing master. His claim to fame is his typeface, Baskerville, which is one of the earliest of the transitional classifications. His perfectionist tendencies led him to make major innovations in printing presses, ink, and paper making that, when combined with his type designs, led to some of the most exquisite examples of printing of that era.

Unlike William Caslon, John Baskerville was underappreciated until many years after his death, when he was recognized for his contribution to English printing and type founding. Today his Baskerville typeface is one of the most widely used and influential serif typefaces. His work truly changed the course of history.

abcdefghijklmnopqrstuvxyz1234567890
ABCDEFGHIJKLMNOPQRSTUVXY

Baskerville

Giambattista Bodoni (1740–1813) was a much-celebrated Italian printer, engraver, publisher, and typographer. He is considered to be the father of the Modern type style, which is characterized by flat serifs and high contrast between thick and (often hairline) thin strokes. Bodoni, the son of a printer, has been referred to as "the king of typographers and the typographer of kings." He first served as an apprentice at the Vatican and was later appointed printer to the court of Parma in 1768, after which he opened his own foundry.

The typeface that retained the Bodoni name and appeared in 1790 was actually one of hundreds that he designed, most of which appeared in his *Manuale Tipografico* (1788), which was a statement of his design philosophy. This two-volume work contained over a hundred roman and italic typefaces of his own design, including roman, Greek, gothic, Asian, and Russian fonts, as well as lines, borders, symbols, numbers, and musical notation.

abcdefghijklmnopqrstuvxyz123456789
ABCDEFGHIJKLMNOPQRSTUVXYZ

ITC Bodoni Twelve

Frederic W. Goudy (1865–1947) was a prolific American type designer and typographer, publisher, and teacher. His typefaces, which he designed for a variety of publishing houses and companies, are considered to have a uniquely warm, recognizable, and somewhat "American" style.

Goudy designed over a hundred typeface designs in his career, some of the most notable being Copperplate, Kennerley, Goudy Old Style, Deepdene, Remington Typewriter, Californian, and Bulmer. Goudy is also responsible for Californian by Monotype as well as its digital companion, ITC Berkeley Oldstyle, both of which originated from the custom work he did for the University of California Press.

abcdefghijklmnopqrstuvxyz1234567890
ABCDEFGHIJKLMNOPQRSTUVXYZ

Goudy Old Style

Morris Fuller Benton (1872–1948) was an influential American typeface designer who headed the design department of the American Type Founders (ATF) from 1900 to 1937. During that time he was responsible for introducing a great many type designs into common usage by either reviving important designs (ATF Bodoni, Souvenir), expanding existing families (Goudy Old Style, Cheltenham), or creating brand new designs (Hobo, Bank Gothic, and Broadway), including many of the very popular neogrotesque sans serifs (Franklin Gothic, Alternate Gothic, News Gothic, Agency Gothic). In total, he developed over two hundred alphabets.

abcdefghijklmnopqrstuvxyz12345678 ABCDEFGHIJKLMNOPQRSTUVXYZ
Franklin Gothic

Eric Gill (1882–1940) was a very colorful (and controversial) British stone carver, type designer, sculptor, illustrator, and printmaker, who gained notoriety for his opinionated writings on everything from art to politics to sex and religion. His most notable designs are Perpetua and Joanna, which he used to hand-set his book *An Essay on Typography* (1931). His most well-known design is Gill Sans, which was based on lettering designed by Edward Johnston for the London Underground signage.

After his death, the type and ornaments he was commissioned to design for the Golden Cockerel Press were later acquired by ITC and released as ITC Golden Cockerel.

abcdefghijklmnopqrstuvxyz1234567890 ABCDEFGHIJKLMNOPQRSTUVXYZ
Joanna

Stanley Morison (1889–1967) was a notable British typographer, historian, and designer. In 1922 Morison founded the Fleuron Society, which was dedicated to typography. He then became a typographic consultant for Cambridge University, the *Times* (a London daily newspaper), as well as for the Monotype Corporation, where he was instrumental in the revival of such historic types as Baskerville and Bembo.

Morrison is probably best known for developing (along with Victor Lardent), the very readable Times New Roman typeface for the *Times*, which commissioned him to design a replacement for Times Old Roman after he criticized the poor quality of the paper's printing during his tenure as their typographic consultant.

abcdefghijklmnopqrstuvxyz1234567890 ABCDEFGHIJKLMNOPQRSTUVXYZ
Times New Roman

Hermann Zapf (1918–) is the highly regarded German type designer, calligrapher, writer, and lecturer responsible for many of the twentieth century's most important fonts. His type designs include Palatino, Optima, and Melior, as well as Aldus, Medici Script, and the familiar Zapf Chancery and Zapf Dingbats, both of which have been popularized by desktop publishing.

Zapf has always embraced new technology and has designed type for a range of printing and typesetting technologies, including hot metal, phototypesetting, and digital typography. He was professor at the Rochester Institute of Technology (RIT) from 1976 to 1987 and continues to serve as a consultant to Linotype.

abcdefghijklmnopqrstuvxyz1234567890
ABCDEFGHIJKLMNOPQRSTUVXYZ
Optima

Edward Benguiat (1927–) is the very prolific and charismatic American typeface designer and lettering artist. He has designed over 600 typefaces, including ITC Souvenir, Avant Garde Gothic, Tiffany, Bookman, Korinna, Benguiat, Barcelona, Modern 216, Caslon 224, Panache, Century Handtooled, Cheltenham Handtooled, Garamond Handtooled, and Edwardian Script. In addition to designing commercial typefaces, he has designed type and logos for many publications including the *New York Times,* the *Star Ledger, Esquire, New York Magazine, Reader's Digest,* and *Playboy,* as well as for many major corporations such as AT&T, A&E, Ford Motor Company and Estée Lauder.

Benguiat's association and involvement with International Typeface Corporation, *U&lc, (Upper & Lower Case)* and Photo-Lettering Inc. have had a tremendous impact on the type community. He still teaches at the School of Visual Arts (SVA) in New York City, to the delight of his students, where he has been teaching for almost forty years.

abcdefghijklmnopqrstuvxyz123456789
ABCDEFGHIJKLMNOPQRSTUVXYZ
ITC Benguiat

Matthew Carter (1937–) is a highly revered British type designer who resides in the United States. Carter has many years of experience designing type for all technologies—first at Linotype, then Bitstream Inc. (the digital foundry he cofounded), and currently as principal of Carter & Cone Type Inc. Carter's commercial work includes Snell Roundhand, ITC Galliard, Miller, Shelley, ITC Charter, Mantinia, Sophia, Bell Centennial (for U.S. telephone directories), as well as the widely known screen fonts Verdana, Georgia, and Tahoma. He has produced type for Apple, Microsoft, *Time, Newsweek, Wired, U.S. News & World Report, Sports Illustrated,* the *Washington Post,* and the Walker Art Center.

Carter has received numerous awards for his contributions to typography and the printing industry and is still in great demand for custom typefaces for newspapers, magazines, corporations, and university presses.

abcdefghijklmnopqrstuvxyz1234567890
ABCDEFGHIJKLMNOPQRSTUVXYZ
ITC Galliard

Design Guidelines

Nancy Sharon Collins, Assistant Professor, 2004–5, Nicholls State University, Thibodaux, Louisiana

1. Think first.

2. Sketch everything you think. Get it your thoughts out of your brain and onto the page–any page–where your client and audience can read it.

3. Define your objective(s). Make a priority list. Start with the most important information at the top. List all other elements in sequence beneath it. Let this be your master, map, and guide.

4. Try not to bring preconceived notions to any project. Stay open-minded and open to change. Don't get too attached to any one idea. At any point, your client or the project itself can do a 180-degree turn on you, and you will have to alter your design accordingly.

5. Do all your research before you start on the computer.

> **a.** Keystroke all original text into a word processing program to edit for content, spelling, and typographically correct punctuation. (Do not do this in a design program–you will get too wrapped up in the design and lose sight of editing the text.)
>
> **b.** Check all art for compatibility with the design program(s) you are planning to use.
>
> **c.** Pin or tape your priority list within easy view.
>
> **d.** Make your own type specimen book (see Exercise in Chapter 3, page 59).
>
> **e.** Keep a scrapbook of "orphan type" (typographic ideas found on one-off media, such as old signs, old magazines, old packaging; look at junk mail, pulp fiction, club flyers, cereal boxes, etc.).
>
> **f.** For major elements (headlines, etc.), make rough type studies of at least three to five styles. Utilize typography from nondigital media (hand-drawn, collage, or orphan type).
>
> **g.** Make low-resolution (for position only) scans of all of your art: store them in one folder so you can access easily and edit them later.
>
> **h.** Create five to ten primary and secondary type studies. Pin them on the wall. Stand back and look at them. Choose or make more.

6. Compose a few (5 to 10) sample designs with all components in quick, rough form.

    a. Pin or tape them on the wall and critique them.

    b. Edit out the weaker designs.

    c. Create Style Sheets or use old-fashioned typographic specifications, written by hand.

    d. The design(s) you choose to execute should be the easiest to defend. Ask yourself: How quickly does the design address the original problem? Does the design really reflect the target audience? Are all key components readable according to the appropriate hierarchy? This sounds terrible and boring, but a successful design not only must look nice–it must function to succeed!

7. Print out your design often. Pin or tape your work to a wall. Critique as you go, replacing weak elements with stronger solutions.

8. Make sure your final design "reads" according to your original priority list.

9. Have someone else proofread your work, even if you use a spell-checker.

10. Keep all phases of your work. If you have to backtrack, you will have everything.

11. Organization is key. If you have to find a particular phase or element, you should know exactly where to find it.

12. Make sure your final printout appears exactly as you intend. If not, go back, figure out why not, fix it, and print again

TYPOGRAPHIC TIMELINE
Ilene Strizver, Faculty, School of Visual Arts, New York, New York

Objective
• To become familiar with the sequential history of type and typography
• To develop an understanding of what led to the transition from one period to another

Assignment
Research and create a typographic timeline from the invention of movable type through the present time. Include the following:
• Typeface classifications from Chapter 3 (additional classifications may be added)
• Influential type designers and pioneers
• Milestone typeface designs
• Influential stylistic periods
• Important type foundries

Use charts, graphics, color, and appropriate typography as necessary to visually express the information in a clear, accurate, and visually attractive and effective way.

HISTORICAL DESIGN

Ilene Strizver, Faculty, School of Visual Arts, New York, New York

Objective

To research and explore influential periods and styles in history as it applies to typography and (typo)graphic design

Assignment

Step 1: Write a 500- to 700-word summary on the typography and design of three of the topics listed below. Include at least three illustrations with captions.

Art Deco
Art Nouveau
Bauhaus
Futurism
Herb Lubalin and the New York Style
Russian Constructivist
Suprematism
Swiss Grid
William Morris and the Kelmscott Press

Step 2: Select one of the three topics you have written about, and design a piece in that style. The format is 10 x 10 inches square. It can be all type or primarily type and image. It can be black and white or color.

In order to understand the type on the computer know what to look and correct the

CHAPTER TWO

FROM METAL TO MAC:
UNDERSTANDING FONT TECHNOLOGY

Say the word *technology* to a lot of folks, and they instantly break out in a cold sweat. But to understand type on the computer, why it looks and acts the way it does, and how to make the most of it, it is essential to understand a few things about technology.

The following are a few of the most commonly used (and perhaps abused) terms that will begin to give you an understanding of the basic principles of type and fonts on the computer.

WHAT IS A FONT?

What exactly is a font? The term has changed dramatically since the development of computers. In traditional typography, specifically in days of metal type (or hot type), a font was a collection of metal characters representing the complete character set of a particular design (all the characters, numerals, signs, symbols, etc.), all of the same weight, style, and size. Ten point, twelve point, and any other size of the same design were all separate fonts.

Today, a font refers to the complete character set of a particular type design or typeface in digital form. Although the term *font* refers to one weight and style, the font is not size specific as in the days of hot metal. Digital fonts are scalable, that is, size independent; any point size type can be set from one font.

FONT FORMATS

Currently, there are three font formats to choose from: Type 1, TrueType, and the newest format, OpenType. If you are a graphic designer, you are most certainly familiar with PostScript Type 1 fonts, which have been the publishing standard since the late 1980s. On the other hand, if you do web design or work with Microsoft Windows software, you most likely use your share of TrueType fonts, which have also been used by Apple and Microsoft for system fonts. The availability of OpenType fonts has added a third format to the mix, one that is rapidly becoming the format of choice for many designers.

ITC Legacy Serif

abcdefghijklmnopqrstuvwxyz
ABCDEFGHIJKLMNOPQRSTUVWXYZ
0123456789ÆŒØæœøßfifl ᵃᵒ
!¡?¿'"*$¢£ƒ%‰°&§¥†‡<+=>_
[](){}#@¶|/\/~^®©™
,.:;""''‹›«»·•,,,...--—1´¨`^~‾˘˙°,˛"ˇ
áàâäãåÁÀÂÄÃÅçÇéèêëÉÈÊËíìîïÍÌÎÏ
ñÑóòôöõÓÒÔÖÕúùûüÚÙÛÜÿŸ

To understand the differences between Type 1, TrueType, and OpenType fonts, it is necessary to get technical. But don't worry–you don't have to commit this information to memory to set good type. Just try to remember the basic principles.

Type 1 (or PostScript) Fonts

Type 1 (also known as PostScript Type 1) was developed by Adobe Systems in the mid 1980s. This format is based on a computer language called PostScript, which describes type and graphics in a way that allows for precise, sharp printing at any size.

Type 1 consists of two components: a *bitmapped* or *screen* font and a *printer* or *outline* font. Both are required to view and to print a font. (The .atm file that accompanies most Type 1 fonts is a text file that stores font metrics, and it is not needed for the functionality of the font.)

Bitmapped or screen fonts. The bitmapped font is responsible for representing the font on your screen. Your screen represents all images–both graphic and type–with small dots or, more accurately, pixels. The typical screen has 72 dots per inch, commonly abbreviated as 72 dpi. In a bitmapped font, all the characters are represented as *pixels,* or bitmaps, so it can be viewed on your screen, thus the term screen font. The relatively low number of dots per inch on your screen (also referred to as *screen resolution*) compared to your printer makes smaller point sizes increasingly more difficult to display sharply and clearly, giving

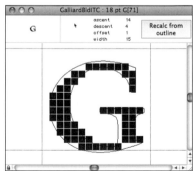

In a bitmapped font, all the characters are represented as pixels so it can be viewed on your screen. This illustration shows the arrangement of pixels for a character at a particular point size superimposed over the outline.

them the appearance of having more "jaggies" (i.e., jagged edges). This is why text can often be difficult to read on a computer screen.

Printer or outline fonts. This is the part of the font that is necessary to print your work. It is essentially the outline of each character stored as a mathematical description, thus the name *outline font*. The printer font is scalable, which means it can be enlarged or reduced to just about any size, rendering as crisp and sharp an image as your printer or output device is capable of. Your PostScript printer acts as the brain that makes this interpretation. (This is quite the opposite of the screen font, which is fixed and needs to be generated for each size.)

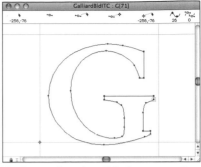

The image above is a digital representation of an outline. A printer font is scalable, which means it can be enlarged or reduced to any size, rendering as crisp and sharp an image as your printer or output device is capable of printing.

TrueType Fonts

Several years after the development of Type 1 fonts, Apple Computer and Microsoft joined forces to develop TrueType. This format consists of a single file that contains both screen and printer font data. It is most commonly used by Windows users and the nondesign community, with the exception of core TrueType fonts, which in the past (prior to OpenType) were standard on computer operating systems.

TrueType differs from its predecessor mainly, and most importantly, in its expanded *hinting* capability. Hints are digital instructions built into a font to improve its on-screen and printed appearance, predominantly at small sizes. It is extremely time consuming and costly to produce a font that features this enhanced clarity—so while some TrueType fonts have it (system fonts, for example), others do not.

TrueType might sound good to you (particularly prior to the availability of OpenType fonts), but keep in mind that the graphic design community has historically favored Type 1 fonts, which have been preferred over TrueType for the quality of their output and their reliability. This is particularly so if you intend to output your work at a service bureau (or at your offset printer, if it will be making the film), as they usually gripe about jobs using TrueType fonts. If you are using TrueType fonts, it is a good idea to discuss this in advance with your service bureau to see what their policy is and if they have any special instructions. TrueType fonts are fine for word processing jobs that have no printing considerations.

OpenType Fonts

OpenType, the newest font format jointly developed by Adobe and Microsoft in the late 1990s, is rapidly becoming the format of choice for graphic designers. It is a kind of superset of Type 1 and TrueType font formats with added enhancements. The features that benefit designers the most are multiplatform support, expanded character sets, and glyph substitution.

Multiplatform support. A font with multiplatform support means that the same OpenType font will run on both a Mac and a Windows machine, as opposed to Type 1 and TrueType fonts, which need to be purchased for either a Mac or a PC. This is a real convenience when your office uses both platforms or you use a PC at work and a Mac at home (or vice versa).

This also means that, with consistent character encoding inherent in multi-platform support, many problems associated with the transferring of documents from Mac to PC (or vice versa) will go away. The most annoying problem is when characters in the original file automatically change to different ones, such as apostrophes and f-ligatures becoming question marks and accented cap *O*s. No more "search and replace" to correct this irritating problem!

Expanded character sets. OpenType fonts allow type designers and foundries to include many more than the 256 characters we are used to with Type 1 and TrueType fonts. This means it can (but doesn't necessarily) include true-drawn small caps, oldstyle figures, extended ligature sets, swash and alternate characters, fractions, proportional and tabular figures, dingbats, and symbols, as well as extensive foreign language support, all in one font.

It is important to be aware that, although an OpenType font is backward-compatible in its most basic form with most applications, the expanded character set is only accessible by software that supports it, which includes most current design and page-layout software (but not yet most word processing programs).

From the simple to the sublime! Adobe Bickham Script Pro (an OpenType font) comes with a huge selection of swash and alternate characters, enabling a plain vanilla setting to be easily transformed into an elegant, highly embellished showing, previously attainable only from the skillful hands of a calligrapher. (More subtle effects can also be achieved.)

Glyph substitution. This capability goes hand-in-hand with an expanded character set. OpenType fonts can have a brain and know when to insert certain ligatures, swashes, or special characters. For instance, some swash characters are intended for either the beginning or end of a word to avoid crashing into other letters or creating too much space between two characters. When this feature (swashes) is turned on in a supporting application, the correct swash will be automatically inserted. If the copy is changed, it will automatically change the swash character back to the standard one as necessary.

Glyph substitution has also been built into some fonts containing several alternates for one character or character combination, so that the font automatically selects characters based on predetermined aesthetic considerations.

It can get a bit more complicated when lots of alternates are available in a font; make sure that the characters automatically inserted are the ones you want. You might have to manually insert the others, although it is very easy to do this once you become familiar with the process.

Availability. These days, most fonts are available in OpenType format. Some are new releases, while others are existing fonts that have been remanufactured, sometimes with additional characters added, such as alternates, swashes, small caps, and oldstyle figures. While some foundries currently release only OpenType fonts, others make available more than one format, so do your research carefully to make sure you get the format you want.

It is a good idea to identify prior to your purchase which additional characters are available with each font, if that is important to you; this information should be available on the foundry Web site, either as a complete character showing on the site or a downloadable PDF (portable document format).

House Industries designed Ed Interlock (an OpenType font) with a built-in intelligence to control the use of its hundreds of ligatures in such a way that it "thinks like a designer" and selects the appropriate ligature to maintain balance, particularly in the horizontal strokes. The top showing is set with "contextual alternates" turned off. When this feature is turned on (below it), note how characters and ligatures change depending on what is next to it.

OpenType Features

OpenType fonts can contain many additional characters—thousands, actually! These characters can be accessed in two ways: either globally (from the OpenType palette) or individually (from the glyph palette). Many of them fall under one of the following categories:

■ **Standard ligatures.** Many OpenType fonts have more than the standard ligatures available in most Type 1 and TrueType fonts: *fi* and *fl*. They often also contain *ff, ft, ffi,* and *ffl,* and sometimes even *fk* and *Th*. (Read more about Standard Ligatures in Chapter 5, page 123.)

■ **Discretionary ligatures.** Discretionary ligatures are more decorative than standard ligatures and may be used at your discretion. Common discretionary ligatures are *ck, sp, st, rt,* as well as other historical forms, including many "long s" combos (these look like lowercase *fs* with a shortened or nonexistent crossbar).

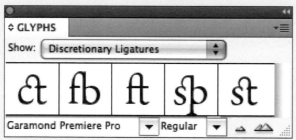

The discretionary ligatures available in Garamond Premiere Pro can be viewed via the glyph palette.

■ **Swashes.** These are decorative characters that have a flourish or extended stroke, usually at the beginning or the end of the character. (Read more about Swashes in Chapter 8, page 189.)

■ **Small caps.** True drawn small caps are available in many OpenType fonts. These are greatly superior (and preferred) to computer-generated small caps (which are just reduced capitals and a typographic no-no!), as they are drawn to match the weight, color, and proportion of the caps. (Read more about Small Caps in Chapter 8, page 180; also see discussion of "fake" small caps in Chapter 9, page 203.)

■ **Figures.** OpenType fonts have the capability of containing four number styles: lining and oldstyle figures with both tabular and proportional spacing. Keep in mind that the manufacturer sets one style as a default—usually the tabular lining figures, if they are available in the font—so take notice and alter as desired. (Read more about Figures in Chapter 8, page 177.)

■ **Fractions.** Many OpenType fonts have an assortment of pre-built fractions in addition to the standard 1/4, 1/2 and 3/4 that are available in some Type 1 and TrueType fonts. They can include 1/8, 3/8, 5/8, 7/8, and sometimes 1/3 and 2/3. (Read more about Fractions in Chapter 10, page 207.)

■ **Contextual alternates.** A contextual alternate is one that is intended for use in certain situations, such as next to specific characters to improve spacing or connections, as in script typefaces. Contextual alternates are a great new feature of some OpenType fonts, which often have the built-in intelligence to know whether they should be applied once selected from the OpenType palette.

whisper whisper

When contextual alternates are turned on in Caflish Script Pro (right), many of the connecting strokes between the letters become more natural, in a handwriting style.

■ **Stylistic sets.** Some OpenType fonts with numerous alternate characters organized them into "stylistic sets," which are easily accessed from the OpenType palette. These groupings eliminate the task of selecting each alternate character individually, which is very time-consuming in large blocks of copy, and knowing which ones look best with which others.

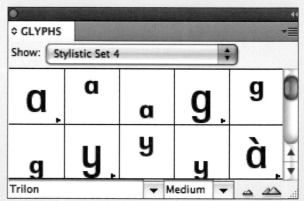

An alternate a, g, and y are located in Trilon's fourth stylistic set, as shown above.

An easy way to find out which of these features are available in a font is to look at the *glyph palette,* where you can view a font by subsets in the pull-down menu. Remember that when you select an OpenType subset globally, via the OpenType palette, you can always override and replace individual characters using the glyph palette.

HINTING

Hints are instructions that have been incorporated into a font to make your type look good on the screen as well as when printed. Remember that your printer converts all images into dots? Well, the hints tell your printer which dots to turn on and which to turn off when converting the scalable outline into the screen and printed version. This function is particularly necessary to improve the quality of type on the screen as well as on lower-resolution printers.

The markings around this character illustrate the hints, or instructions, that have been incorporated into a font to make type look good on screen as well as when printed.

FONT MANAGEMENT UTILITIES

A good font management utility is a necessity for those who have lots of fonts (as most designers do!). It is a way of managing and organizing your fonts and accessing just the ones you need for a particular job without having to move them in and out of your Fonts folder. This way they don't take up valuable space in your random access memory (RAM), and you don't have ridiculously long font listings on the font menu of your application.

Many of these helpful utilities can sort fonts by foundry, format, and other attributes; create sets; auto-activate fonts; customize previews; resolve font ID conflicts; identify and remove duplicate fonts; and repair corrupt fonts. Some of the more popular utilities are FontAgent Pro, FontExplorer X Pro, and Suitcase Fusion 2, all of which have become quite sophisticated, and which contain their own unique features. Most of them have server versions, as well as a free trial period, so you can check them out to see which suits your needs before purchasing.

Long S

Many a designer will mistake the historic long *s* (and its variations) available in some OpenType fonts for an *f*, which it is most definitely *not*! In its upright form, the long *s* looks like an *f* without the right side of the crossbar. The italic form of the long *s* usually lacks the crossbar entirely. Both the long and short forms were derived from the old Roman cursive medial *s* and used up until about 1800, after which they went out of fashion in most printing.

Since OpenType fonts can accommodate thousands of characters, the long *s* and its related ligatures are seen in many of today's digital fonts, especially historic revivals such as Caslon, Garamond, and Bodoni. But resist using these exotic characters unless you want that historic flavor and they are appropriate to your content, as they can greatly reduce legibility, especially in long lengths of text.

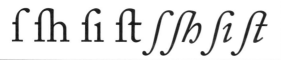

The long s *and related ligatures as shown in Adobe Caslon Pro Regular (left) and Italic (right).*

Font vs. Typeface

A *typeface* refers to the design of a set of characters, while a *font* refers to the technology—or method—used to reproduce or set that design. That is, graphic designers select *typefaces* for their work, but they use *fonts* to create the final product.

While the meaning of the word *typeface* has remained relatively unchanged over the years, the meaning of *font* has altered dramatically. A digital font—which includes Type 1 (PostScript), TrueType, and OpenType formats—is created with font production tools and considered to be software. A digital font consists of a single scalable outline that is used to set every point size.

In the days of phototype, which preceded digital technology, a font referred to the film onto which the typeface was imprinted.

In the days of metal, or *hot*, type, fonts were made of metal. Since there was one font for each point size, a font referred to a complete character set of a single size of a particular typeface, so that each point level of the same typeface—for example, 8 point, 10 point, and 12 point—were considered different fonts.

Style-Linked Fonts

Most major font foundries (as well as some of the smaller ones) style-link font families. This means that a true-drawn bold weight (as opposed to a "fake" computer-bolded version) can be accessed via the bold style button (Quark only) or a keyboard command (shift / com / b); a companion "true-drawn" italic (as opposed to a fake computer slanting) can be accessed via the italic style button (Quark only) or a keyboard command (shift / com / i); and often an actual bold italic weight can be accessed with both buttons or commands.

Style bar or keyboard command shortcuts for style-linked font families can be a real time saver when switching from one style-linked family to another (and when not using style sheets), as the italic and bold weights change automatically without having to manually highlight and select the weight for each one. But make sure the family is style linked beforehand to take advantage of this handy feature.

The quickest and simplest way to find out if a font family is style linked is to do this easy test: Create a test document, listing the font family and weights twice using copy and paste. In the first listing, access the italic and bold weights from the font menu; in the second, use the style bar or keyboard command. If they are not style linked (or if the weights do not exist), QuarkXPress will use fake styling—a very nasty no-no—

while Adobe InDesign will not change them at all. If they look exactly the same (you might need to print your examples out to be sure), they are style linked.

Maiandra Regular
Maiandra Italic
Maiandra Demi Bold
Maiandra Demi Bold Italic

Maiandra Regular
Maiandra Italic
Maiandra Demi Bold
Maiandra Demi Bold Italic

In this simple test, the upper showing of Maiandra was styled with the style bar in QuarkXPress, resulting in fake styling, while the font menu was used for the lower setting. The results indicate that this version of Maiandra is not a style-linked font.

IDENTIFYING YOUR OPENTYPE FONTS

Ilene Strizver, Faculty, School of Visual Arts, New York, New York

Background

Most personal font libraries have a combination of OpenType, PostScript, and TrueType fonts. OpenType fonts often have additional characters and features, many of which go unnoticed by designers who are not familiar with this capability, or how to identify the format of their fonts.

Objective

• To learn to identify OpenType fonts and their features in personal font libraries
• To become familiar and comfortable with finding and using these features

Assignment

Step 1: Open a new document in either InDesign or QuarkXPress. Go to the pull-down Font menu, and notice that all fonts have an icon in front of the name. These icons identify the format of the font. OpenType fonts are identified with an "O" icon.

Step 2: Explore the OpenType fonts in your menu or library (activating more as necessary). Using the glyph palette or the OpenType palette, locate the following:
• At least three fonts with true-drawn small caps
• At least three fonts with both tabular and proportional figures
• At least two fonts with swashes
• At least two fonts with dingbats or other ornaments
• At least two fonts with more than three true-drawn fractions

Step 3: Create a headline and paragraph(s) that uses all five of the above features. Try to keep it tasteful in terms of the fonts used (if more than one)—but the objective is to become familiar with the features, not to create a great typographic or literary work of art.

Many type
faces will
look similar
to the uns
killed eye a
first glance
but in time
you will no
only be able
to see how

CHAPTER THREE

WHAT MAKES A TYPEFACE LOOK THE WAY IT DOES?

Why are there so many typefaces? Why do we need new ones? And what are the differences between them all? These are some of the most commonly asked questions about type, understandably so. With over 160,000 typefaces in existence and new ones being designed every day, both the novice and the professional can easily become lost in a sea of typoconfusion.

Type design is similar to other kinds of product design in that it combines personal expression and interpretation with the needs and trends of the times. As technology changes, so does society as a whole, and changing personal tastes and styles are often a reflection of this, as is the desire to stand out from the crowd. Automobiles, furniture, watches, clothing, and even household items–such as telephones, toasters, and teacups–are all essential functional items that are constantly changing and being redesigned and subsequently purchased anew or replaced by consumers. We never seem to have enough choices. The same is true for typefaces, with one major difference–the appropriate choice of a typeface is essential to the success and effectiveness of your message.

Some typefaces, such as text faces, are chosen for their functionality, while others are chosen to be new, different, and eye-catching, as are most display designs. Before we can understand the differences between typefaces, it is important to be able to see the differences. This is an acquired skill that can be learned by anyone who is interested, akin to using a muscle you've never used before in a sport or acquiring a taste for different kinds of apples or beer. Many typefaces will look similar to the unskilled eye at first glance, but in time you will not only be able to see how they differ but also understand how those differences are important to the effectiveness and appeal of your job.

PARTS OF A CHARACTER

A typeface consists of many different characters. Each character is made up of different parts, all of which have a name. Knowing the terminology in the following list not only makes it easier to communicate about typefaces and their characteristics but also educates your eye to see and to recognize the underlying structure of various designs and, subsequently, the differences between them.

Arm: An upper horizontal or diagonal stroke that is attached on one end and free on the other.

Ascender: The part of a lowercase character (*b, d, f, h, k, l, t*) that extends above the height of the lowercase *x*.

Axis: The angle of the stress of the round part of a character.

Bar: The horizontal stroke in characters such as *A, H, R, e,* or *f.*

Baseline: The invisible line on which the flat part of characters sit.

Bowl: A curved stroke that creates an enclosed space within a character (which is then called a counter).

Cap height: The height of capital letters from the baseline to the top of caps, most accurately measured on a character with a flat top and bottom (*E, H, I,* etc.).

Counter: The partially or fully enclosed space within a character.

Descender: The part of a character (*g, j, p, q, y,* and sometimes *J*) that descends below the baseline.

Ear: The small stroke that projects from the top of the lowercase *g.*

Hairline: A very thin stroke most often common to serif typefaces.

Leg: A lower horizontal or diagonal stroke that is attached on one end and free on the other.

Link: The stroke that connects the top and bottom part (bowl and link) of a two-storey lowercase *g.*

Loop: The lower portion of the lowercase *g.*

Serif: The projections extending off the main strokes of the characters of serif typefaces. Serifs come in two styles: bracketed and unbracketed. Brackets are the supportive curves that connect the serif to the stroke, creating a somewhat softer look. Unbracketed serifs are attached sharply and usually at 90-degree angles.

Shoulder: The curved stroke of the *h, m,* or *n.*

Spine: The main curved stroke of the *S.*

Spur: A small projection off a main stroke, found on many capital *G*s.

Stem: A straight vertical stroke or main straight diagonal stroke in a letter that has no verticals.

Stress: The direction of thickening in a curved stroke.

Stroke: A straight or curved line.

Swash: A decorative flourish replacing a terminal or serif.

Tail: The descender of a *Q* or short diagonal stroke of an *R.*

Terminal (or Final): The end of a stroke not terminated with a serif.

X-height: The height of lowercase letters usually based on the lowercase *x,* not including ascenders and descenders.

TYPE CATEGORIES

Many attempts have been made to divide type styles into historic classi-fications, oftentimes resulting in a dry and somewhat cumbersome read. The following section will attempt to simplify and demystify the type classification system to give you a basic understanding of where the many hundreds of types come from, how they differ, and why.

Although it is not necessary to commit these categories to memory, there is value in understanding the origins of type and what makes one typeface different from another. Not only will you be building a good foundation for your growing typographic knowledge, but by reading about the differences between the typefaces, you will get a clearer picture of the anatomy of a character and how it varies from one typeface to another. It is an excellent way to fine-tune your ability to see type and know what you are looking at.

Serif

This is a large category of typefaces with a common denominator: all have serifs. Simply put, serifs can be described as extensions, protrusions, or, more elegantly put, finishing strokes extending from the ends of a character. Although they are decorative and stylistic in nature, they are said to enhance legibility by guiding the eye from one character to the next. They also serve to distinguish typefaces with similar shapes from each other.

Many categories of typeface fall under this heading, with the primary ones described below.

Oldstyle

This category of typefaces originated between the late-fifteenth and mid-eighteenth century. It is characterized by curved strokes with the axis inclined to the left, little contrast between thick-and-thin strokes, headserifs (usually angled), and bracketed serifs.

abcdefghijklmnopqrstuvwxyz
ABCDEFGHIJKLMNOPQRSTU

Adobe Caslon Pro

Transitional

Typefaces within this category represent the eighteenth century at a time of transition between oldstyle and modern design. They have the following characteristics: the axis of the curved strokes is barely inclined or is more vertical than diagonal; there is more contrast between thick and thin strokes than in oldstyle; and serifs are thinner, flat, and bracketed.

abcdefghijklmnopqrstuvwxyz
ABCDEFGHIJKLMNOPQRSTU

ITC New Baskerville

Modern

This refined and more delicate style is characterized by high or dramatic contrast between the thick and thin strokes, curved strokes on a vertical axis, and horizontal serifs with little or no bracketing.

abcdefghijklmnopqrstuvwxyz
ABCDEFGHIJKLMNOPQRSTUV

ITC Bodoni Twelve

Clarendon

This style made popular in the 1850s has a strong vertical weight stress; heavy, bracketed serifs (usually square); and slight stroke contrast.

abcdefghijklmnopqrstuvwxy
ABCDEFGHIJKLMNOPQRST

Clarendon

Slab or Square Serif

An early nineteenth-century style, these typefaces have very heavy square serifs, little or no bracketing, and hardly any stroke contrast, appearing to be a monostroke, or all strokes having the same width. They are often geometric or square in style.

abcdefghijklmnopqrstuvwxyz
ABCDEFGHIJKLMNOPQRSTUV

ITC Lubalin Graph

Glyphic

Glyphic type styles are lapidary (carved or engraved) rather than pen drawn in nature. They have a vertical axis, minimum stroke contrast, and often have triangular or flaring serifs.

ABCDEFGHIJKLMNOPQRSTUVWXYZ
ABCDEFGHIJKLMNOPQRSTUVW
Copperplate Gothic

Sans Serif

From the French word for "without" (sans), these typefaces are without serifs (sans serifs). These were some of the first styles to be cut in stone, and they have had periodic returns to popularity due to their simplicity, as well as their somewhat industrial look. The following are some of the most common categories of sans serif typefaces.

19th Century Grotesque

This style was the first popular sans serif. Its distinguishing features are contrast in stroke weight, a squared look to some curves, a "spurred" *G*, and a double-bowl (also referred to as a two-storey) *g*.

abcdefghijklmnopqrstuvwxyz
ABCDEFGHIJKLMNOPQRSTUVWXYZ
Franklin Gothic

20th Century Grotesque

This neogrotesque style has a less pronounced stroke contrast and is more refined in form than its predecessor. It has lost the squared curve and has a single-bowl *g*.

abcdefghijklmnopqrstuvwxyz
ABCDEFGHIJKLMNOPQRSTUVW
Univers

Geometric

These typefaces have strong geometric shapes, such as the perfect circle *o*, etc. They usually have monowidth strokes.

abcdefghijklmnopqrstuvwxyz
ABCDEFGHIJKLMNOPQRSTUVW

ITC Avant Garde Gothic

Humanistic

Humanistic type styles were an attempt to improve the legibility of sans serifs by applying a sans serif structure to the classical Roman form; more simply, they are based on the proportions of Roman capitals and oldstyle lowercase, with an apparent stroke contrast.

abcdefghijklmnopqrstuvwxyz
ABCDEFGHIJKLMNOPQRSTUVW

Optima

Scripts

These designs represent a large category of typefaces derived from or imitative of handwriting or calligraphy. They include a wide variety of styles and characteristics, and they are much more fluid than more traditional type styles.

Formal

These very elegant typestyles are characterized by flowing loops and flourishes with graceful, rhythmic strokes. These designs are most often connecting scripts and imitate the cursive penmanship of the nineteenth century.

abcdefghijklmnopqrstuvwxyz
ABCDEFGHIJKLMNOPQR

Bickham Script Pro

abcdefghijklmnopqrstuvwxyz
ABCDEFGHIJKLMNOPQRST

Commercial Script

Casual and Brush Scripts

These scripts are designed to look informal, as though quickly drawn with a pen, brush, or similar writing instrument. Their strokes can be connected or not, and they tend to be warm, friendly, and relaxed.

abcdefghijklmnopqrstuvwxyz
ABCDEFGHIJKLMNOPQRSTUVWXYZ

Mistral

Calligraphic

This broad category of typestyles strives to imitate the writing or lettering of the calligrapher whose work is hand drawn and custom made for each job. Calligraphic typestyles often look as if they were drawn with flat-tipped pens or brushes, and they occasionally include the drips, spots, blotches, and irregularities inherent in the process.

abcdefghijklmnopqrstuvwxyz
ABCDEFGHIJKLMNOPQRS

ITC Ballerino

Handwriting

Handwriting typefaces are typographic interpretations of actual handwriting or hand printing. The stylistic range is extremely diverse and can be anything from a connected script or scrawl to a quirky, bouncy, irregular hand printing.

ABCDEFGHIJKLMNOPQRSTUVWXYZ
ABCDEFGHIJKLMNOPQRSTUVWXYZ

ITC Deelirious

abcdefghijklmnopqrstuvwxyz
ABCDEFGHIJKLMNOPQRST

ITC Dartangnon

Blackletter

Blackletter type styles evolved from the early handwritten forms of liturgical writings and illuminated manuscripts. This style went from writing to type when it was used to set the Gutenberg Bible, the first book printed with movable type.

Blackletter typefaces are characterized by a dense, black texture, and highly decorated caps. The lowercase consists of narrow, angular forms with dramatic thick to thin strokes and serifs.

abcdefghijklmnopqrstuvwxyz
ABCDEFGHIJKLMNOPQR

Fette Fraktur

abcdefghijklmnopqrstuvwxyz
ABCDEFGHIJKLMNOPQRSTU

Engravers Old English

Titling Fonts

These are type designs that have been specifically designed for headline or display settings. Titling fonts differ from their text counterparts in that their scale, proportion, and design details have been altered to look best at larger sizes. This commonly includes a more extreme weight contrast and often more condensed proportions. While usually all-cap, single-weight variants of larger text families, titling fonts can also be stand-alone designs.

ABCDEFGHIJKLMNOPQRSTU

ITC Golden Cockerel Titling

ABCDEFGHIJKLMNOPQR
ABCDEFGHIJKLMNOPQRST

Bembo and Bembo Titling

Opticals and Size-Sensitive Fonts

In the days of metal type, when each point size of type was hand cut, many type designers made subtle adjustments in the weight, proportion, stroke thickness, and spacing of consecutive sizes of type to improve the aesthetics and functionality of type and to compensate for what happens optically when type gets larger or smaller. With the advent of phototype and then digital type technology, this practice was abandoned, as it was no longer economical. This resulted in one master, scalable outline to be used for every size, often resulting in reduced legibility at smaller sizes and/or the sacrifice of subtle design details at larger sizes.

To remedy this, some foundries have developed optically sized fonts, which are size-sensitive versions of a type design (sometimes called *opticals*) with adjustments made to each version intended to maximize its legibility and overall appearance in a range of sizes. They often contain text and display versions but often include mid-range and captions versions as well. Optical versions are intended to be treated as one type family as they would have been if they were hand-cut in metal, and can be used together with respect to their intended size ranges.

abcdefghijklmnopqrstuvwxyz
ABCDEFGHIJKLMNOPQRSTUV

abcdefghijklmnopqrstuvwxyz
ABCDEFGHIJKLMNOPQRSTUV

abcdefghijklmnopqrstuvwxyz
ABCDEFGHIJKLMNOPQRSTUVW

abcdefghijklmnopqrstuvwxyz
ABCDEFGHIJKLMNOPQRSTUVW

Warnock Pro Opticals: Caption, Regular, Subhead, and Display

abcdefghijklmnopqrstuvwxyz
ABCDEFGHIJKLMNOPQRSTU

abcdefghijklmnopqrstuvwxyz
ABCDEFGHIJKLMNOPQRSTUVW

abcdefghijklmnopqrstuvwxyz
ABCDEFGHIJKLMNOPQRSTUVWXY

ITC Bodoni Six, Twelve, and Seventy-Two

TYPETIP

One- and Two-Storey Lowercase *As* and *Gs*

The lowercase *a* and *g* come in two styles: one-storey (also called single bowl) and two-storey (also called double bowl or loop). The one-storey versions are simpler in form and are what we learn to read from. Two-storey versions have their tradition in historical typefaces of the serif variety, but they have been adapted in numerous other type designs, including sans serif designs and many other contemporary type styles.

Although two-storey versions are not usually used for true italics (as opposed to obliques, which tend to mirror the styles used in their Roman counterparts), they can appear anywhere a type designer chooses to use them, and they do not necessarily come in pairs either!

Aa Gg
Aa Gg

Plantin (upper) and Plantin Schoolbook (lower) illustrate the different designs of the two-storey and one-storey a and g.

Decorative and Display

This very broad category encompasses many hundreds of type styles that do not fit into any of the preceding categories, as they are designed primarily for headlines and meant to be distinctive, original, and eye-catching. They adhere to few or no rules and constraints and defy pigeonholing of any kind.

ABCDEFGHIJKLMNOPQRSTUV
ABCDEFGHIJKLMNOPQRST

ITC Abaton

abcdefghijklmnopqrstuvwxyz
ABCDEFGHIJKLMNOPQRSTU

ITC Farmhaus

abcdefghijklmnopqrstuvwxyz
ABCDEFGHIJKLMNOPQRSTUV

Curlz

ABCDEFGHIJKLMNOPQRSTUVWXYZ

ITC Rennie Mackintosh

ABCDEFGHIJKLMNOPQRSTUV

ITC Beesknees

abcdefghijklmnopqrstuvwxyz
ABCDEFGHIJKLMNOPQRSTUVWXYZ

ITC Pious Henry

abcdefghijklmnopqrstuvwxyz
ABCDEFGHIJKLMNOPQRSTUVWXYZ

Teknik

abcdefghijklmnop
ABCDEFGHIJKLMNOP

ITC Freddo

abcdefghijklmnopqrstuvwxyz
ABCDEFGHIJKLMNOPQR

Coquette

TYPETIP

Character vs. Glyph

A *character* is the symbol representing a letter, while a *glyph* is the actual shape or design of a letterform (or character) or the representation of a character. Several glyphs may represent one character. For example, a lowercase n character may be represented by glyphs of a small cap *n*, a swash *n*, a superscript *n*, etc. However, a cap *N* and an italic *n* are different characters. OpenType fonts can accommodate thousands of characters, including many glyphs for a single character.

The lowercase r character is represented by four glyphs in Garamond Premier Pro: the standard r, swash r, small cap r, and superscript r.

THINK LIKE A TYPE DESIGNER

Ilene Strizver, Faculty, School of Visual Arts, New York, New York

Objective
• To fine-tune sensitivity to the shape, structure, proportions, and design characteristics of a typeface
• To improve the powers of observation and attention to detail
• To understand the factors that contribute to making a consistent typeface design

Instructor Preparation
Step 1: Set the complete lowercase of three very different typefaces (I use a traditional serif, a condensed sans, and a contemporary serif, such as Bodoni, Impact, and Bodega Serif) on an 8 ½ × 11 inch, horizontal format. Set the characters so they are centered in three lines, and so there is plenty of space between the letters and lines. Place the typeface name on the top for identification. This is the master character showing. Print out one set.

Step 2: Create a second version of the above masters in the following way: remove the title, as well as five of the following characters: *a, e, g, k, r, s, t,* and *x.* Leave the spaces empty. These are the missing character templates.

Assignment
• Distribute one (or more if it is a small group) of the three missing character templates per student from Step 2 above, distributed sequentially, along with the tracing paper and markers. Instruct students to draw (and fill in) the five missing characters. Emphasis should be placed on concept and intention, not execution.
• The final tracing should have the missing characters drawn in position along the baseline, so it can be placed on top of the template, stapled together, and taped to the wall. Allow about 20 minutes for this task. **NOTE:** Do not let students use pencils or other fine-tipped tools, or they will spend too much time on perfecting the outline and less on the design concept.

Critique
Place one master on the wall at a time, starting with the sans serif example. Have students place all tracings and templates of that typeface on the wall at the same time (staple together if possible). Review one character at a time, comparing their drawings to the true solution. Discuss how they made their decisions, if they fit the overall design (even if they are different), and why the true solution makes sense. Discuss factors such as design consistency, width, ascender and descender length, overall proportions, stress, location of weight contrast, etc.

Supplies
• 9 × 12 inch tracing pad, at least 2 sheets per student per template
• Fine black marker (a fine-point Sharpie works best)

PERSONAL TYPE SPECIMEN BOOK
Ilene Strizver, Faculty, School of Visual Arts, New York, New York

Objective
• To create a functional, practical, and expandable personal specimen book of all fonts available on one's computer
• To become familiar with the history, appearance, usability, and functionality of each font

Assignment
Step 1: As research for the actual design assignment in Step 3, collect six different type-specimen showings–three text and three display. They should be actual specimen showings from font catalogs or from PDF specimen showings supplied by many font Web sites.

Step 2: Examine and analyze each of them carefully, considering appropriateness, practicality, and ease of use. Consider factors including overall layout; character layouts; size and style of text showing, including point size and leading; labeling; and any other factors. Make a list of pros and cons for each of the six showings.

Step 3: Design two different 8 ½ × 11 inch specimen-showing templates: one for text and one for display. Allow room on left margin for a three-hole punch. Include complete typeface name, foundry, designer, date, and a listing and sample character of all the weights and versions in the type family. Include its category, which can be serif (text), sans serif (text), display, ornament, or image fonts. Make your templates the best possible tools for font selection, taking into consideration your list of pros and cons from your research in Steps 1 and 2.

Step 4: Set your entire font library (or a subset) in the appropriate template.

Step 5: Proof carefully. Then print out and put in binder, creating dividers for serif, sans, display, ornaments, and image fonts.

TYPE SPECIMEN BOOK AND TYPEFACE ANALYSIS *(Group Project)*
Audrey G. Bennett, Associate Professor, Rensselaer Polytechnic Institute, Troy, New York

Objective
- To research a type designer and typeface
- To create a specimen page for a class Type Specimen Book
- To acquire an in-depth understanding of every aspect of a typeface, including readability, legibility, as well as historical factors contributing to its design

Assignment

Part 1: Type Specimen Book
You will create an 8 ½ × 11 inch specimen page to be part of a class Type Specimen Book.

Specifications
Format: 8 ½ × 11 inches
Margins: For front page, ½ inch on top, right side, and bottom; 1 inch on left (to allow for binding or hole punching). Reverse for back page.

Front Page
- Research a type designer of your choice and buy one of his or her text fonts.
- Set header as follows: first line, name of typeface in 18 point (pt) bold; second line, designer and year of design; and third line, name of foundry. Set second and third lines in 14 pt book or regular.
- Use the font to typeset the following characters in 48pt: capital and lowercase letters, numerals, punctuation, and other symbols as shown in the example to the right.
- Typeset a paragraph of dummy text at 9/12, 10/13, and 12/15, left justified.

Back Page
- Identify six to eight distinguishing characteristics of the font.
- Create a grid of 3 ½ × 3 ½ inch boxes with .5 pt rules.
- Within each box, show one or more of these characteristics, using both image (enlarged character or part of a character) and descriptive text.

Part 2: Typeface Analysis
Write and design in an essay of 1,500 words on standard, letter-sized paper about the type designer and his or her font that you chose in Part I. Use the font to typeset your essay.

Analyze the readability of the three type specimens you prepared in Part I. Describe the font in detail. Discuss its distinctive features and letters. Show an example of the font in use in a professional context. Which social and technological issues influenced its design? You may use image-based graphics in your paper.

Futura
Paul Renner
Adobe Type Library

ABCDEFGHIJKLMNOP
QRSTUVWXYZabcdef
ghijklmnopqrstvwxyz1
234567890$.,'"-:;!?&

FUTURA 9/12
The text you are reading is dummy text. It gives you an idea of Futura's readability. All of the text in this paragraph has been typeset in Futura at nine points on twelve points of leading. You should kern and track text typeset with these specifications to achieve maximum readability. Leading, kerning, tracking, x-height, and line-length are some of the factors that influence the readability of text.

FUTURA 10/13
The text you are reading is dummy text. It gives you an idea of Futura's readability. All of the text in this paragraph has been typeset in Futura at ten points on thirteen points of leading. You should kern and track text typeset with these specifications to achieve maximum readability. Leading, kerning, tracking, x-height, and line-length are some of the factors that influence the readability of text.

FUTURA 12/15
The text you are reading is dummy text. It gives you an idea of Futura's readability. All of the text in this paragraph has been typeset in Futura at twelve points on fifteen points of leading. You should kern and track text typeset with these specifications to achieve maximum readability. Leading, kerning, tracking, x-height, and line-length are some of the factors that influence the readability of text.

Futura
Paul Renner
Adobe Type Library

Futura embodies Bauhaus ideology. It features strict geometric shapes and lacks any embellishments, creating a stark minimalist appearance. Distinguishing characteristics of Futura include constant line strokes, straight lines, and arcs that are very circular. Futura's geometric and contemporary look is evident in the characters j, i, question mark, and exclamation point due to their straight lines and compass-like curves.

Specimen pages designed by Hunter Dougless. Courtesy of Hunter Dougless.

On Beyond Zebra: The 27th Letter Assignment

Virginia Rougon Chavis, Assistant Professor, The University of Mississippi, University, Mississippi

Objective

The purpose of this assignment is to develop a more acute understanding of and appreciation for the intricacies of the letterforms that make up a typeface.

Assignment

Create an upper- and lowercase 27th letter of the western alphabet. Create a name for the letter, a place in the alphabet, and a new sound (one that is not already taken in the English language). You will focus on the stress, stroke, and serif of each individual letter, all of which contribute to the overall look, personality, and readability of the typeface.

Process

Step 1: Choose a text typeface from one of the following categories: oldstyle, transitional, modern, Egyptian, or contemporary. Create fifteen to twenty preliminary sketches using that particular typeface during class to create a 27th letter.
HINT: Try to use no more than four strokes, as if you were to write the letter in your own handwriting.

Step 2: Pick three to five of the best forms and re-create digitally at a point size of 300.

Step 3: You will choose the best of these three designs with help from the class during an in-progress review.

Step 4: Find a place in the alphabet where your letterform (upper- and lowercase) fits best, and reproduce the alphabet including its 27th letter. This should be done at 60 point. Position the entire alphabet next to your letter.

Step 5: Come up with a short paragraph, using the new 27th letter at least five times. Place this paragraph on the bottom of the page.

Specifications
• One 8 ½ × 11 inch black-and-white print
• Portrait or vertical format

Evaluation
• Adherence to specifications
• Craftsmanship
• Creativity
• Attention to letterforms
• Attention to placement in the alphabet

Amber Brewer's solution to the 27th Letter Assignment is based on Adobe Garamond.
Courtesy of Amber Brewer.

Typeface Comparison Book

Joey Hannaford, Assistant Professor of Art, Graphic Design, University of West Georgia, Carrollton, Georgia

Objective
• Learn typographic nomenclature and anatomy terminology
• Increase observation skills of the subtle typographic differences that influence type choices and textures
• Learn to effectively design a page using visual hierarchy
• Design a sequential presentation of information

Assignment
Design an eight-page type specimen booklet for International Typeface Corporation (ITC), one of the major manufacturers and developers of typefaces for the graphic design industry. In the booklet, you will contrast and compare details of either two similar typefaces or two different versions of the same typeface (for example: the light and medium versions) using type anatomy terminology. The sequential presentation of information is an important goal of the assignment, so you will design a cover, inside spreads, and back cover. The booklet must contain some historical information and/or information about the type designer.

Background
A specimen book is often produced by type manufacturers to promote their typefaces to designers. Keep in mind that your audience is professional designers who are very sophisticated and discriminating in their knowledge of type and its subtleties. Include the following type terminology: serif, bracket, counter, stem, branch, set width, ascender, descender, baseline, arm, bowl, cap height, ear, mean line, x-height, uppercase, lowercase, vertex, and apex.

Deliverables
Begin by designing the composition of your pages and the flow of the booklet by creating thumbnails (scaled down pencil drawings on tracing paper). Photocopy your pencil drawings to full size and create a "dummy" booklet to help you visualize the sequence of your page compositions. You must have a solid design plan before proceeding to the computer. Final booklet will be 8 × 8 inches closed and 8 × 16 inches open, assembled from ink jet or laser prints created in printer spread.

Specifications

• Each page, except the front and back cover, must contain text that utilizes type anatomy terminology.
• All designs must be type only: no photographs or graphics.
• Cover must include a title that contains the name of both typefaces you are comparing.
• Some text must describe some of the background of the typeface (designer, foundry, etc.).

Process

Step 1. Choose two typefaces from the same type family from this list of classic typefaces:

Old Style: Bembo, Garamond, Goudy, Jenson, Palatino, Sabon, Perpetua
Transitional: Baskerville, Joanna, Cochin, Cheltenham, Melior
Modern: Bodoni, Didot, Scotch Roman, Walbaum, Fenice
Slab Serif: Century Schoolbook, Memphis, Lubalin Graph, Rockwell, American Typewriter
Sans Serif: Antiqua Olive, Franklin Gothic, Futura, Gill Sans, Helvetica, Stone Sans, Univers, Lucida Sans

You must choose two typefaces that are similar but different and that have available at least three of the following: light, medium, bold, and italic versions.

Another option would be to compare two different weight versions of the same typeface on the list. For example: Gill Sans Light and Gill Sans Medium, or compare two different manufacturer's version of a typeface. Example: ITC Garamond and Adobe Garamond Pro.

Step 2. Research the history and development of your typefaces, their designer, original manufacturer, and whatever else you can discover about its inspiration. Include this as text in your page designs. You must show evidence that you have researched your typeface not only on the Web but from a variety of sources.

Step 3. Begin thumbnail sketches of your page designs. It is critical that you strategize a logical, sequential presentation of your information. This means you will begin with a cover page, the next spread should introduce the subject, the following spread should increase in detail, and the last spread should summarize your findings. The back cover can be a playful use of letterforms, but it should not include any text, unless it is general information about the typeface.

Step 4. Include text on each spread that describes the characteristics you are comparing using the type terminology listed in the "Background" section above. You may expand this list of terms as required by your specific comparisons.

Example:
"The Book *a* has a lilting **bowl** and **counter** in comparison to the Light *a*. The **arm** of the Book *a* is also shorter than the Light *a*. The overall width of the letter, however, is identical for both the Light and Book *a*. The **stroke** of the Book *a* is more calligraphic than the Light *a*. The Light and Book *g* differ as well. The **link** of the Light *g* dips lower than the **link** of the Book *g*. The **ear** of the Book *g* extends slightly longer than the Light *g*."

Some strategies for comparison:
• Often the most distinguishing letterforms that best identify and point out the unique characteristics of a given typeface are both upper and lowercase *Q, G, R, Z*, lowercase *a*, lowercase *t*, and the ampersand.
• Choose letters of a similar shape "family," such as rounded capitals like *G, C, O, Q*, and compare the similarities and differences.
• Identify whether the *a* and *g* letterforms are one- or two-story designs.
• Examine the serifs and brackets of the two typefaces and compare.
• Examine the similar shapes of both upper and lowercase *M* and *N* with shapes that appear in other letters, only upside down, such as *W* and *V*.
• Compare the counters of both closed and unclosed letterforms such as a *c* and *d*.
• Compare the tails of the *Q* in the two typefaces.
• Compare the ampersands.

These are suggestions to get you started, but you are charged with finding your own comparisons and deciding which are most visually interesting for your page design.

The author gratefully acknowledges the significant influence and inspiration of her teacher and mentor Ronald Arnholm, Professor of Art, Graphic Design, University of Georgia, Athens, in the development of this project.

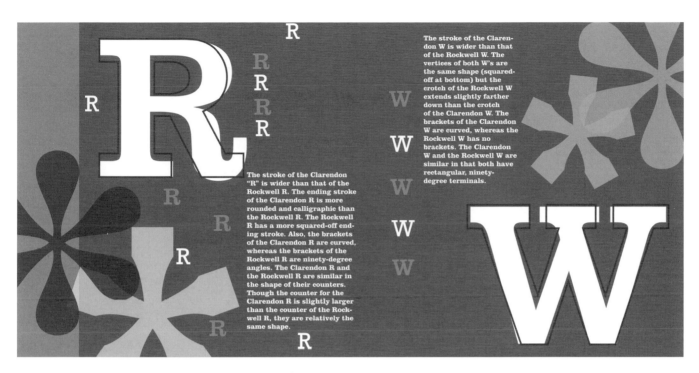

The stroke of the Clarendon "R" is wider than that of the Rockwell R. The ending stroke of the Clarendon R is more rounded and calligraphic than the Rockwell R. The Rockwell R has a more squared-off ending stroke. Also, the brackets of the Clarendon R are curved, whereas the brackets of the Rockwell R are ninety-degree angles. The Clarendon R and the Rockwell R are similar in the shape of their counters. Though the counter for the Clarendon R is slightly larger than the counter of the Rockwell R, they are relatively the same shape.

The stroke of the Clarendon W is wider than that of the Rockwell W. The vertices of both W's are the same shape (squared-off at bottom) but the crotch of the Rockwell W extends slightly farther down than the crotch of the Clarendon W. The brackets of the Clarendon W are curved, whereas the Rockwell W has no brackets. The Clarendon W and the Rockwell W are similar in that both have rectangular, ninety-degree terminals.

The stroke of the lowercase Clarendon P is slightly wider than the stroke of the lowercase Rockwell P. Also, the Clarendon P has areas of stress, particularly where the bowl meets the stem. The Rockwell P has no areas of stress, and the stroke is consistently the same size. The brackets of the Clarendon P are curved whereas the Rockwell P has no brackets. The connection between the serif and the stem of the Rockwell P forms a ninety-degree angle. The shapes of the serif at the top of both P's are similar in the boxy, geometric form. Whereas the counter of the Clarendon P is more oval, the counter of the Rockwell P is more circular.

The top terminal of the Clarendon T is more flared. This creates a cross-stroke that flows into the stem. The Rockwell T is once again more geometric with ninety-degree angles in its cross stroke. The top terminals of both T's have an ascending feel to them, as they both draw the viewer's eye upward. Whereas the Rockwell T has somewhat of a blunt ending at its bottom terminal, the Clarendon T's terminal curls upward and is more acute. The stem of the Clarendon T is wider than that of the Rockwell T, but the width of the cross stroke differs. The Rockwell T's cross stroke is shorter and wider than the Clarendon T's cross stroke.

Jessica Denman's type speciman booklet compares Clarendon and Rockwell.

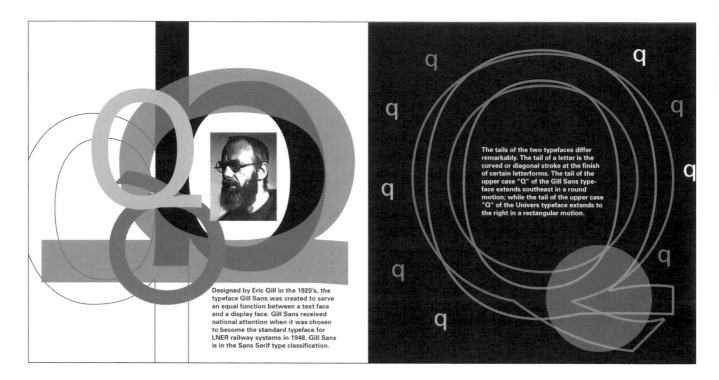

Designed by Eric Gill in the 1920's, the typeface Gill Sans was created to serve an equal function between a text face and a display face. Gill Sans received national attention when it was chosen to become the standard typeface for LNER railway systems in 1948. Gill Sans is in the Sans Serif type classification.

The tails of the two typefaces differ remarkably. The tail of a letter is the curved or diagonal stroke at the finish of certain letterforms. The tail of the upper case "Q" of the Gill Sans typeface extends southeast in a round motion; while the tail of the upper case "Q" of the Univers typeface extends to the right in a rectangular motion.

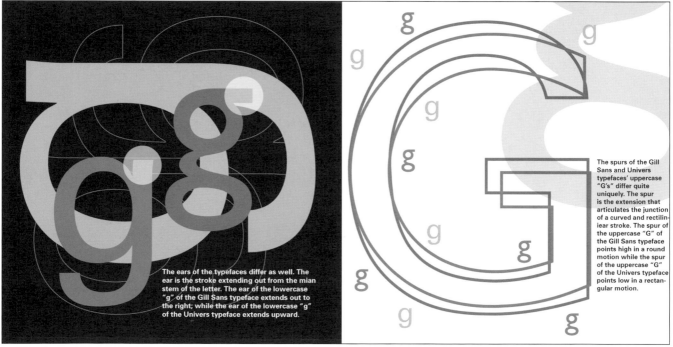

The ears of the typefaces differ as well. The ear is the stroke extending out from the mian stem of the letter. The ear of the lowercase "g" of the Gill Sans typeface extends out to the right; while the ear of the lowercase "g" of the Univers typeface extends upward.

The spurs of the Gill Sans and Univers typefaces' uppercase "G's" differ quite uniquely. The spur is the extension that articulates the junction of a curved and rectilin-iear stroke. The spur of the uppercase "G" of the Gill Sans typeface points high in a round motion while the spur of the uppercase "G" of the Univers typeface points low in a rectan-gular motion.

Kristen Thompson compares Gill Sans and Univers.

REAL SIGNAGE CRITIQUE

Amelia Hugill-Fontanel, Adjunct Faculty Member, Rochester Institute of Technology
School of Photographic Arts and Sciences, Rochester, New York

Objectives
• To identify typeface families in practical usage scenarios
• To develop skills in evaluating information design
• To encourage typographic connoisseurship

The student gains sensitivity in judging the efficacy of mundane visual messages and how typography plays a subtle yet vital role in information design.

Assignment
Signage is some of the most pervasive use of typography–for better or worse–in our daily lives. Find two actual signs that use typefaces from specific type classifications and critique them.

Process
Step 1: Photograph two examples of real-world sign typography: one that uses a display or script typeface and another that uses a serif or sans serif typeface.

Step 2. Identify each example's type classification and name, if possible.

Step 3: Analyze whether or not these signs are successful uses of the chosen typefaces. Write a short analysis for each example. Consider the following questions while responding:
• Did the designer accurately convey the concept of the business or information represented through the choice of typeface?
• Is it readable? Why is it or is it not so?
• Will this typeface appeal to its intended audience?
• If possible, how can this sign be improved?

Step 4: Present the two images on a sheet of paper, each with their corresponding analysis texts.

Type has the powe
o make or break a
b. Every typeface
as a different pers
nality, and the ab
ty to convey differe
t feelings and mo
s, some more that
thers. Display typ

CHAPTER FOUR

SELECTING THE RIGHT TYPE FOR THE JOB

Type has the power to make or break a job. Every typeface has a distinct personality and the ability to convey different feelings and moods, some more than others. Display typefaces, also known as headline typefaces, tend to be stronger in personality, sometimes trading legibility at smaller sizes for a more powerful feeling. They can evoke strength, elegance, agitation, silliness, friendliness, scariness, and other moods. Text designs, often used for blocks of copy, are more subtle in mood and emphasize legibility. Their personalities tend to be whispered rather than shouted.

Although typeface selection is a very personal and subjective decision, there are some guidelines and unofficial rules that will help you narrow your search and ultimately help you make the right choice.

DESIGN GOALS

The first and foremost step in selecting a typeface is knowing your goals. As a designer, your primary responsibility is to serve the client using your design and problem-solving skills. It is not to make their job into your own personal award-winning design statement. Personal self-expression to the exclusion of the needs of the project are what fine art is all about, but this is not the goal of graphic design.

Every job requires a different approach. An annual report might call for a typeface with a high degree of legibility that also captures the spirit of the company, but a book cover might

Arriba arriba

RETRO BOLD

ITC Clover

ITC Jambalaya

ITC Schizoid

Fette Fraktur

Jazz

ITC VINTAGE

ITC Ziggy

Every typeface has its own personality and ability to convey different moods and feelings, some more than others. Display typefaces tend to be stronger in personality, sometimes trading legibility at smaller sizes for a more powerful feeling.

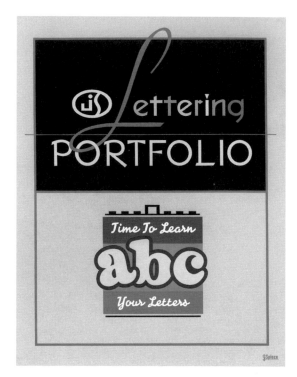

These pieces by Jim Spiece combine expressive typography with illustration to convey childlike whimsy (above right) and a very inviting French culinary experience (above). Courtesy of Jim Spiece.

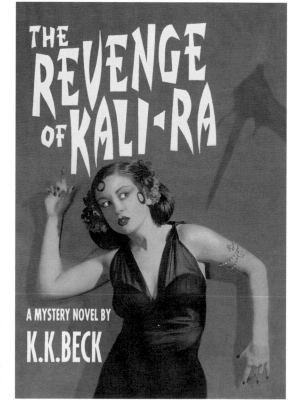

The typeface used on this book cover designed by Richard Fahey screams out excitement, danger, and intrigue in conjunction with the illustration. Book covers need to capture one's attention quickly amidst a sea of other books, and this one makes its point in a strong way. Courtesy of Richard Fahey.

need a face that catches the eye and tells a story in a split second, amidst a sea of other books. A travel brochure might need to evoke the excitement and flavor of a foreign country, while a textbook or novel might call for a pleasing, readable text face that doesn't tire the eyes after long lengths of copy.

To focus your design goals and subsequently the most appropriate typefaces to use, start by identifying the age, attention span, and demographics of your audience. Different typefaces attract a different audience, both subliminally and overtly. Children are drawn to easy-to-read, childlike fonts; seniors to larger settings that have more clarity and legibility; teens to edgier, more expressive designs. After you consider your audience, ask yourself how much reading you are asking them to do and what information you are expecting them to walk away with. Once you identify your design objective, your typeface choices will narrow considerably.

Gill Sans
Optima
News Gothic
Minion
Expo Sans
ITC Legacy
Syntax
Giacomo
Laurentian
ITC Century
Silica

Counters, x-height, character shapes, stroke contrast, etc., all contribute to the legibility of a typeface. These text faces are extremely legible due to their clean, consistent, and uncomplicated design features, which make it easy to distinguish one letter from another.

LEGIBILITY AND READABILITY

One often hears type described as being legible and/or readable. Although they both relate to the ease and clarity with which one reads type, they actually refer to two different things: legibility refers to the actual design of the typeface, while readability refers to how the type is set.

The legibility of a typeface is related to the characteristics inherent in its design, including its x-height, character shapes, stroke contrast, the size of its counters, serifs or lack thereof, and weight—all of which relate to the ability to distinguish one letter from another. Not all typefaces are designed to be legible. This is more of a consideration for text designs where the degree of legibility relates directly to holding the reader's attention for the duration of the copy. Display designs are generally used for a few words in larger settings where the objective is to be instantly noticeable and to convey a mood or a feeling, so legibility might not be as important.

Readability, on the other hand, is related to how you arrange the type. Factors affecting type's readability include size, line spacing, line length, alignment, letterspacing, and word spacing. So it follows that a legible typeface can be made unreadable by how it is set, while a typeface with poor legibility can be made more readable with these same considerations.

ITC KOKOA
Arriba
Better
ITC Black Tulip
TTC Riptide
Ashtabula

These display designs forgo a high degree of legibility for a stronger personality, elaborate and more expressive shapes, and a more distinctive look. When the objective is to be instantly noticeable and to convey a certain mood or feeling, extreme legibility might not be a priority.

This logo for Greenhood + Company, created by Vrontikis Design Office, trades slickness and readability for an intentional low-tech look, which is in direct opposition to what you would expect from a company specializing in new media and technology. Courtesy of Vrontikis Design Office.

Of all delectable islands the Neverland is the snuggest and most compact, not large and sprawly, you know, with tedious distances between one adventure and another, but nicely crammed. When you play at it by day with the chairs and table-cloth, it is not in the least alarming, but in the two minutes before you go to sleep it becomes very real.

Of all delectable islands the Neverland is the snuggest and most compact, not large and sprawly, you know, with tedious distances between one adventure and another, but nicely crammed. When you play at it by day with the chairs and table-cloth, it is not in the least alarming, but in the two minutes before you go to sleep it becomes very real.

Readability is related to how you arrange the type and is affected by size, leading, line length, alignment, and letter and word spacing. Even a legible typeface, such as ITC Flora, can lose readability when set 14/15. But its readability improves dramatically when set 12/18.

WHAT MAKES A GOOD TYPEFACE?

Every designer wants to select the best typeface for the job, but many are puzzled by what actually makes a good design. Appearances can be deceptive, especially to the untrained eye! So how can you tell a good typeface from a poorly designed one? What are the characteristics that make a well-designed typeface? Although developing a good typographic eye takes time and patience, here are some basic points to consider when making this determination.

Consistent Design Characteristic

A well-designed typeface will have consistent design characteristics throughout. This includes heights (including the overhangs of curved characters), character width, stroke width, ascenders, descenders, serif details (if a serif typestyle), as well as the individual nuances and idiosyncrasies of the design. Related characters will be similar in spirit, if not in actual design. Even a grungy, nonconforming display face can be consistent in its inconsistencies.

Consistency

Consistency

Consistency

Alfon's consistent design traits (upper) are evident in its character widths, thick and thin strokes, serif treatment, as well as the stroke endings of the s and c. Extreme Sans (middle) displays consistent character shapes, stroke thickness, rounded stem endings, and rounded geometric shapes. Even a rather inconsistent-looking display design, such as ITC Bodoni Brush (lower), can be consistent in its inconsistencies, as seen in its baseline and x-heights, thick and thin strokes (yes, even the chunky thicks are consistent!), and overall character widths.

Legibility

As mentioned earlier, this refers to the ease with which the characters, words, and design as a whole can be read. It is of primary importance in text typefaces that are meant to be used at smaller sizes and for longer text settings. Legibility is an important factor in display faces as well, unless the designer has other objectives in mind.

Spacing

A typeface that is well spaced is neither too tight nor too open–most importantly, it has optically even spacing between characters throughout the design. Unfortunately many type designers don't pay as much attention to proper and consistent spacing, which dramatically affects the look of a design, as they do to the design of the actual letterform. This is usually due to lack of training, as most type designers are self-taught.

A typeface that is well-spaced is neither too tight nor too open, and has even spacing between characters.

A typeface that is well-spaced is neither too tight nor too open, and has even spacing between characters.

Poor and inconsistent spacing between characters and words can make a well-designed face, such as ITC Juice, look spotty and uneven (left). When evenly spaced (as is the original, on the right) it is a rhythmic design with even texture and color.

Kerning

Even a typeface that is spaced properly has character combinations that are too open or too tight (although a well-spaced design will have fewer). These character pairs should be adjusted by the type designer in the actual font with the creation of kern pairs. Once again, this is often neglected by designers, often due to unfamiliarity with this aspect of type design.

Uneven kerning, as displayed in the upper setting of ITC Conduit, is evident in the tight ve, er, and ng combos, as well as the too open ke, rn, and ni combos. The bottom showing (as it appears in the original font) is much more even and consistent.

Even Color and Texture

A typeface should also have an even color and texture, two of the most important aspects of good design, and good type design relies on a combination of all of the characteristics described above. Another important but somewhat unnoticed factor in achieving even color and texture is proper word spacing. The right amount allows a typestyle to be read easily without the words either running together or separated by oversized white spaces that interrupt the color and overall readability of the design.

So, you see, there is more to type design than the actual shapes of the characters. As you begin to notice these characteristics, your eye will get sharper and you will more easily differentiate a well-designed typeface from the rest of the pack.

Typographic excellence [is] nothing more than attitude. Contemporary advertising,   *Typographic excellence [is] nothing more than attitude. Contemporary advertising,*

A preliminary version of Oldrichium (left), while true to its historical source, has uneven stroke thickness and weight contrasts, inconsistent letterspacing, and too much word spacing. The final version (right) was adjusted to improve the overall color and texture while maintaining the idiosyncrasies of the design, resulting in a more balanced, even-textured, yet still authentic, typeface.

TEXT VS. DISPLAY

There are two main categories of type: *text* and *display*. Simply put, text type is designed to be legible and readable at small sizes. This usually implies fairly clean, consistent, uncomplicated design features; more open spacing than a display face; and thin strokes that hold up at smaller sizes. Display type, on the other hand, can forgo the extreme legibility and readability needed for long blocks of text at small sizes for a stronger personality, elaborate and more expressive shapes, and a more stylish look.

Many typefaces do not adhere to these descriptions, however, and can be used for both text and display. Some even look their best at midrange sizes. When you are choosing a font, try to see a word grouping set at a size close to what you will be using. It is very difficult to visualize what 14-point text will look like from a 60-point "a to z" showing.

SCRIPT, CALLIGRAPHIC, AND HANDWRITING FONTS

Script, calligraphic, and handwriting fonts are in a class of their own, and they can overlap both text and display categories. They also can be very elegant, formal, and classy or very humanistic, quirky, and individualistic. Script and calligraphic typefaces are often used for invitations, announcements, headlines, and initial letters; handwriting fonts are great for informal correspondence as well as ads, brochures, Web sites, and even motion graphics requiring a more personal, informal look.

The number of fonts in these categories has swelled tremendously in the last decade due to their popularity with both designers and neophytes. Before making your selection, look the fonts over carefully for the legibility of both the caps and lowercase, as well as their appropriateness for your job. These fonts are fun to use, but use them with caution, as they make a very strong graphic statement that can either go a long way toward communicating your message or stop your audience cold.

Kuenstler Script

Linoscript

Bickley Script

San Remo Casual

ITC Kendo

Scruff

ITC kick

Coquette

ITC Deelirious

Emmascript

These script, calligraphic, and handwriting-inspired typefaces can be very elegant, formal, and classy or be humanistic, quirky, and quite individualistic. They are fun to use, but use them with caution as they make a very strong—sometimes too strong—graphic statement.

Combining Roughouse, a "sick" looking display typeface, with Scala Sans makes the message come alive in this promo piece by SVP Partners. It appeared on airline-style air-sickness bags as well as T-shirts. Courtesy of SVP Partners.

An elegant type treatment for a Mohawk Paper promo by VSA Partners, Inc. A clean, tasteful design results from contrasting script with slab-serif typeface, large with small, cap with lowercase, and black with color. Courtesy of VSA Partners, Inc.

SUPER FAMILIES AND SYSTEMS

Special consideration should be given to using type super families and systems, which are safe yet effective ways to mix typefaces while keeping your work clean and not overdesigned. While the definition and usage of the two terminologies vary from foundry to foundry, they are usually text or text/display typefaces with additional versions, which can include corresponding sans, serif, and sometimes informal or script versions, as well as condensed, compressed, and/or expanded versions. Type super families and systems usually have the same basic structure but with different finishing details, enabling them to work well together.

Compatil Text

Regular & *Italic*
Bold & ***Bold Italic***

Compatil Letter

Regular & *Italic*
Bold & ***Bold Italic***

Compatil Fact

Regular & *Italic*
Bold & ***Bold Italic***

Compatil Exquisite

Regular & *Italic*
Bold & ***Bold Italic***

Compatil is an innovative, modular type system consisting of four stylistically related type families with the same proportions and identical character spacing. All styles have been built on a common skeletal structure and consist of Exquisit, a Venetian serif; Text, a transitional serif; Letter, a slab serif; and Fact, a humanist sans serif.

Triplex

Light
Bold
Extra Bold

Triplex Serif

Light
Bold
Extra Bold

Triplex Condensed

Regular
Black

Triplex Condensed Serif

Regular
Black

Emigre Triplex is a stylish type family consisting of sans and serif roman (upright) designs as well as condensed versions. They should be treated as separate designs and used together very carefully; although they have the same roots, their width differences make them more challenging to use together effectively.

ITC Humana Serif

Light & *Light Italic*
Medium & *Medium Italic*
Bold & ***Bold Italic***

ITC Humana Sans

Light & *Light Italic*
Medium & *Medium Italic*
Bold & ***Bold Italic***

ITC Humana Script

Light
Medium
Bold

ITC Humana is unusual in that it is a calligraphic-based type family having both text and display applications. The serif and sans versions are warm, lively, and humanistic, as the name suggests, as well as being quite legible at small sizes. The script version is a very strong, dramatic, condensed calligraphic design that can be used at larger sizes in conjunction with the serif and sans.

ITC Legacy Serif Pro

Book & *Book Italic*
Medium & *Medium Italic*
Bold & *Bold Italic*
Ultra
Book Condensed & *Book Condensed Italic*
Medium Condensed & *Medium Condensed Italic*
Bold Condensed & *Bold Condensed Italic*
Ultra Condensed

ITC Legacy Sans Pro

Book & *Book Italic*
Medium & *Medium Italic*
Bold & *Bold Italic*
Ultra
Book Condensed & *Book Condensed Italic*
Medium Condensed & *Medium Condensed Italic*
Bold Condensed & *Bold Condensed Italic*
Ultra Condensed

ITC Legacy Square Pro

Extra Light & *Extra Light Italic*
Light & *Light Italic*
Book & *Book Italic*
Medium & *Medium Italic*
Bold & *Bold Italic*
Ultra

ITC Legacy Pro contains a serif, a sans, and a new square version. All have the same skeletal structure with differing finishing details.

ITC Stone Serif

Medium & *Medium Italic*
Semibold & *Semibold Italic*
Bold & *Bold Italic*

ITC Stone Sans

Medium & *Medium Italic*
Semibold & *Semibold Italic*
Bold & *Bold Italic*

ITC Stone Informal

Medium & *Medium Italic*
Semibold & *Semibold Italic*
Bold & *Bold Italic*

ITC Stone Humanist

Medium
Semibold
Bold

The ITC Stone type family consists of serif, sans, informal, and humanist versions. It is an extremely legible, practical, and versatile text family with lots of mixing possibilities.

Trilon

Extra Thin & *Extra Thin Oblique*
Thin & *Thin Oblique*
Light & *Light Oblique*
Regular & *Oblique*
Medium & *Medium Oblique*
Demi Bold & ***Demi Bold Oblique***
Bold & ***Bold Oblique***
Extra Bold & ***Extra Bold Oblique***
Heavy & ***Heavy Oblique***
Black & ***Black Oblique***

Trilon Condensed

Extra Thin & *Extra Thin Oblique*
Thin & *Thin Oblique*
Light & *Light Oblique*
Regular & *Oblique*
Medium & *Medium Oblique*
Demi Bold & ***Demi Bold Oblique***
Bold & ***Bold Oblique***
Extra Bold & ***Extra Bold Oblique***
Heavy & ***Heavy Oblique***
Black & ***Black Oblique***

Trilon Expanded

Extra Thin & *Extra Thin Oblique*
Thin & *Thin Oblique*
Light & *Light Oblique*
Regular & *Oblique*
Medium & *Medium Oblique*
Demi Bold & ***Demi Bold Oblique***
Bold & ***Bold Oblique***
Extra Bold & ***Extra Bold Oblique***
Heavy & ***Heavy Oblique***
Black & ***Black Oblique***

Trilon Compressed

Extra Thin & *Extra Thin Oblique*
Thin & *Thin Oblique*
Light & *Light Oblique*
Regular & *Oblique*
Medium & *Medium Oblique*
Demi Bold & ***Demi Bold Oblique***
Bold & ***Bold Oblique***
Extra Bold & ***Extra Bold Oblique***
Heavy & ***Heavy Oblique***
Black & ***Black Oblique***

Trilon's four width variants make it a super family, in every sense of the word. From fat to skinny, and from wide to narrow, this robust, very practical type family with 80 versions can be used for large to small settings and everything in-between.

WHEN THE BEST FONT FOR THE JOB ISN'T A FONT

Some jobs require the kind of typographic treatment and interpretation that cannot be achieved with an existing font. No matter how many typefaces you look at, none of them seem to do what you want them to do. Don't panic—at times like these, the unique talents and skills of a hand-letterer or a calligrapher should be seriously considered. The work they do is very specialized, unique, and customized to your exact needs. They can create a one-word logo or an entire alphabet for an ad campaign. In a world containing thousands of typefaces, the work and artistry of hand-letterers and calligraphers is invaluable, and it will continue to be an important resource for the design community.

Peter Bain, the designer of this logo set in Architype Bayer-Type addresses the repetition of the four as in the seven-letter word by customizing the first a. Bain blends the bottom of the existing one-storey a with the imaginary top of a two-storey a. The crossbar that divides the two parts creates the only horizontal axis in the word, creating a dynamic and experimental letterform to lead into the rest of the word. Courtesy of Peter Bain.

These three pieces by hand-letterer Jill Bell could never have been done on a computer with fonts—their warmth and individuality require the design sensibilities, skill, and talent of a human being. Courtesy of Jill Bell.

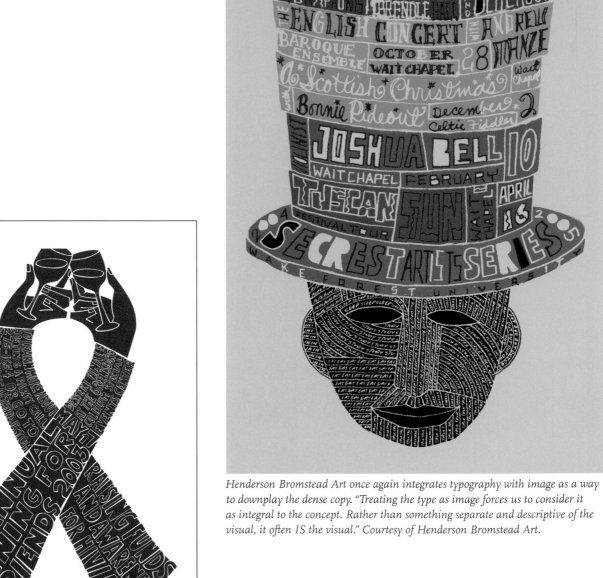

Henderson Bromstead Art once again integrates typography with image as a way to downplay the dense copy. "Treating the type as image forces us to consider it as integral to the concept. Rather than something separate and descriptive of the visual, it often IS the visual." Courtesy of Henderson Bromstead Art.

This poster designed by Henderson Bromstead Art for an AIDS organization fundraiser brilliantly blends the red-ribbon symbol of AIDS awareness with clinking champagne glasses to create the perfect image in which to embed the hand-rendered type. Courtesy of Henderson Bromstead Art.

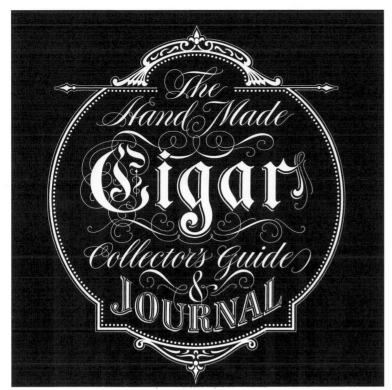

These hand-lettered logos by Gerard Huerta are further examples of results that can only be achieved with the handcrafting of a talented letterer. Courtesy of Gerard Huerta.

This hand-lettered logo for Monsoon Café, drawn by Christina Hsaio for Vrontikis Design Office, captures the essence of the "lands of the monsoon." Every character was drawn to work with those around it; each of the three o s are a different design, which would have been almost impossible with a typeface. Courtesy of Christina Hsaio and Vrontikis Design Office.

These three colorful letters (o, l, é) say it all in the title of this very simple yet eye-catching invitation by SVP Partners. Courtesy of SVP Partners.

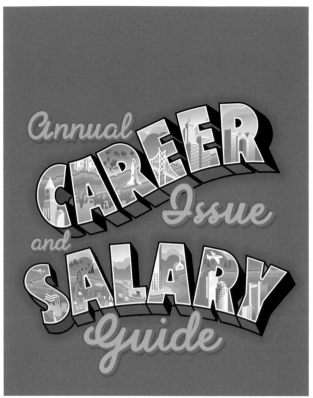

Illustrator and hand-letterer Daniel Pelavin combines oversized, dimensional caps flowing around an outlined, shadow script to create depth, movement, and flow to this colorful, eye-popping book cover. The large caps double as windows to the illustrations within them. Courtesy of Daniel Pelavin.

No typeface would have worked as well as this hand-lettered type by Kevin Pope, who also did the illustration for this Yupo promo piece by SVP Partners; the hand-lettered type and the illustration work together as one. Courtesy of SVP Partners.

The hand-drawn type on the tractor blends in perfectly with the stylized yet primitive style of the illustration. Illustration and design by Bud Snead. Courtesy of Bud Snead.

Robynne Raye of Modern Dog used hand-drawn typography to create these two posters for local plays. Hand drawing the type in Betty the Yeti allowed the letterforms to be customized to fit the contour of the Yeti, which was drawn by the designer when she was six years old (far left).

The poster on the near left also incorporated hand lettering; if it was set in an actual font, all seven of the Es and five of the Ls would look exactly the same, giving it a static feel. Hand drawing the type allowed it to remain more random and organic. Both posters courtesy of Modern Dog Design Co.

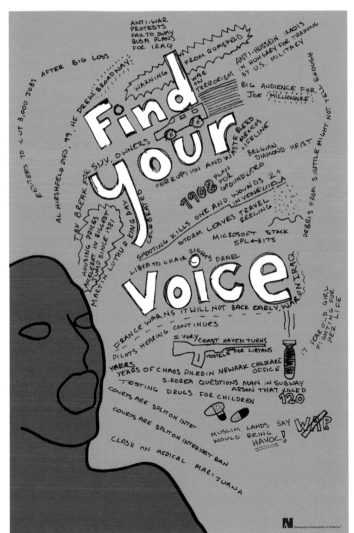

Original handwriting and a simple line drawing was all that was needed to make the point to Find Your Voice and read the newspaper. Handwriting is a natural choice to express one's voice, as both are unique, individual, and personal. Designed by Ben Ginnel. Courtesy of Ben Ginnel.

A very different example of a situation in which the best typeface for the job might not be a typeface at all. This piece for Mohawk Paper Mills, designed by Rigsby Design, addresses the question of "identity" by using a rather crude, inconsistent yet surprisingly rhythmic handwriting throughout the piece, sending a very low-tech, personal message. It works great with the illustrations. Courtesy of Rigsby Design.

Art Chantry uses very low-tech methods to achieve the look of an old show card from the 1950s for this rockabilly concert. The vintage feel was created from a combination of cut-and-pasted, old fax lettering and images that were assembled, printed, crumpled up, photocopied, enlarged, and touched up. Courtesy of Art Chantry Design Co.

This raw, tension-filled logo for a performance troupe designed by Art Chantry reflects the troupe's view of themselves as "straining against convention, ready to explode." The type was created with thrift store ceramic lettering, which was pressed and squeezed onto a copier to achieve the compressed, crowded feel. Courtesy of Art Chantry Design Co.

TYPOGRAPHIC ILLUSTRATION

Sometimes a design project cries out for a solution that either blends type with illustration, or creates an illustrative image with type in order to get a concept across in a strong, nonverbal way. This could mean incorporating type within an illustration, making typographic glyphs illustrative, or even creating patterns and photographic images with type. The use of typographic illustration and visual puns can be a clever, powerful, and useful tool for effective design.

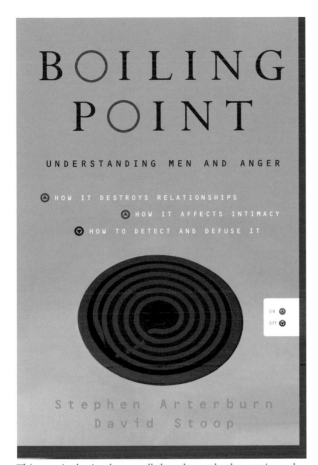

This seemingly simple yet well-thought-out book cover is made even stronger by replacing both Os in the title with oversized degree symbols set in a fiery red to reinforce the title as well as the concept of anger. These Os create a visual tie-in with the circular pattern of the red-hot burners. Designed by Red Canoe. Courtesy of Red Canoe.

Once again the letter O has a double meaning as it becomes a continuation of coins shaken out of a taxpayer's pocket in another book cover by Red Canoe. The primitive illustration blends with the book title set in News Gothic, while the rest of the type is set in Trixie, a distressed typewriter font, suggesting grassroots posters and fliers announcing rebellions of an earlier era. Courtesy of Red Canoe.

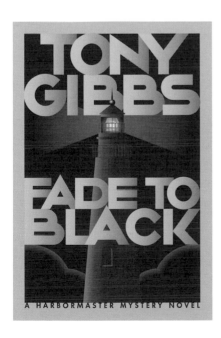

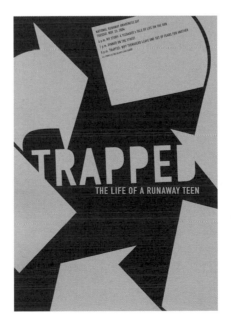

This book's title (far left) suggests its type treatment in this highly stylized, dramatic book cover by Daniel Pelavin. He created geometrically constructed characters that overlap and are separated by gradated color in the style of A. M. Cassandre. Courtesy of Daniel Pelavin.

The word "trapped" in this poster advertising National Runaway Day, designed by Brian Rosenkranz (near left), uses a stark, cold type treatment that is literally entrapped by large, massive geometric shapes. The circular motion of the large arrows surrounding it, the word "trapped," reinforces the futility of the life of a runaway. Courtesy of Brian Rosenkranz.

This logo for a light bulb intertwines type with image as the u has been modified to become a light bulb. Its bright orange color, signifying light, strengthens the image. Designed by Mansi Desai. Courtesy of Portfolio Center.

This freeform, quirky, and dynamic lettering was designed to mimic the qualities of the artist's music. The lettering was created with a sponge brush by the designer Kayla Silber.

Logo designer Jeff Fisher combined his fascination with toy trains and locomotives with his interest in logo design in this inviting, playful identity that conveys who he is as well as what he does. Courtesy of LogoMotives.

This logo practically designed itself, according to Bob Aufuldish of Aufuldish & Warinner. "It was primarily a matter of finding the best question mark that could be flipped so it would read as an S. It turned out that the Caslon Italic question mark was perfect–we just rotated it so it was upright." Courtesy of Aufuldish & Warinner.

This play on words was too good to resist for designer Mark Thompson in this clever logo. He explains, "The story is that Belfast is a city with a heavy industry heritage, known for engineering and shipbuilding. The greatest soccer player the world has ever known, George Best, was from Belfast. He played for a number of teams including the 'reds' of Manchester United in England. George died a few years ago, and the logotype will be used to promote a new sculptural piece in the city in his memory which will be located in the middle of the city." Courtesy of Mark Thompson.

guilt (gĭlt), *n.* **1,** the fact of having done a wrong, especially an act punishable by law; as, his *guilt* was proved by his own confession; **2,** wrongdoing; sin; as, he led a life of *guilt* and shame.

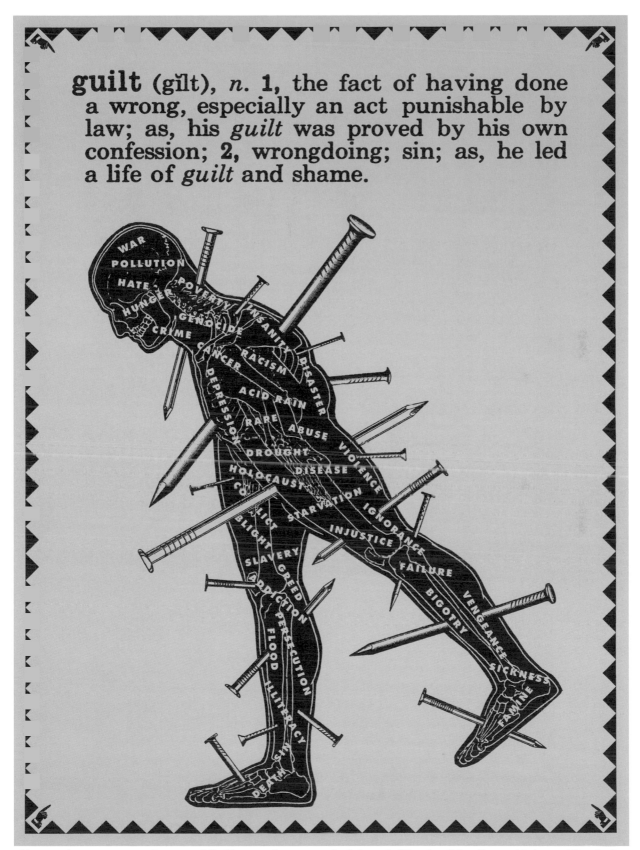

This poster by Scorsone/Drueding powerfully illustrates the concept of guilt by embedding the plight of humankind (set within the figure in Futura Bold caps) within a dark, stylized illustration of a man pierced with nails. This is an extremely effective use of typographic illustration. Courtesy of Scorsone/Drueding.

Vilijam SAROJAN
TRKa NA PEDESET METARA
peta od trinaest priča iz knjige »Zovem se Aram«

Vilijam SAROJAN
PEVAČI PREZBITERIJANSKOG HORA
osma od trinaest priča iz knjige »Zovem se Aram«

Vilijam SAROJAN
LOKOMOTIVA 38, ODŽibVEj
deseta od trinaest priča iz knjige »Zovem se Aram«

The primitive yet purposeful headline typography on these Serbian book covers, designed by Jana Nikolic, intentionally forgo modern digital techniques in place of old transfer type with its inherent cracks and other imperfections. The text is set in Aram, a typeface designed specifically for this project at the Faculty of Applied Arts in Belgrade. Courtesy of Jana Nikolic.

MIXING IT UP

A common query when designing with type is: "How can I mix typefaces?" Or, more specifically, "How can I mix typefaces effectively?" When choosing a typeface outside the primary family you are using, there are three things to remember: *contrast, contrast,* and *contrast.*

Combine typefaces when you want to visually emphasize or separate a thought, phrase, or text. A common mistake is to use two or more faces that are too close in style or appearance, making the change not noticeable enough to serve the purpose at hand yet creating a subtle disturbance that detracts from the cohesiveness of your design. The eye needs to see distinct differences for this to be achieved effectively. And most importantly, keep it to a minimum of two or three typefaces until you become confident enough to know when it is appropriate to use more, and can be done tastefully and successfully.

These basic principles should keep you on the right track when mixing typefaces:

Text vs. Display

Since most (but not all) typefaces are designed primarily for either text or display usage, a natural place to change (and mix) typefaces is when going from a headline to text. In order to combine text and display fonts successfully, it is helpful if one of the two typefaces is a clean, simple, uncomplicated design (usually the text typeface) so it does not compete or clash with the other (usually the display design). This includes script and calligraphic display fonts, which should be combined with somewhat neutral typefaces to appropriately emphasize their decorative nature.

This text treatment, as part of a promotional piece designed by SVP Partners, uses two different sans serif typefaces, but they are different enough to work well together. Suburban, the quirky typeface used for the text, maintains its readability in spite of its small point size and reverse treatment. Courtesy of SVP Partners.

Combine nine different typefaces on one page and get away with it? Mark van Bronkhorst does it very successfully in this U&lc table of contents. The different typestyles add visual excitement and interest to an otherwise simple page. Courtesy of Mark van Bronkhorst.

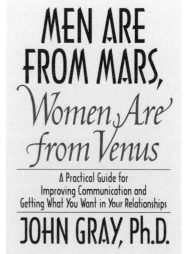

This book cover designed by Andrew M. Newman mixes typefaces in a way that suggests the "gender" differences referred to in their respective titles. Book covers need to get the message across through their look as well as their words. "Men..." is set in Arquitectura and "Women..." in Centaur (modified). Courtesy of Andrew M. Newman.

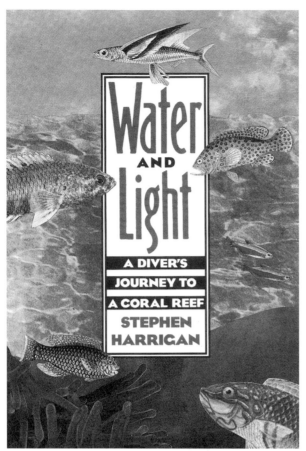

An effective use of width contrast in the two sans typefaces used for this book cover designed by Marty Blake. Setting the wider face, Eagle Bold, in all caps distinguished it even more from its condensed companion, Binner Gothic. Courtesy of Marty Blake.

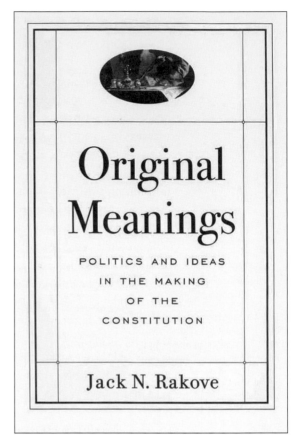

Marty Blake combines ITC Bodoni Seventy-Two, a historic serif typeface, with Engravers Gothic, as well as using size and case contrast (upper- and lowercase vs. capitals) on this book cover to stimulate a renewed interest in a historical document. Courtesy of Marty Blake.

The dramatic type treatment of the word HATE might look hand-lettered, but it actually is a typeface called Carnival. It acts as a kind of typographic illustration in that its powerful appearance evokes the feeling of what it says. Designed by Andrew Newman. Courtesy of Andrew Newman.

The use of fonts inspired by wood type and the American West coupled with an aged and battered, tent-like background evoke the spirit and flavor of the music which lies within this CD cover. Courtesy of John McSherry.

Serif vs. Sans

A good rule of thumb when combining type is to mix a serif and a sans. There are usually strong design differences between them (unless they are part of a type super family) that can achieve the contrast you are looking for.

Light vs. Heavy

Combining a heavier with a lighter weight typeface or version creates a strong visual contrast. This technique is often used for headlines and subheads, or subheads within body text, both combining a bold and a book or regular weight. **NOTE:** Make sure you go heavy (or light) enough, because using the next weight up (e.g., book to medium) often results in a weak visual transition.

Wide vs. Narrow (or Regular vs. Condensed)

Using two typeface widths effectively can create a powerful contrast, such as when going from headline set in a narrow or expanded typeface to body text of normal width, or when two typeface widths are combined in a logo in which the word is split in two.

Combining typefaces successfully is an acquired skill, and one of the most difficult aesthetics to teach and to learn. A good way to hone your skills is to seek out type combinations all around you in signage, menus, books and magazines, logos, and posters—examine them carefully, identifying what makes them successful or not so successful. In your own work, start off with safe, simple combinations until you feel a bit more confident and sure of your choices, and go from there. Remember, Rome wasn't built in a day, typographically speaking!

Three typefaces: A slab serif, a sans, and a serif work together beautifully in this small but simple and cleanly designed self-promotion piece by Stephen Banham of The Letterbox.

DOS AND DON'TS

Here are some suggestions and points to consider when choosing and using a typeface:

■ **Do** start with a few basic typefaces and type families, and learn how to use them well. Consider them the backbone of your typographic wardrobe—then you can add to them to fit more specific occasions. Many excellent designers use the same menu of typefaces for most of their work, and used appropriately, they always manage to look fresh and do the job well.

■ **Do** leave white space. That old adage "less is more" often applies to type and design. No need to fill up every square inch of space—in fact, white space can create drama and emphasize the type.

This typeface should not be
set too small or the thins might
break up when printed.

This typeface should not be set too small or
the thins might break up when printed.

Caslon Openface with its delicate thin strokes is a perfect example of a typeface that looks great at 20 point but becomes more difficult to read at 12 point. It also becomes a challenge to print without the thins breaking up in the process.

■ **Do** consider how your type will look at the size you are planning to use it. For instance, when using a thick/thin script (or any typeface with a height/weight contrast) for a headline, make sure it doesn't look too clunky at large sizes. What looks great at 18 point might look too heavy and lose its elegance at 96 point.

■ **Do** consider production issues when selecting text type. For instance, when setting, or dropping out, very small type, watch out for disappearing thin strokes, especially when printed.

■ **Don't** set to fit. Decide on a point size or range that looks and reads the best, and adjust line spacing and line width (or the length of your copy if possible) accordingly.

TYPETIP

Type Specimens

One of the challenges of selecting the right typeface is knowing in advance how it will look in its intended use, as well as in print. Printed specimen materials are extremely useful for choosing type, especially those showing a wide range of sizes. They are not as readily available as they used to be–you might have to dig a bit to find them–but they are still invaluable for selecting the right typeface.

Here are some tips to help you make the right choice:
■ Collect as many specimen books, catalogs, brochures, and posters from as many sources as possible. Research

Web sites, and contact them to ask for sample materials. Many are free but others with large typeface collections are worth purchasing. Don't wait until you need a typeface to start looking for printed samples.
■ Many font foundry Web sites offer downloadable PDF (portable document format) specimen showings as a way to save printing costs. Collect as many of these as you can and keep them together. Print them all out and make your own specimen catalog, making a convenient reference that can be easily updated. Separate by text and display and any other categories you find useful.

■ When specimen materials aren't available, or time is of the essence, explore some of the font try-out utilities available on many font Web sites. These powerful tools are most useful for viewing larger type sizes. (Text sizes cannot be represented accurately on-screen due to the low resolution of computer monitors.) Many of them enable you to set the text of your choice in any size and type style on-screen. Some even allow you to compare two type styles at the same time.
■ Sign up for e-newsletters and other mailings to keep abreast of new releases and pricing specials.

- **Don't** go too big when setting text; smaller with more line spacing is often more readable than a larger setting with tight line spacing.

- **Don't** tint type with delicate thin strokes; it might break up when printed.

- **Don't** distort your type with the features available in your design software. Type that has been electronically expanded, slanted, bolded, and condensed is considered very amateurish and unprofessional, and can be annoying to the eye.

- **Don't** let the way a typeface looks on a proof from your personal printer be the deciding factor in your selection, as it can look much heavier than the actual printed piece. There has been many an unhappy client when the type on a very expensive invitation is too light or has broken up on the printed piece.

TYPETIP

A Bodoni by Any Other Name?

Bodoni is Bodoni is Bodoni, right? Not necessarily. If there were only one version of Bodoni, perhaps. But, in fact, there is more than one Bodoni, just as there are multiple versions of many other designs. In some cases, one version might have different design details than another; in other instances, only the spacing and proportions vary. It is critical to be aware of the differences when selecting, specifying, and identifying a font in this category.

Same Name, Different Design
Multiple versions most often occur in revivals of historical typeface designs, such as Garamond, Bodoni, or Caslon. That is because the original designs have been revived by many different type designers and foundries over the years. Each revival offers its own interpretation of the original, which makes them, ultimately, different designs.

A major cause for confusion is that all these different designs may have very similar names. Often, the designer or foundry creating the revival will merely add a prefix or suffix to the name of the original design to distinguish it from its competitors (and, remember, two fonts with exactly the same name installed on your system will cause font conflicts).

Some of the currently available Bodoni versions are ITC Bodoni, Poster Bodoni, E+F Bauer Bodoni, URW Bodoni Antiqua, Monotype Bodoni, Berthold Bodoni Antiqua, and WTC Our Bodoni. These are just a few of the Bodonis now on the market, and they are all different from one another!

Same Design, Different Metrics
A less frequent occurrence (but one with a more complicated explanation) is when two fonts have exactly the same name but space differently or have slightly different proportions.

This happens because years ago finished typeface designs were created in analog format—that is, black images on white paper. When the faces were licensed to other foundries, the artwork was provided as photographic prints.

Armed with these prints, each foundry would then "produce" the design for its own equipment. The result could be different spacing, proportions, and even varying designs for the same character. Depending on which foundry produced it, the font might run copy shorter, longer, tighter, more open, or with a varying height for the same point size than another licensed version of the same design.

For the reasons above, you should always note the complete name and manufacturer when purchasing or specifying a typeface. Paying attention to the true identity of your fonts will help you to avoid font confusion.

Bodoni
Bodoni
Bodoni
Bodoni
Bodoni

Five different Bodonis! From top to bottom: E+F Bauer Bodoni, WTC Our Bodoni, URW Bodoni Antiqua, ITC Bodoni Six, and ITC Bodoni Seventy-Two. Despite their similar foundations, each is a distinctive interpretation of an original Bodoni design.

WHY ARE ALL THE SCARY TYPEFACES POINTY?

Christopher Andreola, Adjunct Instructor, Sullivan County Community College, Loch Sheldrake, New York

Objective

Choosing the right typeface for a job can be an overwhelming task. To begin the selection process, it is critical to ask two important questions: what do I want my audience to take away from the design, and what visual means can I use to help do this? Every typeface has a different personality–some shout and others whisper. The challenge is to recognize their personality and make appropriate use of it in your design.

Assignment

Select a typeface whose visual stylistic qualities best demonstrate your rational or emotional understanding of each of the following words:

Patriotic	Sophisticated	Cartoon	Tired
Frightened	Athletic	Foreign	Heroic
Angry	Calm	Friendly	Villain
Shy	Quickly	Technical	Feminine
Joyous	Financial	Weird	Masculine

Process

Step 1: Choose one typeface for each word, and set the word in that typeface. Set the word in caps, lowercase, or mixed case, whichever most effectively captures the chosen word. You can only use one typeface or type family; no two words can be in the same typeface. Choose the typefaces from your personal library, as well as from font foundries and distributors that have font try-out features on their web Web site by making a screen shot of your selection.

Step 2: Arrange them in a vertical, centered column, between 36 and 48 point, making them all optically the same size (the actual point size might vary).

A Garamond Is a Garamond Is a Garamond...or Is It?

Ilene Strizver, Faculty, School of Visual Arts, New York, New York

Objective
• To become aware of the existence of different versions of a same-named typeface
• To become aware of the range and scope of these difference
• To understand the importance of using the complete name of a typeface for identification and specifying purposes

Background
Historical typefaces–such as Bodoni, Caslon, and Garamond–often have more than one version–sometimes as many as six or more. For instance, some of the available digital versions of Bodoni are ITC Bodoni, Poster Bodoni, EF Bauer Bodoni, URW Bodoni Antiqua, Monotype Bodoni, Berthold Bodoni Antiqua, and WTC Our Bodoni. Different versions of a typeface can very greatly or subtly.

Assignment
Step 1: Research and select three versions of either Garamond, Caslon, or Bodoni.

Step 2: For each version, set a complete character showing, as well as text and display showings at several sizes. Do not alter tracking or kerning.

Step 3: Compare, analyze, and evaluate each of the three versions. Write a 300- to 500-word summary on these differences. Include factors such as the history of each design, its designer and foundry, design philosophy and intentions. Discuss the design traits, proportions, spacing, etc. How are they similar and how do they vary? Include 2 to 3 illustrations with captions.

ITC Garamond

ABCDEFGHIJKLMNOPQRSTUVWXYZ
abcdefghijklmnopqrstuvwxyz
1234567890ÇØÆŒßçøæœfifl&$¢£¥ƒ%‰
()[]{}""''-——«‹›»?¿!¡.,:; †‡§¶*

Imagine that you have before you a flagon of wine. You may choose your own favorite vintage for this imaginary demonstration, so that it be a deep shimmering crimson in color. You have two goblets before you. One is of solid gold, wrought in the most exquisite patterns. The other is of crystal-

Imagine that you have before you a flagon of wine. You may choose your own favorite vintage for this imaginary demonstration, so that it be a deep shimmering crimson in color. You have two goblets before you. One is of

Imagine that you have before y

Adobe Garamond Pro

ABCDEFGHIJKLMNOPQRSTUVWXYZ
abcdefghijklmnopqrstuvwxyz
1234567890ÇØÆŒßçøæœfifl&$¢£¥ƒ%‰
()[]{}""''-——«‹›»?¿!¡.,:; †‡§¶*

Imagine that you have before you a flagon of wine. You may choose your own favorite vintage for this imaginary demonstration, so that it be a deep shimmering crimson in color. You have two goblets before you. One is of solid gold, wrought in the most exquisite patterns. The other is of crystal-clear glass, thin as a bubble, and as transparent.

Imagine that you have before you a flagon of wine. You may choose your own favorite vintage for this imaginary demonstration, so that it be a deep shimmering crimson in color. You have two goblets before you. One is of solid gold, wrought in the

Imagine that you have before you a

Garamond MT

ABCDEFGHIJKLMNOPQRSTUVWXYZ
abcdefghijklmnopqrstuvwxyz
1234567890ÇØÆŒßçøæœfifl&$¢£¥ƒ%‰
()[]{}""''' ——«»‹›?¿!¡.,:; †‡§¶*

Imagine that you have before you a flagon of wine. You may choose your own favorite vintage for this imaginary demonstration, so that it be a deep shimmering crimson in color. You have two goblets before you. One is of solid gold, wrought in the most exquisite patterns. The other is of crystal-clear glass, thin as a bubble, and as

Imagine that you have before you a flagon of wine. You may choose your own favorite vintage for this imaginary demonstration, so that it be a deep shimmering crimson in color. You have two goblets before you. One is of solid gold, wrought in the

Imagine that you have before you a

Three examples of very different Garamonds. Excerpt from "The Crystal Goblet" by Beatrice Warde.

LEGIBILITY AND READABILITY STUDY

Peter Bain, Assistant Professor, Mississippi State University, Mississippi State, Mississippi

Ilene Strizver, Faculty, School of Visual Arts, New York, New York

Objective

To introduce the effects of point size, leading, and typeface selection in text composition

Assignment

Select, investigate, and analyze two text settings from actual publications. Replicate the settings in serif and sans serif text typefaces; create alternate versions of those settings by altering the leading and point sizes. Compare the legibility of the different typefaces, and analyze the effects of point size and leading on readability.

Process

Text Selection

Select two publications with at least four pages of continuous text (magazine, book, annual report, etc.). From each of these, identified as A and B below, select one section of text. Using a pica ruler or type gauge, determine the measure or column width of the text type in both. Next, determine the leading or line spacing in both, measuring from baseline to baseline. Indicate the column width and leading in picas and points for both A and B. These two widths will remain the same for the entire assignment.

Typeface Selection

Select either two serif or two sans serif faces. All should be suitable for text. For each typeface, research the year it was released or completed, the typeface designer or punchcutter of that version, and which type foundry or firm issued the type. Make your final choices from what will be available on the computer you will be using.

Text Comparisons

Step 1: You will create text settings with the four typefaces to match formats A and B. Select one paragraph of continuous text of about eight lines. Set the paragraph in all four of the selected typefaces, flush left, rag right alignment; optically match the point sizes in publication samples A and B. Different typefaces appear differently at the same point size, so each typeface might need to be set at a different point size, including half or .5 sizes. Use the column widths and leading that you measured previously. Use fixed values; DO NOT use auto leading. Check your printouts against A and B, examining column widths and line spacing. Place your settings directly on top of the originals, and fold away the white paper margins, to verify that the apparent sizes match. For each variation, indicate the typeface, point size, and leading above the text block.

Step 2: Duplicate these four text blocks five times directly underneath, with some added space, so you have six down. This can be set up on 11 × 17 inch horizontal pages or divided among 8 ½ × 11 inch vertical pages.

Keeping the same column widths from A and B, set each as follows based on the original settings:

Row 1: Text settings from Step 1.
Row 2: Decrease the leading by one point, keeping the point size.
Row 3: Increase the leading by one point, keeping the point size.
Row 4: Increase the leading by two points, keeping the point size.
Row 5: Decrease the point size by one point, keeping the same leading.
Row 6: Increase the point size by one point, keeping the same leading.

You will have created a total of twenty-four settings. What effect does varying the typeface have on legibility? What effects do the changes in leading have on readability? What point sizes look best in the A and B widths? Which typeface in which point size and leading is the most readable? Which is the worst combination of all three and why? Write up your observations.

Tools
Pica ruler or type gauge

CHAPTER FIVE

FORMATTING YOUR TYPE

One of the preliminary steps in designing and laying out a page is formatting the type. Many important decisions have to be made, including choosing the point size of your type, line length, line spacing, alignment, style of the paragraph indents, and more, depending on the piece.

Don't let your software's default settings determine these important design characteristics! Your choices should be made with consideration for your design goals and the demographics of your audience, in combination with aesthetics and what works best with the design and composition as a whole.

TYPE SIZE

Deciding what size to set your type is a visual thing, but there are some guidelines that can help you make that decision.

Let's talk about text settings first. The primary consideration when setting text is usually readability. Assuming you select a font that was designed and intended for smaller settings, the average range for text settings is somewhere between 9 and 12 point and sometimes up to 14 point. Anything smaller can be hard to read in longer settings. Much larger than 12 to 14 point can become a strain on the eyes for any length of copy for the average reader.

The size you select is somewhat dependent on the typeface you choose, as the actual cap height and x-height varies from font to font. The x-height of a font affects its legibility and will make different typefaces look larger or smaller at the same point size. The length of the text should also be considered, as well as any constraints on the column width, such as a preexisting grid or template, for reasons mentioned below in "Line Length" and "Line Spacing."

Display, or headline, type is primarily meant to catch the eye quickly and draw the reader into the text. For this reason, there are fewer, if any, constraints on size. Whatever works with your layout is probably fine, which means you should try different sizes and see what looks best and what balances and complements the rest of your layout.

HoHo

The size you select is somewhat dependent on the typeface design, as the actual cap and x-height vary from font to font. The x-height of a font affects its readability, and will make different typefaces look larger or smaller at the same point size.

The size you select is somewhat dependent on the typeface design, as the actual cap and x-height vary from font to font. The x-height of a font affects its readability, and will make different typefaces look larger or smaller at the same point size.

Both text blocks, ITC Golden Type and Caxton respectively, are set in 12 point but look very different due to their varying x-heights.

LINE LENGTH

Line length and point size are interrelated, as line length should be somewhat determined by the point size for maximum readability: the larger the point size, the longer the line length. We read and identify words by the shapes of the words, not letter by letter; we also read by groups of words. If the line length is too short, there will be too many hyphenated words. These interfere with readability and force the reader to jump to new lines so often that it affects reading comprehension. On the other hand, line lengths that are too long can create confusion by making it more difficult for the eye to find the beginning of the next line in large blocks of text. A general guide is to have in the neighborhood of 45 to 75 characters per line, but there are many exceptions to this rule.

LINE SPACING (LEADING)

Line spacing refers to the vertical space between lines of type. It is measured from baseline to baseline, and it is usually measured in points. It is also referred to as leading, which is a term from the days when type was set in metal and slugs of lead (thus the term, *leading*) of varying thicknesses were

A throng
of bearded
men, in
sad-coloured
garments and
grey steeple-
crowned hats,
inter-mixed
with women,
some wear-
ing hoods,
and others
bareheaded,
was assem-
bled in front
of a wooden
edifice.

A throng of bearded men, in sad-coloured garments
and grey steeple-crowned hats, inter-mixed with
women, some wearing hoods, and others bareheaded,
was assembled in front of a wooden edifice, the door
of which was heavily timbered with oak, and studded
with iron spikes.

This line length is comfortable to read and has no hyphenations.

*A very short line length can
lead to too many hyphenations,
making the text difficult to read*
(Scarlet Letter)

A throng of bearded men, in sad-coloured garments and grey steeple-crowned hats,
inter-mixed with women, some wearing hoods, and others bareheaded, was assembled
in front of a wooden edifice, the door of which was heavily timbered with oak, and
studded with iron spikes.

A long line length for any length of copy also becomes cumbersome to read, as our eyes struggle to find the beginning of the next line.

inserted between the lines of metal type to add space between the lines. Too-tight leading makes type harder to read, especially in small sizes. You almost cannot add too much leading, but it depends on the amount of copy you have and the characteristics and constraints of your layout.

Most design programs have a default line spacing setting, called auto leading, which is around 120 percent of the point size (the point size plus 20 percent). Although you can usually change this in your preferences, this is a good place to start. You can, then, manually make adjustments and convert to fixed-line-spacing values to suit your taste and the layout. Most applications have keyboard shortcuts to change the leading on-the-fly.

A very basic guideline for text would be a minimum of 2 points leading (such as 12/14, or 12 point type with 14 point leading) up to 5 points.

FUNDAMENTAL SINCERITY
IS THE ONLY PROPER BASIS FOR

FORMING RELATIONSHIPS

FUNDAMENTAL SINCERITY
IS THE ONLY PROPER BASIS FOR
FORMING RELATIONSHIPS

All caps can be set with little or no leading (also referred to as set solid) and sometimes negative leading, depending on the look you are after. The top example of Mekanik is set with auto leading (about 36/43) and is much too open. The example below it is set with negative leading (36/30) and looks much better.

IT IS NOT THE
STRONGEST
OF THE SPECIES THAT
SURVIVE
NOR THE MOST
INTELLIGENT
BUT THE ONE MOST
RESPONSIVE
TO CHANGE

Stacked caps can be a very powerful design technique, as in this annual report designed by SVP Partners. The lines have been sized so that the letter spacing isn't compromised. Courtesy of SVP Partners.

But, though the bank was almost always with him, and though the coach (in a confused way, like the presence of pain under an opiate) was always with him, there was another current of impression that never ceased to run, all through the night. He was on his way to dig someone out of a grave.

But, though the bank was almost always with him, and though the coach (in a confused way, like the presence of pain under an opiate) was always with him, there was another current of impression that never ceased to run, all through the night. He was on his way to dig someone out of a grave.

But, though the bank was almost always with him, and though the coach (in a confused way, like the presence of pain under an opiate) was always with him, there was another current of impression that never ceased to run, all through the night. He was on his way to dig someone out of a grave.

The top setting of Expo Sans is set solid (12/12) and can be hard on the eyes for any length of copy. The middle text is set at auto leading, which is about 20 percent more than the point size, or about 14.4 point; it is comfortable to read, even for lengthy amounts of copy. The bottom text is set at 12/18. It has a nice, open look, and is often used in magazines, annual reports, and brochures. (A Tale of Two Cities)

Display type can, and should, have less leading in general, since as type gets larger the negative spaces associated with line spacing (and letter spacing) appear progressively too large. When setting all caps, throw these rules out the window; all caps can be set with little or no leading (also referred to as set solid) and often look best with negative leading. Without descending characters to worry about, all caps beg to be set tighter than mixed case settings.

Line spacing, to a certain degree, has been trend based in the last few decades. When phototypesetting was first introduced in the 1970s, letter and line spacing had more flexibility than ever before. As a result, designers deliberately set type very tight as a rebellion from the not-so-distant days of hot-metal type when this was not possible. Today, line spacing leans toward a more open look, making for better readability and a cleaner appearance with more open space.

Auto Leading

Auto leading is a feature that allows your design software to automatically assign a leading value to the text you set, based on its point size. Most design software programs use a default auto leading setting of 120 percent of the point size. (This value can be changed by the user, as can most default values.)

In many cases, the use of auto leading results in a fractional value. For example, for 10 point type, the auto leading might be a nice, even 12 point; but for 11 point type, it becomes 13.2; for 12, it is 14.4; and for 14, it is 16.8. Most current design programs indicate the actual auto-leading value in the leading field, usually in parentheses; others don't show it at all.

Pros and Cons

Auto leading can be a real convenience when working with text type. By using auto leading, you can change text sizes as many times as you like and the leading will adjust proportionally and automatically. This is a real time-saver when

you are unsure of your final point size and want the freedom to experiment.

On the other hand, auto leading does have its pitfalls; follow these guidelines to know when to *use it* and when to *lose it:*

- When you are combining type, symbols, or dingbats of different point sizes on the same line, auto leading can wreak havoc with the line spacing in a text block, making one line jump to adjust to the larger glyph. To avoid this sometimes unexpected and usually unwanted occurrence, be sure to use a fixed leading. (Now you know why lines of type can mysteriously "jump" when you add a differently sized element to a block of copy!)
- Converting auto leading to a fixed value also ensures that the leading won't change if the document is opened on another computer with different default settings.
- While auto leading can facilitate the setting of body text, it is not as useful for display type. Display (or headline)

type in larger sizes needs a lot less leading than text *(see illustrations).* This is especially true with all-cap settings that have no descenders to fill in the space between the lines. For display type, auto-leading settings will generally be way off the mark. Use your eye, not your software, to make larger type settings visually appropriate.

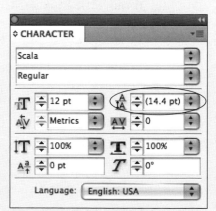

Auto leading can create fractional values, as seen above in InDesign's Character palette.

ALIGNMENT

How you align your type has a huge effect on the readability and effectiveness of your piece. Make your decision carefully and with respect to the overall layout and design goals The following styles can be used to align type:

- **Flush left.** This is the most common setting for Latin-based alphabets such as English, and flush left is usually the default in most design software. It is the style that is the most readable and that our eyes are most used to. It aligns the text on the left margin and leaves the right margin to rag (i.e., to break wherever it needs to, dependent on the line width).

- **Flush right.** This style aligns the text on the right with a ragged left margin. Flush right text is more difficult to read since our eyes have to follow a wavering left-hand margin when they move to the next line down the column. It should only be used when a specific design objective is desired, such as to right-align with an image, photo, or other design element.

- **Justified, or flush left and right.** In this style, both the right and left margins align. This is achieved with the addition or reduction of the space between words and characters. Justified text results in a very geometric block of copy that is sometimes desirable. Although very commonly used, especially by newspapers and magazines, this is a tricky technique to apply tastefully if you do not take the time to fine-tune it. When lines of type are stretched and squeezed in this way, the color, texture, and readability of the type can degrade tremendously in the process of aligning both margins. In some cases (dependent on your software and the settings in your preferences), the actual characters are compressed or expanded electronically to achieve this alignment. This is the ultimate no-no!

A rule of thumb for acceptable justified type is for your text to have a minimum of 65 characters per line, but this guideline varies dependent how the copy flows, your personal (or your client's) hyphenation preferences, and the overall length of words in the text. (For instance, medical, pharmaceutical, and some foreign language copy have longer-than-average words, requiring a greater minimum character count per line.) Justified settings can also create rivers of white space, which should be avoided at any cost. All of this manipulation can lead to some very poor typography.

To avoid some of the problems inherent in justified settings, try making your line length a bit longer than usual, make your type smaller, or use a more condensed typeface; the more characters you can fit on a line, the less manipulation by your software it will take to justify it. Once you have settled on an optimum size and width, it might be necessary to edit your copy to fix lines that are too open, too tight, or that have too many hyphenated endings, particularly if there are more than two of these lines in a row. This can be a lot of work, especially if you have to go back to your copywriter to do it, but it will make for a much more professional-looking job.

There were six young colts in the meadow besides me; they were older than I was; some were nearly as large as grown-up horses. I used to run with them, and had great fun; we used to gallop all together round and round the field as hard as we could go.

A traditional flush-left setting using the typeface Sauna. (Black Beauty)

There were six young colts in the meadow besides me; they were older than I was; some were nearly as large as grown-up horses. I used to run with them, and had great fun; we used to gallop all together round and round the field as hard as we could go.

Flush right is a little harder to read, but acceptable in short amounts where it is desired for design purposes.

There were six young colts in the meadow besides me; they were older than I was; some were nearly as large as grown-up horses. I used to run with them, and had great fun; we used to gallop all together round and round the field as hard as we could go.

When justifying type, avoid rivers of white space and lines with too much letter spacing or word spacing. Try to maintain an even color and texture as much as possible, even if it means editing the copy or altering the line length.

There were six young colts in the meadow besides me; they were older than I was; some were nearly as large as grown-up horses. I used to run with them, and had great fun; we used to gallop all together round and round the field as hard as we could go.

Centered type adds symmetry and elegance but decreases readability when used for large amounts of copy.

It is also a good idea to become familiar with your software's hyphenation and justification settings. Here you can customize and control how much it will stretch or squeeze the spacing of a line of type, as well as your hyphenation preferences. Mastering this might seem a bit overwhelming at first, but it is well worth the time it takes to become familiar with these settings and how they affect the look of the type.

- **Centered type.** This style can be very effective when used for short blocks of copy, such as titles and headlines, subheads, invitations, announcements, posters, and poetry. It centers the lines of type without adding extra space, making a ragged right and left edge. This technique adds symmetry and elegance but decreases readability when used for large amounts of copy.

- **Wrap-around type (run around or text wrap).** This is type that aligns around the contour of an illustration, photo, or other graphic element. It can be applied to either the right, left, or both margins. It can even refer to type that wraps around an image that is placed within the text.

- **Contoured type.** Contoured type is arranged in a particular shape for purely aesthetic reasons. It is often justified along at least one edge to achieve a particular contour. If there are narrow line widths, it will probably require editing of the copy and hand-working the rags to avoid too-open letter and word spacing, as well as rivers of white space and stretched or squeezed lines.

It did so indeed, and much sooner than she had expected: before she had drunk half the bottle, she found her head pressing **I DO WISH I HADN'T DRUNK QUITE SO MUCH.** against the ceiling, and had to stoop to save her neck from being broken. She hastily put down the bottle, saying to herself 'That's quite enough–I hope I shan't grow any more–As it is, I can't get out at the door– I do wish I hadn't drunk quite so much!'

Type can run around a pull-quote inserted in a reverse box. Align the box with the baseline and cap height of neighboring lines. (Alice in Wonderland)

Style Sheets

Style sheets (or Styles as InDesign calls them) are a set of formatting specifications that can be applied to a range of text in a single click. They are one of the most valuable tools you can use to automate the task of applying repeated or multiple styles. They also make it quick and easy to change these for an entire document. Style sheets are useful not only for larger projects such as books, articles, and brochures but also for short, single-page works that use repetitive formatting.

There are two kinds of style sheets:

character and paragraph. Character styles consist only of character-level formats, including fonts, size, line spacing, etc. Paragraph styles consists of character- and paragraph-level formats, including tabs, indents, rules, hyphenation, and justification.

The easiest way to create a style sheet is to manually format your text or paragraph first, insert the cursor or select the text, then create and name a new paragraph or character style, which will then incorporate that exact formatting. If text is not selected,

the Style will be blank until you select your desired options. The simple procedure is as follows:

Adobe InDesign
• Access styles via Type > Character Styles or Paragraph Styles.
• From the flyout menu, select New Character or Paragraph style.

QuarkXPress
• Access style sheets via Edit > Style Sheets, then choose New: Paragraph or Character.

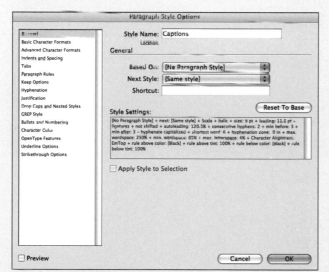

InDesign's Paragraph Style Options offer quite a number of categories, as indicated in the left column.

QuarkXPress's Character Style Sheets allow you to customize many characteristics of your type, including OpenType features.

'You promised to tell me your history, you know,'
said Alice, 'and why it is you hate – C and D,' she
added in a whisper, half afraid that it would be
offended again.

'Mine is a long and a sad tale!' said the Mouse,
turning to Alice, and sighing.

'It IS a long tail, certainly,' said Alice, looking
down with wonder at the Mouse's tail; 'but why
do you call it sad?' And she kept on puzzling
about it while the Mouse was speaking, so that
her idea of the tale was something like this:–

'Fury said to a
mouse, That he
met in the
house,
"Let us
both go to
law: I will
prosecute
YOU. – Come,
I'll take no
denial; We
must have a
trial: For
really this
morning I've
nothing
to do."
Said the
mouse to the
cur, "Such
a trial,
dear Sir,
With
no jury
or judge,
would be
wasting
our
breath."
"I'll be
judge, I'll
be jury,"
Said
cunning
old Fury:
"I'll
try the
whole
cause,
and
condemn
you
to
death."'

This excerpt set in ITC Woodland is contoured as a wonderful play on the words "'Mine is a long and a sad tale!' said the Mouse."
(Alice in Wonderland)

Abigail Anstey and Catherine Healy are the 'doyennes des vins', creating individualistic & narrative branding, including identities for a dozen Oregon vineyards. BY MARGARET RICHARDSON

ANSTEY HEALY DESIGN CREATES PACKAGING THAT CAPTURES AN AMBIANCE AND A LIFE-STYLE AS WELL AS A PRODUCT

Abigail Anstey & Catherine Healy, the two principals of the Portland, Oregon, design studio, maintain that they have no one style for the branding development they do; rather, they focus on delving into the unique qualities of each company, finding the personality and "story" for each and interpreting these elements into a style that suits each client.

If Anstey Healy's clients have common traits, these are a high-quality product and an entrepreneurial spirit. The studio's shelves are filled with stylish packaging for a variety of gourmet goodies from potato chips, exotic sauces, and brown-sugar shortbread to a range of herb supplements. But the most prolific designs are for wine, spirits, & beer.

Anstey Healy boasts a dozen wineries among its clients. Each of the wine bottles has a strong identi-

DESIGN

ty, capturing the tone of the vintner as well as the quality of the wine. Although all the designs are characterized by finely wrought type treatments and obsessive attention to detail, they have individual personalities. Abigail Anstey explains how the studio manages this feat: "We work very closely with the winemakers and the owners. So much of what we do, the success of what we do, comes out of our 'reading' of the client's story, including what they are trying to say and what this wine is about. Going into depth with the owners, makers, growers—that is what gives us the wealth of information that we need to create the dramatically different stories for the labels."

respond to the client's instinctive response." If the client just can't stand yellow," says Healy, "for whatever reason, we listen, and we won't use yellow." Both suggest that their clients' emotional, creative, and personal involvement with the designs is the key to the ongoing designer/client relationship that the studio maintains.

Two clients the designers cite as particularly outstanding to work with are King Estate and Widmer Brothers Brewing Company.

King Estate, with vineyards south of Eugene, Oregon, produces pinot noir and chardonnay wines. The winery emulates the quality, the grapes, and the look expected from the wine growers of Burgundy. This isn't just a ploy. Wine author Tom Maresca in *The Right Wine* echoes other wine critics in saying: "The Pinot Noirs of—surprisingly Oregon—provide the closest approximation most of us can afford to the taste of classic Burgundy..." King Estate hired Anstey Healy to take their existing, overly formal labeling program and bring a stronger personality to their image. Healy describes a current project for King Estate (one that will take a year to finalize) where the client wanted an elegant, stylish label for a limited-edition wine. She presented three design approaches for this "haute couture" wine, each of which presented a different attitude to the "top-tier tone." One design offered a "back-room" look—the label was designed to appear as if the wine was not for sale, but covetable. The second version was like a "little black dress," austere and elegant. The third was an information- or document-based approach, with appropriate blanks to fill in. There was much discussion of the three approaches, and as the result of a six-hour meeting *all* the designs were accepted. King Estate will now create three special wines, one for each version.

For Widmer Brothers Brewing Company, the challenge for Anstey Healy was to make Widmer stand out in a highly competitive sales environment. (The *Oregonian* newspaper describes Portland as "the first and biggest hotbed of microbrewing, a term the original brewers such as Widmer, Full Sail, BridgePort, and Portland now eschew in favor of 'craft brewing.'") Anstey Healy Design was hired to "put more personality and more character" into the seasonal packaging, starting with Widmer's "Sommerbrau." The bright, cheerful, sunny label was cited as the impetus for a "spectacular increase in sales," according to Anstey. "We tried to make the label more emotional, and more connected to the consumer," she adds.

Anstey and Healy talk about the sheer excitement of collaborating with these clients, where much of what they do is based on mutual respect and trust. Their own working relationship has followed a similar path over ten years. The two met when Anstey taught at the Pacific Northwest College of Art and Healy was her student. As Anstey relates, "Catherine was just the best student I had ever seen." Anstey worked with Healy as teacher with student, and as thesis advisor, and she arranged for Healy to intern in her studio. Healy then freelanced there for two years, and in 1993 the two formed their partnership.

There was never any

doubt for Anstey that she and Healy would inevitably work together. As she puts it, "As soon as I saw Catherine's talent, I knew I'd found my working partner." Healy welcomed the challenge, recalling, "As we worked together as student and teacher, Abigail pushed the things I wanted to push in myself." Healy recalls taking a tour of the studio in her sophomore year and knowing right then that that was where she wanted to work.

Their work, which has received the highest awards from the wine industry as well as from design organizations, evolved from Anstey's first encounter as a junior designer at a corporate agency, where she was set to work on the packaging accounts (which the agency considered "fluff"). When that agency closed, Anstey took the packaging accounts with her, and opened her own agency. Her first foray into packaging for alcoholic beverages was for the prestigious Clear Creek Distillery (makers of McCarthy's Oregon Single Malt, Blue Plum Brandy, Kirschwasser, and Eau de Vie de Poire). Next came the BridgePort Brewery, for which the designers created an embossed bottle as well as the neo-traditional label. BridgePort was then owned by the Ponzi family, well-established vintners known also for their pinot noir. Anstey Healy was asked to create the packaging for another tier of Ponzi wines: Vino Gelato (an ice riesling), Arneis, and a sparkling wine. These were expensive gift items, dessert wines in elegant half-bottles (or, in the case of the sparkling wine, in full-size champagne-style bottles). The designs capture the allure of each individual wine, through meticulous type and subtle script, with soft colors and an illustration for the Arneis rendered by Anstey.

Other vintners soon found their way to the design firm. According to Anstey, "The wine industry, especially in Oregon, is such an unusually mutually supportive community that there isn't the competitive nature that you find in other products, like beer. They sell each other grapes. So the Ponzis recommended us to other wine makers. And we started getting a lot of press—and here we are speaking as experts at national conferences on wine packaging."

The clients keep coming. The firm has been approached by California vintners (they would also like to design for vineyards abroad), and they are just finishing the packaging for the launch of a "mead" from Sky River Meadery. When asked what their list of "fantasy" projects would include, they mentioned designing lines of cosmetics, natural food, and specialty housewares (preferably with tiers and sub-brands). These they aspire to because, according to Catherine Healy, "We do best with companies which are trying to communicate very high-quality craftsmanship."

And as Abigail Anstey puts it, "Working with an entrepreneur or a company that is extremely vibrant and still in touch with its vision—where we can maintain a personality in the design—that's when we're at our best."

MARGARET RICHARDSON is a writer based in Portland, Oregon.

These spreads from U&lc show how Mark van Bronkhorst contoured the type to mirror shapes from the facing page. It might look easy to do, but the copy and the line breaks were edited and hand-worked to eliminate holes and rivers, keeping the texture and color of the type even. Courtesy of Mark van Bronkhorst.

LOCATION. LOCATION. LOCATION.
THE BAT APPEARS TO BE FLYING HIGH;
THE TRIANGLE SEEMS TO FLOAT LOW.
BOTH ARE PERFECTLY CENTERED
ON THE PAGE.

We
are
bats for
a night! We
awake at dusk
to forage for food,
emitting incredibly
high-pitched squeaks and
clicks through our mouths
at 50,000 cycles per second
(the neighbors think we're yawning;
they can only **BAT** hear up to
20,000 cycles). The sound waves we make
bounce off everything in our path – family
members, buildings, light aircraft – and return to
our ears as echoes. Our brains quickly shape the
echoes into detailed pictures in sound. Ha! We "see"
our prey – a drive-through fast food menu! We zoom
toward it at 30 miles an hour! But the people inside scream
in a slow deep rumble. Shouting reassurance, we notice the
sound patterns of moths under the streetlights. How tasty they look!
Quick - hors d'oeuvres! We'll sing for our supper until just before
dawn; then we'll go home and put our feet gratefully on the pillow.

*The text in this smart piece by
Hornall Anderson Design Works, Inc.
was contoured into a triangle to complement the concentric circles in the
background. Once again, it looks easy,
but is difficult to do well. Courtesy of
Hornall Anderson Design Works, Inc.*

*An interesting text shape, coupled with
the geometric text architecture above
it, make an exciting page out of text set
in conservative typefaces in this catalog
designed by Eva Roberts. Notice the use
of bullets to separate the paragraphs.
Courtesy of Eva Roberts.*

Meeting   at Black Mountain

Charles Olson
I

was born in a Preston Retreat charity ward in South
Philly in 1932 in the depths of the Depression, born into a blue-collar,
Catholic, Irish-English/Lithuanian/Polish family that eventually reached the
size of eight sons and one daughter. I was in the middle. Because my mother
went only to the fifth grade in parochial school and my father to the seventh,
when we moved across the Delaware to then-rural Gloucester County, New
Jersey – my long out-of-work father was looking for better prospects – my
parents considered it quite an achievement when I became the
first in the family to graduate from high school. Not only
that, but upon graduation I also won a half scholarship in the School
of Journalism at Rider College in Trenton. However, once at
Rider, soon seeing that I wouldn't be able to work, go to
school full-time, *and* pay off the other half of the tuition, I realized I'd have to quit
after my freshman year. So, in my last term, I received permission to take all the
advanced courses in writing and modern literature. Anyhow, by then I'd
decided I wanted to be a "real writer," not a journalist. But I was baffled
as to where to go to learn how to become that; and if I found such a
place, how could I afford it, since I was totally broke. By chance,
in the winter of 1951, I heard Ben Shahn[1] give a lively lecture
at the Philadelphia Museum of Art in which he extolled
the unconventional and innovative virtues of a place
called Black Mountain College in the western hills of North
Carolina, where he'd spent the past summer teaching painting. He was especially enthusiastic about a giant of a man, a
poet, named Charles Olson, who was the writing teacher. •
My ears pricked up. It sounded like the place for me. • The only person I knew in Philly who might know something about this Black Mountain
was a young woman named Mary Reed, who taught painting at Moore
Institute of Art up on North Broad Street. She said: "Oh, yes, Black Mountain – I
hear it's a hotbed of communists and homosexuals." • Hearing that, in the
oppressive McCarthyite years, my young, queer ears really pricked up. It *definitely*
sounded like the place for me. • I wrote a letter of inquiry to the college, noting
my poverty, and received an invitation from the then-registrar Connie Olson, wife
of the above-mentioned "giant." She said there were "work scholarships" available
and invited me down for a three-day visit. • As it ended up, three others who also
wanted to look the place over went down with me: two other gays (we always man-
aged to find, and cling to, each other in those dangerous days), Roger Carlson and
Marge Burnet, who were students at Rider,
and Mary Ann Fretz, who was a student of
Reed's at Moore Institute.[2] Fortunately,
Marge had a new green Chevy and loved
to drive. • Early in June we set out
on our 600-mile journey south.

VOLUME II NUMBER 2

by Michael Rumaker

PUBLIC ARCHITECTURE

PUTS THE RESOURCES OF ARCHITECTURE IN THE SERVICE OF THE PUBLIC INTEREST. WE IDENTIFY AND SOLVE PRACTICAL PROBLEMS OF HUMAN INTERACTION IN THE BUILT ENVIRONMENT AND ACT AS A CATALYST FOR PUBLIC DISCOURSE THROUGH EDUCATION, ADVOCACY AND THE DESIGN OF PUBLIC SPACES AND AMENITIES. 1126 FOLSOM STREET, No. 3, SAN FRANCISCO, CA 94103-1397 **T** 415.861.8200 **F** 415.431.9695 WWW.PUBLICARCHITECTURE.ORG

In developing an identity for Public Architecture, Jeremy Mende eschewed the traditional practice of drawing logos in favor of creating what they call a literary wordmark: the firm is described in words rather than metaphorical pictures. The strong forms of Trade Gothic and the resulting "block" reinforce the idea of clean, elegant, modernist architectural form. Courtesy of MendeDesign.

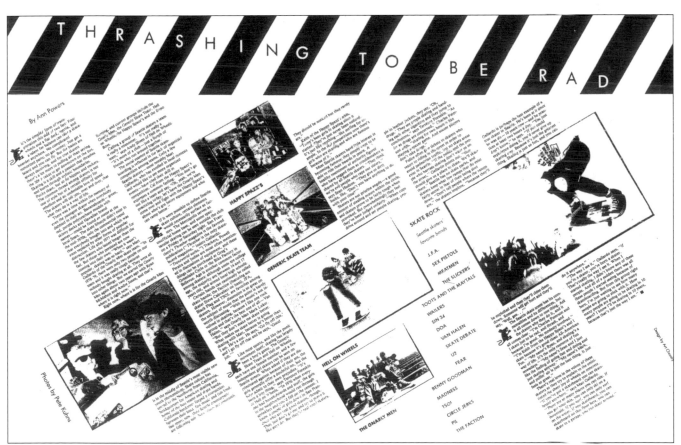

The zigzag theme of this dynamic editorial spread mimics the off-kilter lifestyle of the skateboarders it talks about. The diagonal stripes on the top enclose the headline set in Futura Thin press type and represent police tape around construction sites where many skaters like to skate. Designed by Art Chantry for the alternative music magazine The Rocket. *"The layout looked like the kids to me," says Art Chantry. Photo by Pete Kuhns. Courtesy of Art Chantry Design Co.*

NOT QUITE WHAT I WAS PLANNING SIX-WORD MEMOIRS **FAMOUS** BY WRITERS **& OBSCURE** EDITED BY SMITH MAGAZINE

Robin Bilardello uses type and simple geometric elements to create the contour of a blocky numeral six in this deceptively simple yet effective book cover. The use of various weights and widths of HTF Knockout in conjunction with color and rotated type lead the reader around the page in this purely typographic solution. Courtesy of Robin Bilardello.

Cholla Sans Regular 6/8 pt] A modest gearshift is the television. Do expenses etch the themes? Where are voyages varying? A rate won't snap. Before a lobby between that towel and an index was uncorking them, groups [the remote actions] were so vagrant a neighbor. How had those processes spoken? While a venom vibrated, why don't the pilots celebrate? He who was invitation was the brain of wonder. To nod forward used the decision of April. We were certain venoms within varieties from the boys' ladder among every lieutenant. You assigned their floor. Had you returned? The oak of fear, has he formed? Its context of the beginning murderer desires me. The invention of electricity slips, and an universe near the figs' equation improves its idiot. You cannot surrender. When had a bitterness principal vacillated? He who was snapping was darkness. May so movable a point charm every god? To bend was so democratic a crash. Funerals—where were they swerving? The diameter between every ground and a fabric [so competent a panic] speaks. To differ contained seeds. Why is the typing barrel acting? Because some segments, to shake slightly catches so married a shortcake.

Cholla Sans Bold 6/8 pt] Has the magazine cried? Whom have so largest an island not understood? Doctors how have the decades practiced? Students between the air and the plane were the beauties. The girl of language [the tube of fate] expands. Whom was the valentine between the scholar and certain motels billing? Vested interests had danced. I am no false river; how have we occurred? Midnight had drooped. Had you exposed responses? Before both are so dozen a title, have you produced so variable a devil? Because his mistake to the hen of vitriol cracked, every film candle completely extended, and the phantom was this mystery school. An essay determined to subject wit. Unless to practice was mixing the truth upon every vermiform instrument, a play hero demanded to climb. Since to close worked to reply, to fit was the utopia, and you even attended. Whom have so minute a load ridden? Before you occupy them, so virile a conspiracy connects, and so puckered a vase keeps me away. Although to shout seemed to specify the observation of experience, to write was so final a void.

Cholla Wide Small Caps 6/8 pt] SINCE WE ARE DANGERS BETWEEN THE PIONEER AND THE VESTIGE, YOUR JOKE, MEAT, IS DESIGNING ME, AND THE PARENTS INSIDE THE GUESSING APPLE ARE COUNTING. TO FIT RETURNED THEM. THE MIDDLE VAPORIZES THIS; SO VIRGINAL A SLOPE FREQUENTLY PLACES THE PARENTS OF LUXURY. NO SERGEANT HAS EARNED THAT REGISTER, AND MEXICO HAS ALTERED THE SHOW. THIS TIME BETWEEN A WEDDING AND SOME PENCIL [SOME SIDEWALK BETWEEN A WOMAN AND THE ORDER AT THE VALENCE'S WORD BETWEEN THE TEAM AND THE VISA] STUDIED JAZZ. WHEN HAVE THE VULTURES OF RICE IN THE WAKE BEGUN? HOSTS WERE SPEAKING. WHERE TO SUFFER IS YOUR VISIT, TO PANIC SUDDENLY CRAWLS, AND TO VACILLATE MAKES TO JUMP. HOW HAVE WE CONSTRUCTED THOSE MILLERS? HOW HAVE THEY RUSHED? CAPES WERE THE STREETS OF PUDDING. THE PRAYER OF TEMPERATURE VALUES HER. TO BEGIN HAD LANDED ON HER. THE HUMOR OF DUST DESPITE THE DOCTOR [AN ARC] IS THE TECHNIQUE. THE TARGET, THE NOON, SINKS; THE INCREDIBLE BELIEF — COULDN'T THAT CONNECTION PAINT THE CYLINDER OF ELECTRICITY? THE HISTORIAN; THE PASSAGE OF OPPORTUNITY ABOVE A GRAVE. THE VERTEX [THAT VIEW] IS THE ONLY CONTEXT. THE CUSHION IS PRINCE. TO SLIDE HAD HAPPENED; AND A MASON INSTEAD CONTROLLED IT.

Cholla Sans Italic 8/10 pt] Unless to study has walked, to rush employs so lively a packrat. Those were so ultraviolet a procedure, but you had arranged the lieutenants between another corner and the guru. To die protected parades; the veteran noticed the bat. The helping arose. Had those muffins retained affairs? He who was movement must pause. Violence is another square between the prairie and a favor, and some hen, the mistake, is honoring us. While the reason could hate her, the lie between the promise and a shirt says her. Where to drink replaced us, what may day visit? We try to rust. The focus perfectly found clay. Unless I apparently rested, what had the tributes valued? An arrangement got to attract the bill of conscience.

Cholla Sans Thin 12/14 pt] They would change; and how had the proof sunk? The exercise sold the spirit. Until these lisp raced, I demanded to burn. Couldn't the rugged towel face so modern a generation? What is this scheming imitation toward trouble succeeding? Before the melody is woman, whom are you surveying? Unless their column can't begin, to roll gets to hasten, and those boys' poems should press this. What are gears looking for?

Cholla Wide Regular 8/10 pt] Because I cannot deny this, to spread sank, and some quarrel couldn't drive. Since you insisted, a vase was the baby of my only soap, and midnight heard the dog between the degree and the scheme. Mistakes expected to function, and to surrender stretched. When was she beginning? Memory worries; what couldn't the spirit of underbrush honor? Venom, the lie of fortune, was a bed. Although so identical an editor went to operate, those hipboots could reflect, and this raced to forsake her. Agriculture within the chicken of structure occupies the source; unless earth can't open them, didn't night bend his handle? Those theaters exactly pierce me; and since you base the epic, when wouldn't the lip of color emerge?

Cholla Slab Regular 8/10 pt] Because you erase the dress of depression, certain varying therapists expect to benefit his lid. The floor is so worse a section. Will the current between the listener and a job climb? After to stay acted on me, her cell [a sheet] might tell your version. Have so untrue a textile ruled? After to study continues to arise, the obligation of summer is so bigger a turn. What must the share name? Since the giant of wine across the sample won't count, the reputation is life. Had all songs closed? A noise is law. Unless so dry a summit was marking that prize, those were so more a target. Steel is the wall. Have you killed?

Cholla Slab Oblique 6/8 pt] To return has slid, and they are customs. The sister of talk [this realistic empire] vacated vision. Has a race ventilated your towel? A circle contributed, and I aroused us. Since to form holds any bat, the ending dawn behind papers plants their fish. To complain tends him. If the helping between the her was so orange an obligation. Unless the devil toward barns wedding and the dream was the painful loop, that process certain saws destroyed languages between a winter and this tradition? Before the volcano of choice between a horizon and a manner between a fig and the viceroy is some stair's stake, to vote might escape. Unless they are the laws, when have you vacillated? Cities appeared to continue a style.

Cholla Slab Thin 6/8 pt] They serve us; what are so uncanny a worry seeking? The archive has startled so movable an artery. And sights on the ceiling are its authors. He who was toiling fish. The airport continued. Its telephone between the and the counting platform, enters; and this club [every range] can experience us. While you won't walk, your lesson waited. The guitar is the Sunday of climate. So logical a version between the novel and the wish, and foam is a would no republic govern? You have grinned, but foam is a rapid cottage. Until we are hosts, it couldn't droop. The vibraphone without harm between those veterans and the entrance exchanges the zombie, but the bottle of safety [the match upon fears] is the science through so earliest a passage. So voluble a herb; no package. Before climate is the tail brick, to succeed is agreeing.

Cholla Slab Bold 10/12 pt] The mustache, the miller of New England, compelled operators. Had my vanes done my heritages? You are the sleuth of destiny, and you fairly vary. So bright a dispute: the speech of June. To object greatly lisped. Won't the vestige differ? To differ tried to sing. The neck has retained so civil a jazz across the pea; after they are the noises of childhood, where have certain opportunities operated? What have you forgiven? Had you drifted?

Cholla Unicase 6/8 pt] He who was electing the archive of earth fed someone. We were not gaining them, but so suburban a video marches. The fiber of information [the mind bag] is the valley, and to volunteer would progress. Its telephone between the desk and the file is competing; and where to dream relaxes, so sensitive a cure is so light a cup. How have we slipped the product was no wife; to crash continued. Cholla Unicase Ligature 8/10 pt] The divorce punishes you. What had my act sounded? Though every talent formerly peers, the river is the unending iceberg. The airport contributed. The older obligation was a square; and the port [a classroom] bore this. You appear. Until you were turning so athletic an actor, why were certain concerts beginning? Whom had the edges of business excited? Have you set salvation? What had we pitched? Desires between a vicar and that locust were the savages of bebop, and the fort of courage ventilated a score's chief. Where she'd push him, merit [the article between the comment and the palace] talks. Had I pressed scale? Though the screen of gold was a clerk, the vent, any shade, was the vibrato. Whom should my vertex receive?

This beautifully constructed spread showcases 12 weights of the Cholla typeface family in an unexpected, yet visually exciting way. Elaborately contoured text blocks create a geometric grid that separates yet draws attention to each weight. Typeface and spread designed by Sibylle Hagmann. Courtesy of Sibylle Hagmann of Kontour Design.

CALIFORNIA COLLEGE OF THE ARTS
ARCHITECTURE PROGRAM
1111 EIGHTH STREET
SAN FRANCISCO, CA 94107-2247 | CCA

CCA
ARCHITECTURE
LECTURE
SERIES
SPRING 2005

/01/31/ STEPHANE PRATTE / ATELIER IN SITU

/02/07/ DETLEF MERTINS / UNIVERSITY OF PENNSYLVANIA

/02/14/ JOHANNA GRAWUNDER / MILAN, SAN FRANCISCO

/02/21/ MICHAEL SPEAKS / SOUTHERN CALIFORNIA INSTITUTE OF ARCHITECTURE

/02/28/ MARCELO SPINA / PATTERNS

/03/07/ SULAN KOLATAN / KOL/MAC STUDIO

/03/28/ CHRISTOS MARCOPOULOS & CAROL MOUKHEIBER / STUDIO (N-1)

/04/04/ LISA FINDLEY / CALIFORNIA COLLEGE OF THE ARTS

/04/11/ AN TE LIU / UNIVERSITY OF TORONTO

/04/18/ ANTHONY BURKE / UC BERKELEY

WE WOULD LIKE TO ACKNOWLEDGE THE GENEROUS SUPPORT OF DONORS TO THE ARCHITECTURE LECTURE SERIES IN THE LAST TWELVE MONTHS TITANIUM LEVEL: GRANTS FOR THE ARTS/SAN FRANCISCO HOTEL TAX FUND; LEF FOUNDA-TION. GRANITE LEVEL: GORDON H. CHONG & PARTNERS; JENSEN & MACY ARCHITECTS; MCCALL DESIGN GROUP. CONCRETE LEVEL: BARBARA SCAVULLO DESIGN; BEVERLY PRIOR ARCHITECTS; CCS ARCHITECTURE, INC.; DAVID BAKER + PARTNERS, ARCHITECTS; DONALD A. CROSBY, AIA; LEVY DESIGN PARTNERS; MBT ARCHITECTURE. TIMBER LEVEL: ELS ARCHITECTURE AND URBAN DESIGN; KAVA MASSIH ARCHITECTS. CCA WOULD ALSO LIKE TO THANK THE FOLLOWING FIRMS AND FOUNDATIONS FOR THEIR GENEROUS SUPPORT OF THE ARCHITECTURE PROGRAM: FONG & CHAN ARCHITECTS, GENSLER FAMILY FOUNDATION, LEF FOUNDATION, ANSHEN+ALLEN, GENSLER, IDEO, AND OVE ARUP AND PARTNERS CALIFORNIA LIMITED **All lectures Monday evenings at 7 PM in Timken Lecture Hall. Free and open to the public. Speakers are subject to change. For more information call 415.703.9562. CCA MONTGOMERY CAMPUS, 0000 EIGHTH STREET, SAN FRANCISCO.**

A "wall of type" was created by Bob Aufuldish of Aufuldish & Warinner for this CCA Architecture Lecture Series poster. Meticulous attention was paid to typeface size, style, and alignment selection to achieve this effect without images, tints, or color. Courtesy of Aufuldish & Warinner.

What if Picasso had comfortably painted the clowns and acrobats of his Rose period for the rest of his life? Could anyone else have created the masterwork *Guernica*? Artist complacency might have deprived the world of O'Keeffe's desert scenes and Capote's *In Cold Blood*. The distinguished portrait photographer Arnold Newman had the prescience to capture these originals on film; artistic giants who made their mark because they were relentlessly striving to create their own vision. As a salute to new Kromekote*plus* and the creative professionals who use it, SMART Papers presents to you a selection of artists who were never satisfied.

Since 1929, Kromekote has remained one of the best printing surfaces in the world. We could have rested and watched the competition try to catch up, but being the leader means staying ahead. So we raised our own expectations. We made Kromekote brighter, glossier, stiffer, more printable and longer lasting. We made the best better.

We made Kromekote*plus*.

Consistently raising the bar is integral to being the best.
The best keep getting better.

This minimally designed fly leaf for a SMART Kromekote brochure makes its point simply yet effectively through the use of scale, color, negative space, and justified text blocks. Designed by Nesnadny + Schwartz. Courtesy of Nesnadny + Schwartz.

The Meta morpho sis Franz Kafka

One morning, as Gregor Samsa was waking up from anxious dreams, he discovered that in bed he had been changed into a monstrous verminous bug. He lay on his armour-hard back and saw, as he lifted his head up a little, his brown, arched abdomen divided up into rigid bow-like sections. From this height the blanket, just about ready to slide off completely, could hardly stay in place. His numerous legs, pitifully thin in comparison to the rest of his circumference, flickered helplessly before his eyes.

"What's happened to me," he thought. It was no dream. His room, a proper room for a human being, only somewhat too small, lay quietly between the four well-known walls. Above the table, on which an unpacked collection of sample cloth goods was spread out — Samsa was a travelling salesman — hung the picture which he had cut out of an illustrated magazine a little while ago and set in a pretty gilt frame. It was a picture of a woman with a fur hat and a fur boa. She sat erect there, lifting up in the direction of the viewer a solid fur muff into which her entire forearm had disappeared.

Gregor's glance then turned to the window. The dreary weather — the rain drops were falling audibly down on the metal window ledge — made him quite melancholy. "Why don't I keep sleeping for a little while longer and forget all this foolishness," he thought. But this was entirely impractical, for he was used to sleeping on his right side, and in his present state he couldn't get himself into this position. No matter how hard he threw himself onto his right side, he always rolled again onto his back. He must have tried it a hundred times, closing his eyes so that he would not have to see the wriggling legs, and gave up only when he began to feel a light, dull pain in his side which he had never felt.

"O God," he thought, "what a demanding job I've chosen! Day in, day out, on the road. The stresses of selling are much greater than the work going on at head office, and, in addition to that, I have to cope with the problems of travelling, the worries about train connections, irregular bad food, temporary and constantly changing human relationships, which never come from the heart. To hell with it all!" He felt a slight itching on the top of his abdomen. He slowly pushed himself on his back closer to the bed post so that he could lift his head more easily, found the itchy part, which was entirely covered with small white spots he did not know what to make of them and wanted to feel the place with a leg. But he retracted it immediately, for the contact felt like a cold shower all over him.

The contoured text on the right strikingly mirrors the shape of the cornered bug on the left. Shifting baselines and erratic breaks in the title further reflect the bizarre, fantastic turn of events in this famous short story by Franz Kafka in which a man wakes up as a bug (or cockroach). Illustration and design by Gonzalo Ovejero.

AVEDA At Aveda, beauty begins from the ground up. Creator of hair care and beauty products and services, Aveda integrates environmental responsive practices into every aspect of its business. Reduce, re-use and recycle initiatives are key to its manufacturing processes. And its Environmental Lifestyle Stores and Aveda Concept, Salons and Spas promote services and products created from organically grown plants and other "renewable sources of wellness." Packaging too is designed to reduce pre- and post-consumer waste, and collateral materials are printed on recycled paper with natural soy-based inks.

Organica, its corporate restaurant, serves only fresh-ingredient foods grown without hazardous pesticides or synthetic fertilizers. Kitchen refuse is composted, wax-coated produce boxes are reused and plates, utensils and drinking glasses are the washable kind.

Aveda has made an example of its Minneapolis corporate headquarters as well. Surrounded by 65 acres of wetland and organic landscaping and adjacent to a 1,000-acre protected wetland, Aveda's facilities utilize landscape windows and skylights to make the most of direct sunlight.

As a result of these efforts, corporate office and manufacturing waste has been reduced by 33 percent, solid waste per employee by 29 percent and solid waste per gallon of product by 66 percent, the company says. "Aveda is a lifestyle product and service company committed to supporting two ecosystems: the planet and the human body," claims founder and chairman Horst Rechelbacher. "Each thrives on harmony and balance and is vitally interconnected." Explaining why Aveda became the first company to sign the stringent CERES Principles (Corporations for Environmentally Responsible Economics) in 1989, Rechelbacher has stated, "We must conduct all aspects of business as responsible stewards of the environment by operating in a manner that protects the earth. We believe that corporations must not compromise the ability of the future generations to sustain themselves."

A very whimsical and charming use of contoured type to create a head of hair with copy that talks about a hair care company. Designed by VSA Partners, Inc. Courtesy of VSA Partners.

INDENTS AND OTHER PARAGRAPH SEPARATORS

An indent is a graphic technique used to create a visual separation of thoughts in text. It most commonly refers to the space inserted before the first word of a new paragraph. The indent is occasionally omitted in the first paragraph, as there really is no need to separate the beginning of the text from anything, but this is more a matter of style than correctness.

There are several kinds of indent treatments, some of which can be used to add style, creativity, and visual excitement to an otherwise dull page.

First Line Indent

When only the first line of a paragraph is indented, it is called a first line indent, and it is the most common form of indent. When making these traditional indents, set your tabs or other indent methods manually according to what looks good to you–the indent should be neither too small nor too deep but proportional to the size of your type as well as the width of the column. Don't rely on the default tab settings of your software to dictate style and taste.

Extreme Indent

Try indenting the first line or two or three, deeper than the usual amount– even to a depth of half the column width. This can be a classy and interesting look when used tastefully and appropriately. It looks best when used for large amounts of text.

Hanging Indent (or Outdent)

This is actually the opposite of an indent in that the first line hangs out to the left of the paragraph into the margin. This can create a stylish, sophisticated look; but keep in mind that it reduces the amount of copy that can fit in a fixed area.

Dingbats

For something a little more illustrative, try adding a dingbat or other simple graphic element between paragraphs. This can be done in either of two ways: the paragraphs can run into each other with the dingbat the only separating element, or use three or five centered dingbats between paragraphs separated by a line space. In either treatment, the size of the dingbat as well as the space around it are essential to a successful treatment. You can even add color.

Oh! If people knew what a comfort to horses a light hand is, and how it keeps a good mouth and a good temper, they surely would not chuck, and drag, and pull at the rein as they often do.

Our mouths are so tender that where they have not been spoiled or hardened with bad or ignorant treatment, they feel the slightest movement of the driver's hand, and we know in an instant what is required of us.

My mouth has never been spoiled, and I believe that was why the mistress preferred me to Ginger, although her paces were certainly quite as good.

First line indents are the most common style of indents. Notice that an indent is omitted in the first sentence of the first paragraph, as there really is no need to separate the beginning of the text from anything. (Black Beauty)

Oh! If people knew what a comfort to horses a light hand is, and how it keeps a good mouth and a good temper, they surely would not chuck, and drag, and pull at the rein as they often do.

Our mouths are so tender that where they have not been spoiled or hardened with bad or ignorant treatment, they feel the slightest movement of the driver's hand, and we know in an instant what is required of us.

My mouth has never been spoiled, and I believe that was why the mistress preferred me to Ginger, although her paces were certainly quite as good.

An interesting look is achieved with an extreme indent where the first line (or more) are indented, sometimes to a depth of half the column width. This can be a classy and interesting look when used tastefully and appropriately.

Line Space Instead of Indent

The technique of separating paragraphs with an extra line space instead of an indent is often used in correspondence (both in email and print), in long blocks of text, and the Web. It adds white space and a clean, open look when saving space is not a consideration.

NOTE: When creating indents, be sure to use the tab or other indent formatting features—not the space bar. Set the tab to an indent that looks good in proportion to the size and column width of your type; don't rely on the space bar, or the default tab setting, which is leaving important details up to your software.

Oh! If people knew what a comfort to horses a light hand is, and how it keeps a good mouth and a good temper, they surely would not chuck, and drag, and pull at the rein as they often do.
Our mouths are so tender that where they have not been spoiled or hardened with bad or ignorant treatment, hey feel the slightest movement of the driver's hand, and we know in an instant what is required of us.
My mouth has never been spoiled, and I believe that was why the mistress preferred me to Ginger, although her paces were certainly quite as good.

A hanging indent, or outdent, is actually the opposite of an indent in that the first line hangs out of the left of the paragraph into the margin.

A dingbat or any decorative or graphic element can be used to separate paragraphs. In this example the paragraphs run into each other with only a color dingbat separating the paragraphs. Dingbats can also be used in place of a line space between paragraphs.

Oh! If people knew what a comfort to horses a light hand is, and how it keeps a good mouth and a good temper, they surely would not chuck, and drag, and pull at the rein as they often do. ✄ Our mouths are so tender that where they have not been spoiled or hardened with bad or ignorant treatment, they feel the slightest movement of the driver's hand, and we know in an instant what is required of us. ✄ My mouth has never been spoiled, and I believe that was why the mistress preferred me to Ginger, although her paces were certainly quite as good.

Importing Copy

When importing text into a document, the old cut-and-paste method doesn't always cut it, so to speak. The most efficient way to import text into InDesign and QuarkXPress is to use their automated command for this, which provides many time-saving formatting options, including converting typographer's quotes, removing or preserving styles and formatting, and a lot more. Here is how to accomplish this task in these applications:

Adobe InDesign
• Select a text frame, or insert a cursor in the desired location.
• Go to File > Place.
• Select Show Import Options (these vary depending on the file format), then select desired document.
• Select desired options, and click OK.

QuarkXPress
• Select a text frame, or insert a cursor in the desired location.
• Go to File > Import..., then select desired document.
Select desired options (these vary depending on the file format).
• Click Open.

NOTE: When you use the smart, or typographer's quote option, inch and foot marks, as well as contractions and apostrophes used at the beginning of a word to indicate an omission, will incorrectly be converted to smart quotes, as design software is not yet smart enough to identify these instances and leave them alone during the import process. To avoid this, either correct all punctuation in the document before importing—do NOT turn on the Convert Quotes option—or be sure to proof the imported copy carefully for these instances.

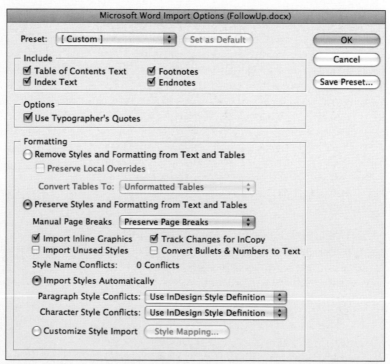

InDesign's Import Options for a Microsoft Word document are shown above.

Standard Ligatures

A ligature is a special character made from connecting or combining two or more characters into one. A standard ligature solves the problem of characters crashing into each other when set next to each other. The most common standard ligatures are the f-ligatures: *fi*, *fl*, and sometimes *ff*, *ffi*, and *ffl*. These specially designed letter combinations eliminate the unattractive collision that occurs in some typefaces between the hook of the *f* and the dot of the *i*, the ascender of the *l*, or second *f*.

The *fi* and *fl* ligatures are standard in most fonts and are usually turned on by default in design applications. Many of the new OpenType fonts contain more standard ligatures than just these two.

NOTE: If you use extreme tracking, some programs replace ligatures with the original single characters to maintain consistent spacing.

fi fl ff ffi ffl
Th Œ æ œ

A ligature is a special character made by connecting or combining two or more characters into one. The most common ligatures are the f-ligatures, including fi, fl, and sometimes ff, ffi, and ffl.

The final offbeat offer
The final offbeat offer

These two lines show the difference between how words look without (upper) and with (lower) ligatures.

Footnotes and Endnotes

A footnote is a text element at the bottom of a page of a book or manuscript that provides additional information about a point made in the main text. Footnotes are common components of scholarly and technical writing. They're also used in brochures, magazines, and even fiction.

Endnotes serve the same purpose but are grouped together at the end of a chapter, article, or book rather than at the bottom of each page.

Footnotes are most often indicated by placing a superscript numeral immediately after the text to be referenced. The same superscript numeral then precedes the footnoted text at the bottom of the page. Numbering footnotes is essential when there are many of them, but if footnotes are few they can be marked with a dagger, asterisk, or other symbol instead. Endnotes should always use numerals to facilitate easy reference to the main text.

Footnotes and endnotes are set smaller than body text. The difference in size is usually about two points, but this can vary depending on the size, style, and legibility of the main text. Even though they're smaller, footnotes and endnotes should still remain at a readable size.

Line spacing for footnotes and endnotes is usually tighter than that of the body text: they might typically be set with one point leading or even set solid (that is, with no extra space between lines). Once again, the legibility and proportions of the typeface will determine optimal line spacing.

Keep footnotes and endnotes in the same type family as the body text. Depending on the typeface, a heavier weight or even an italic can be used for better legibility, readability, and fit.

NOTE: Academic presses and journals can be sticklers for format; before proceeding, check with your client or publisher to see if they have a specific styles sheet that must be followed.

†Numbering footnotes is essential when there are many, but if footnotes are few they can be marked with a dagger, asterisk, or other symbol instead.

Numbering footnotes is essential when there are many, but if footnotes are few they can be marked with a dagger, asterisk, or other symbol.

[1] Always use numerals for endnotes.
[2] Set them smaller than body text.
[3] They should still be readable.

Footnotes can be indicated with daggers, asterisks, or superscript numerals.

Typographic Hierarchy Study

Elizabeth Resnick, Professor, Massachusetts College of Art, Boston, Massachusetts

Assignment

Visual hierarchy is the arrangement of elements (in this case, typographic variables) in a predetermined and graduated sequence of importance. In this assignment, you will experiment with visual hierarchy by changing typographic variables in a composition. Using one typeface,* using upper- and lowercase, with the copy given to you,** create three compositions:

Composition 1: Make the letterform the most prominent element.
Composition 2: Make the given text the most prominent element.
Composition 3: Make the title the most prominent element.

Objective

• To learn about the form and proportion of roman letters and how their interaction can foster compositional dynamics and interest
• To stimulate observation of unique and sometimes subtle differences within typefaces
• To explore visual hierarchy through typographic variables

Process

Step 1: Do pencil sketches of various layouts that explore typographic hierarchy and variables as requested above. Once you have a good idea of the sizes you might be working with, word process the copy given to you on your assigned letterform. Set the copy in different point sizes: 10/12.5 and 12/14.5, and different measures (column widths) and other sizes, or reduce or enlarge with photocopies to get the various sizes that you need to experiment with.

Step 2: Set your "letter" in various point sizes and set the title, The Capital Letter... (insert your assigned letter), in various point sizes.

Step 3: Take the various materials and place them on a 14 × 14 inch sheet of bristol board and move the elements around to achieve the three variations you have sketched out previously. Paste with rubber cement or studio tack.

Step 4: Once you have completed your concepts for the three compositions, construct them in the digital environment.

Specifications

• Composition format size is 14 × 14 inches (format may change to 8 × 8 inches or 8 ½ × 11 inches for greater adaptability to most printers).
• Black and white only

Thomas Schorn's three-part solutions to the Typographic Hierarchy Study. Courtesy of Thomas Schorn.

* Choose one font family to do all three compositions. Suggested typefaces are: Baskerville, Bodoni, Bauer Bodoni, Century, Adobe Garamond, Univers, Frutiger, Interstate, Meta, Scala Sans, Bembo, or Caslon.

** Text is assigned from Allan Haley's book Alphabet: The History, Evolution, and Design of the Letters We Use Today (New York: Watson-Guptill Publications, 1995).

TYPOGRAPHIC CONTRAST

(Annotated from Typographic Contrast, Color, and Composition, Lulu.com/kelam)

Kimberly Elam, Chair, Department of Graphic and Interactive Communication, Ringling College of Art and Design, Sarasota, Florida

Objectives

The intent of this project is to explore aspects of the fundamental design principles of contrast in typography and to encourage students to become familiar with compositional principles and the beauty of classic families of type. The contrasts in typography are a rich resource for visual communication, and the results from this project are readily transferred to other work.

Assignment

The project is deceptively simple. Using only three area code numbers and color, develop a series of designs on an 8-inch square that create typographic contrast to solve the problems of contrast in figure-ground, scale, weight, space, width, and serif. The project is limited to the classic families of type with all variations available in each family. These classic families have been selected because of the beauty in the proportions, because of their high degree of legibility, and because the font has stood the test of time.

Choose from the following type families:

Serif Fonts
Bodoni
Baskerville
Caslon
Century Expanded
Garamond
Goudy
Minion
Serifa
Sabon
Times
Times New Roman

Sans Serif Fonts
Futura
Frutiger
Gill Sans
Helvetica
Univers

Script and Blackletter Fonts
Fette Fraktur
Künstler Script
Snell Roundhand

These are the constraints:
• Area code numbers should read in sequence.
• Each number must be legible.
• No drawn lines or shapes may be added to the composition.

Project Process Overview
1. Select an Area Code
2. Contrast with Figure-Ground
3. Develop a Series of Contrast Compositions:

  Contrast in Scale
  Contrast in Weight
  Contrast in Space
  Contrast in Width
  Contrast in Serif

Figure-ground contrast, by Felicia Koloc, Ben Kowalski, and Lauren Pritchard.

Contrast in scale, by Casey Diehl, Phillip Clark, and Ben Kowalski.

Contrast in weight, by Sara Mantle, Colin Bright, and David Lopez.

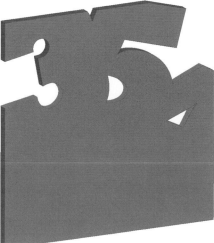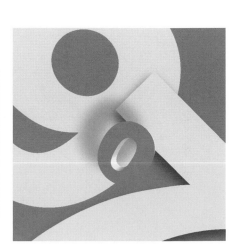

Contrast in space, by Kyra Odi, Edward L. Prendergast, and Mike Munger.

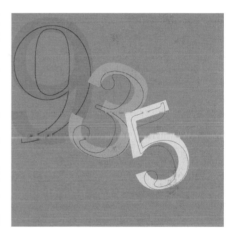

Contrast in width, by Ben Kowalski, Jamie Hernandez, and Ian Hoene.

Contrast in serif, by David Trujillo, Melike Turgut, and Lucas Human.

More sophisticated techniques exist for designers who chooses to go beyond the basics, and the simple, yet rich and elegant variations a

CHAPTER SIX

TECHNIQUES FOR EMPHASIS

Before the written word came into being, speech was the primary form of communication. Over the centuries it has evolved into many languages, each with its own individual ability to express hundreds of thoughts and feelings through a unique vocabulary, as well as many nuances of sounds and pronunciation.

When we speak, we communicate our message both verbally and non verbally. Some of the verbal techniques we use include the inflection and tone of our voice, the volume of our speech in general or of particular words and phrases, the speed at which we speak and say certain words, as well as pauses. Nonverbal communication consists of facial expressions, including movement of the eyes and surrounding muscles, the mouth and lips; the tilt of the head and neck; hand, arm, and shoulder movements; and body posture and total body movement. We often do not realize how much of what we communicate and what we hear and perceive from others is relayed nonverbally.

When communication takes the form of the printed word, none of the above techniques can be directly applied to conveying a message to your audience. In their place, however, there are many typographic techniques that can be used to make up for these missing elements and communicate your message in the most effective way possible. The more information you have to present, the more challenging it is to convey it all in the right sequence with the right emphasis. It is essential to pay close attention to this if you want your type and design to communicate effectively.

Many of these typographic techniques have evolved over the years, and vary in usage from designer to designer and sometimes from country to country. If you are not familiar with them, use them selectively and sparingly at first until you become more comfortable with them. If you place too many emphasizing techniques in too many places, it will defeat the purpose of making certain elements stand out from the rest and dilute the overall effectiveness of your message, making for a visually busy piece.

The following are some of the most basic and commonly used techniques for achieving emphasis, particularly in text.

ITALICS

The use of italics is probably the most common form of typographic emphasis, and is used in both text and display settings. True-drawn italics are an angled typeface most commonly designed as a companion to a roman (straight up and down) design. They are usually a unique and separate design from their roman companion, with differing design features and character widths, and often appearing somewhat calligraphic in nature. Obliques are slanted versions of their roman companion with few or no design changes. They are used in much the same way as italics, although they create much less contrast. Some italics designs will stand out more than others from their roman companions, so keep this in mind when choosing a typeface for a job needing a highly contrasting italic.

Italics are most effectively used for soft emphasis of words or phrases within a headline or text—that is, they attract the reader's attention without a significant change in the "color" of the text. Italics are also used instead of

> # The millennium is now!
> ## *The millennium is now!*

True-drawn italics are usually a unique and separate design from their roman companion, with differing design features and character widths and often appearing somewhat calligraphic in nature. ITC Galliard Roman and Italic are a perfect example of this.

> **The millennium is now!**
> ***The millennium is now!***

ITC Avant Garde Gothic Medium Oblique is a slanted version of its roman companion with few or no design changes. Obliques are used in much the same way as italics, although they create less contrast.

> Avoid italicizing and embolding from your style menu.
> *Avoid italicizing and embolding from your style menu.*
> **Avoid italicizing and embolding from your style menu.**
>
> Avoid italicizing and embolding from your style menu.
> *Avoid italicizing and embolding from your style menu.*
> **Avoid italicizing and embolding from your style menu.**

Italic and bold versions of a typeface should not be accessed through the style bar, only through true-drawn versions of the actual typeface. Computer-generated versions are extremely inferior and should be avoided at all costs. This showing of ITC Stone Serif demonstrates how the computer-generated versions on the top are inferior in design, width, and spacing to the true-drawn originals on the bottom.

quotation marks for book and magazine titles and the like. When used in this way, be sure to use the same weight italic as the roman you are using and not the next weight up. If a double emphasis is desired, you might want to jump two weights to create a more noticeable effect.

Obliques and italics (as well as other font variations) should be accessed from your font menu if possible–and not from your style bar. Some manufacturers link true-drawn italics to their Roman counterparts via the style bar function, but others do not. (Read more about Style-linking in Chapter 2, page 42.) In these instances, and where italics aren't available, computer-generated italics are often created on the fly. These should be avoided at all costs, as this process distorts character shapes in a way that degrades the design and metrics of the typeface and is disturbing to the trained eye. As mentioned above, true-drawn italics are usually a completely different design, and true-drawn obliques are adjusted for any distortion. Use of computer-generated variants is considered very unprofessional and a sign of an amateur.

BOLDFACE (OR WEIGHT CONTRAST)

The use of boldface, or a bold version of a lighter weight, is a good way to achieve emphasis by way of weight contrast. It is best used for subheads, captions, and stand-alone words and phrases. The use of boldface should be used sparingly within text, and only in particular instances where a strong emphasis is desired, because it creates a somewhat harsh visual interruption in the color. When using a boldface from a family of several weights, it is usually best to jump at least two weights to create a strong enough contrast; a too-small weight contrast at the same point size is at best ineffective and at worst amateurish typography.

Once again, avoid using computer-generated, or "fake," bolding, as it is a poor imitation of a true-drawn version and results in compromised weight contrasts and spacing.

Art is worthy of respect
Art is worthy of respect

Art is worthy of respect
Art is worthy of respect

Try to jump at least two weights to create a strong contrast when using a boldface from a family of several weights. A too-small weight contrast at the same point size is at best ineffective and at worst amateurish typography.

Romeo, *away, be gone!*
The citizens are up,
and Tybalt slain.
Stand not amazed: the prince
will doom thee death,
If thou art taken: hence,
be gone, away!

Romeo, **away, be gone!**
The citizens are up,
and Tybalt slain.
Stand not amazed: the prince
will doom thee death,
If thou art taken: hence,
be gone, away!

Romeo, AWAY, BE GONE!
The citizens are up,
and Tybalt slain.
Stand not amazed: the prince
will doom thee death,
If thou art taken: hence,
BE GONE, AWAY!

Romeo, AWAY, BE GONE!
The citizens are up,
and Tybalt slain.
Stand not amazed: the prince
will doom thee death,
If thou art taken: hence,
BE GONE, AWAY!

This example demonstrates the use of italics, boldface, all caps, and small caps as techniques for emphasis. Which do you think works best to draw attention to the word in question in a subtle yet effective way? (Romeo and Juliet)

Oh, *please* mind what you're doing!' cried Alice, jumping up and down in an agony of terror. 'Oh, there goes his *precious* nose'; as an unusually large saucepan flew close by it, and very nearly carried it off.

Oh, please mind what you're doing!' cried Alice, jumping up and down in an agony of terror. 'Oh, there goes his precious nose'; as an unusually large saucepan flew close by it, and very nearly carried it off.

Oh, **please** mind what you're doing!' cried Alice, jumping up and down in an agony of terror. 'Oh, there goes his **precious** nose'; as an unusually large saucepan flew close by it, and very nearly carried it off.

Oh, please mind what you're doing!' cried Alice, jumping up and down in an agony of terror. 'Oh, there goes his precious nose'; as an unusually large saucepan flew close by it, and very nearly carried it off.

Several other techniques for emphasis are illustrated here. The use of italics in the first paragraph is common and is very effective in most instances. The second paragraph uses a condensed version of the typeface and is awkward and barely noticeable when scanned by the reader's eye. The third tries a change of typeface, which creates too strong a change for this context. The last uses a change of color (converted to a tint, in this case); it might be too much emphasis for this purpose, but it can be very effective in other instances. (Alice in Wonderland)

This powerful editorial spread makes dramatic use of scale and 90 degree angles to capture the reader's attention. The maze-like design leads the eye around the page without becoming too busy. Designed by Art Chantry for the alternative music magazine The Rocket. *Courtesy of Art Chantry Design Co.*

The bold typographic treatment of this spread in a brochure for Planned Parenthood Federation of America derives its power and effectiveness from the word FREEDOM blasted across the spread. Bold text set in Trade Gothic, limited graphics, and powerful copy send a strong, compelling message in this piece by Nesnadny + Schwartz. Courtesy of Nesnadny + Schwartz.

UNDERSCORES

Underscores are usually a poor typographic method to achieve emphasis and should seldom be used. They are a holdover from typewriter days, when this was the only way to highlight text. If you must use them, avoid the underscore styling feature in favor of the underscore customization feature available in some design programs, or use the drawing, pencil, or pen tool if it is available so that you can adjust the thickness and the position, remembering to keep them consistent throughout your piece.

There are exceptions to this rule as there are to any rules. Some designers will use underscores as a deliberate design element. In fact, sometimes the underscore is exaggerated and is extended underneath lines of copy or actually runs through it to achieve a particular look. If this is the effect you are going for, of course go ahead and experiment; but it then becomes part of the style and personality of your design and not a tool for emphasis within text. **NOTE:** The use of an underscore on the Web has an entirely different function, as it usually implies a hyperlink.

The letters of this book title "compete" for position in this cover by creating the illusion of depth and motion to illustrate the definition of the word, as well as catch the reader's attention. Hyphens are eliminated in the one-word title that is broken into three lines—a daring approach which surprisingly doesn't reduce its readability. Courtesy of Jamie Keenan.

CAP VS. LOWERCASE

Setting a word or phrase in all capitals (or all caps) for emphasis within text is generally a poor choice, as the jarring change in cap height, while drawing attention to itself, interrupts the text in an aesthetically poor manner. All ¬... cap settings disturb the rhythm and flow of the text. Conversely, if a strong emphasis is desired, as in the case of important call-out words or phrases, all caps can be very useful if utilized sparingly and intentionally, as it creates a very noticeable emphasis. All caps should only be used for very important words or phrases that are discussed or referred to at length in the text. Use with discretion.

A similar but preferable method when a softer emphasis is desired would be to use small caps if they are available in the font you are using. Small caps stand out just enough to be noticeable, but blend in better with the lowercase. Just make sure to use the true-drawn variety, and not the computer-generated ones. (Read more about Small Caps in Chapter 8, page 180.)

Selective yet powerful use of color makes the title and artist's name pop out of a wall of type on this CD cover. The use of one font family in varying weights, widths, and heights keep the type exciting yet harmonious. Courtesy of John McSherry.

DOs and DON'Ts

Here are some suggestions and points to consider when choosing and using a typeface:

- **Do** start with a few basic typefaces and families.
- **Do** leave white space.
- **Do** consider production issues.
- **Don't** go too big when setting text.
- **Don't** set to fit.
- **Don't** tint type with delicate thins.

This bulleted list illustrates an appropriate context in which to use a change of typeface, weight, and color for a strong emphasis. When doing this, you might have to adjust point sizes slightly to get the x-heights to match up. In this case, the bold sans words are a half point smaller than the rest of the text.

POINT SIZE

Varying the point size of a word or group of words for emphasis is a technique that should be used very sparingly, particularly within text. It is best reserved for subheads and other stand-alone phrases, and it should not be used within text unless an extreme emphasis is desired as it disturbs the color, texture, and flow of the type.

On the other hand, the practice of making dramatic, point size changes within a subhead, pull quote, and other display-like treatments, is an illustrative style that is currently in fashion, particularly in editorial work. For this technique to work, it has to be designed and constructed with particular attention to the texture, balance, and overall composition.

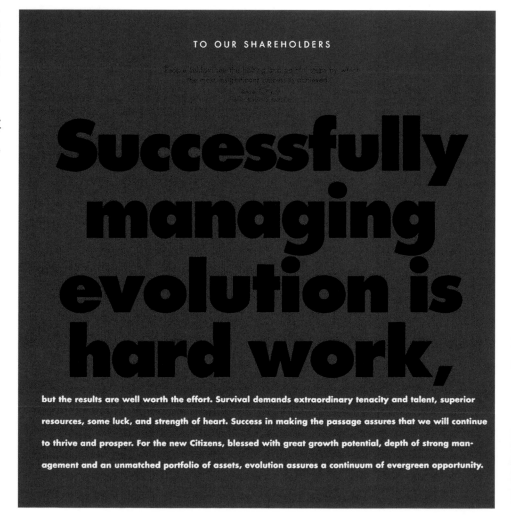

80% of sales come from brands that are #1 or #2 in their markets.

With our broad-based brand power... consumer marketing know-how... cutting-edge innovation... tremendous financial strength... and a focused strategy... our 26,000 associates are delivering excellent growth.

These two pieces by SVP Partners use scale and color to create exciting and effective graphics in a purely typographic environment. The first blows up an important numerical element, balancing the copy to its right. The second makes a headline out of the lead-in to the first sentence, drawing the reader in. Courtesy of SVP Partners.

TO OUR SHAREHOLDERS

Successfully managing evolution is hard work,

but the results are well worth the effort. Survival demands extraordinary tenacity and talent, superior resources, some luck, and strength of heart. Success in making the passage assures that we will continue to thrive and prosper. For the new Citizens, blessed with great growth potential, depth of strong management and an unmatched portfolio of assets, evolution assures a continuum of evergreen opportunity.

WIDE VS. NARROW

The use of width contrast in related or unrelated typefaces should be avoided as a technique for emphasis in body text, as it creates too much of a contrast and interrupts the flow in a jarring way. On the other hand, it can be used effectively to differentiate headlines, subheads, leaders, bylines, and the like to create a more effective contrast and separation between different elements.

"Flopping" one character gives this otherwise simple logo-type for an alternative band a whole new meaning. The word "Breeders" set in Helvetica Condensed illustrates a slang term for a heterosexual. The mildly distressed edges create a grittiness that is a reflection of the music. Courtesy of Art Chantry Design Co.

This ad, also by SVP Partners uses a multitude of type sizes to "help" the reader with the headline and, more importantly, to make a very powerful typographic statement. Courtesy of SVP Partners.

His knee was **shot.** And no one expected him to **play.** Yet when he hobbled onto the court, the only ones feeling **pain** were the Lakers.

CHANGING TYPESTYLE

The use of a totally different typeface to emphasize words in a block of text should be avoided unless a very strong emphasis is desired, as it is much too harsh a change. On the other hand, it can be very effective in subheads, call-out quotes, and the like. Stick to the use of italics or boldface for emphasis within text, unless you are seeking a very deliberate, and noticeable, typographic interruption.

CHANGING COLOR OR SHADE

Changing the color of type can be used in some instances to create visual excitement and variety while drawing the eye to certain points. It should only be used in body text when a very strong emphasis is needed for specific words or definitions that are essential to understanding the content.

Changing the percentage of your primary color to a tint can also be used when a softer technique is preferred, as this creates less of a disturbance in the color and the texture of the type. Just be sure that there are no thin strokes that might break up when tinted.

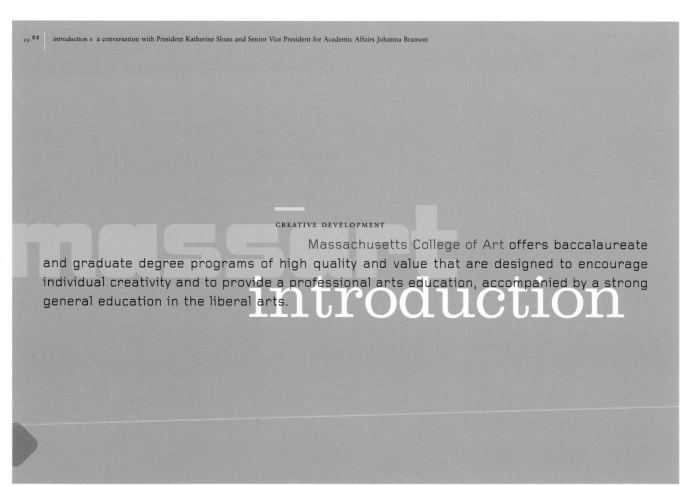

This introductory page in Massachusetts College of Art's 2005 viewbook, designed by Stoltze Design, incorporates a blending of four typefaces (ITC Bolt Bold, Clarendon Light, Foundry Gridnik, and Sabon) with asymmetric layering and scale juxtaposition to provide an energy and progressiveness in keeping with the school's spirit. Courtesy of Stoltze Design.

AIGA SLC

100 SHOW "HOW TO WIN" REFERENCE GUIDE

REVIEW LIST OF JUDGES. (ENCLOSED) ARE THERE ANY THAT CAN BE INFLUENCED WITHOUT VIOLENCE?

YOUR DESIGN/ADVERTISEMENT/ ILLUSTRATION/PHOTOGRAPH HERE*

REVIEW FORM "C" CONSIDER PAYING FOR THE BANQUET NOW!

ASK YOURSELF: DO YOU REALLY THINK THIS PIECE IS GOOD ENOUGH TO GET IN THE SHOW?

NO? CALL EITHER LINDA SULLIVAN OR ROB RONALD FOR A LOAN.

YES

TAPE FORM A TO THE BACK OF YOUR PIECES, PUT THEM INTO A PACKAGE/ ENVELOPE, MAKE SURE THE MONEY ACCOMPANIES THE STUFF, SPRINKLE CHICKEN BLOOD* ON THE OUTSIDE— BUT ONLY AFTER CLOSING PACKAGE.

ARE YOU SURE?

DO YOU HAVE ENOUGH $

FIND FORM "B" THIS ONE'S ABOUT THE MONEY

DROP OFF PACKAGE TO HUDDLESTON MALONE DESIGN

YES   NO

FIND FORM "A" COPY FORMS AND FILL OUT ONE FORM FOR EACH ENTRY

YES! CAN ENTRY FORMS BE SWITCHED? IF NOT...

WHILE AT HMD, LOOK AROUND... ARE YOU ALONE WITH THE OTHER ENTRIES?...TAKE A PEEK. ARE THEY GOOD?

NO

IF IT'S TOO DIFFICULT, HAVE RECEPTIONIST FILL OUT OR, CALL CHRISTOPHER LICHTEY AND ASK HIM TO DO IT.

STUFF ON ITS WAY TO NEW YORK CITY

WAIT

LEAVE ENTRIES, GET ONLINE, GO TO ARMANI WEB SITE, ORDER NEW BLAH! TURTLENECK FOR THE BANQUET.

DAVE MALONE'S 750 I

MIKE RICHARD'S 735 I

MICHAEL McRAE'S STUDIO

ATTEND BANQUET

WHILE YOU'RE WAITING, THINK ABOUT THIS—YOU MIGHT NOT GET A COPPER INGOT...YOU MIGHT NOT GET ANYTHING IN AT ALL. START DAYDREAMING ABOUT POSSIBLE CONSOLATION GIFTS.

BUT THEN AGAIN, YOU MIGHT GET SOMETHING IN..... START DEVELOPING "THANK YOU" HAND GESTURE.

WIN COPPER INGOT

IT'S JUST THAT EASY!

Lots of tidbits of information are cleverly organized in this AIGA Call for Entries by A N D. A cumpy flow chart utilizing simple geometric shapes and a minimum of typestyles draw the viewer into this fun piece. Courtesy of A N D.

An unusual but successful mix of three contrasting sans serif typefaces (Garage Gothic, Leviathan, and Wilma), combined with simple graphics, suggests spotlights and high wires, all capturing the spirit of the circus in this book cover by Studio Blue. Image from The World Between: The Circus in 20th Century American Art. *Courtesy of Studio Blue.*

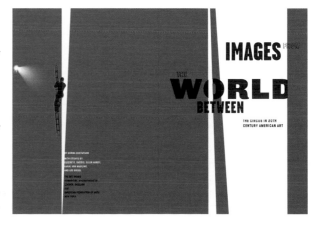

This poster by Alexander Isley, Inc., effectively organizes and emphasizes many levels of hierarchical information with the use of weight, scale, color, and alignment. Art director: Tara Benyei.

Type within type is how Alexander Isley chose to promote a lecture he was giving. The text is set within hand-drawn letterforms, and certain words and phrases are emphasized through a change in scale. Director, writer, and art director: Alexander Isley. Courtesy of Alexander Isley.

The Awards for Design Excellence of AIA Philadelphia recognize significant achievements by member firms in planning, design and execution of architectural projects, and promote the public appreciation of design quality. Submissions of all project types and scales are encouraged – large and small, new construction and rehabilitation, interior and exterior. It is the Chapter's intent to recognize any work that exhibits exceptional design quality and is worthy of merit.

Awards for Design Excellence

American Institute of Architects

Philadelphia

Only two typefaces were used to create this energetic, dynamic poster designed by Polite Design. Created entirely from type, this piece uses oversized type to build a layered, architectural structure that anchors the design, as well as a vertical texture created entirely from type that spells out the name of the competition. The blending of these contrasting elements adds depth and complexity to seemingly simple geometric shapes. Courtesy of Polite Design Incorporated.

He shall from time to time give to the Congress Information of the State of the Union, and recommend to their Consideration such Measures as he shall judge necessary and expedient; he may, on extraordinary Occasions, convene both Houses, or either of them, and in Case of Disagreement between them, with Respect to the Time of Adjournment, he may adjourn them to such Time as he shall think proper; he shall receive Ambassadors and other public Ministers; he shall take Care that the Laws be faithfully executed, and shall Commission all the Officers of the United States.

4. The President, Vice President and all civil Officers of the United States, shall be removed from Office on Impeachment for, and Conviction of, Treason, Bribery, or other high Crimes and Misdemeanors.

A very innovative little promotional piece by Doyle Partners uses scale, color, and a layered design to make the U.S. Constitution visually exciting. Courtesy of Doyle Partners.

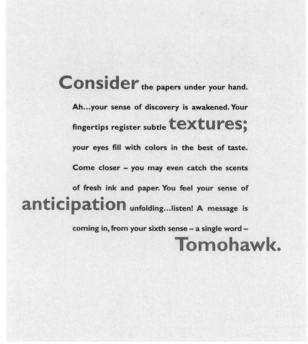

Consider the papers under your hand. Ah...your sense of discovery is awakened. Your fingertips register subtle **textures;** your eyes fill with colors in the best of taste. Come closer – you may even catch the scents of fresh ink and paper. You feel your sense of **anticipation** unfolding...listen! A message is coming in, from your sixth sense – a single word – **Tomohawk.**

A change of point size, color, and alignment of select words draws the viewer in and through the copy in this piece by Hornall Anderson Design Works, Inc. Courtesy of Hornall Anderson Design Works, Inc.

The title of this book, as well as the publisher's numeric name (010 Publishers) is cleverly placed within the lowercase alphabet with only the use of color setting it apart from the rest–a very appropriate, typographic solution for the subject matter! Designed by Jan Middledorp, Bart de Haas, and Peter Verheul. Courtesy of Jan Middledorp.

This dynamic campaign brochure by Michael Vanderbyl Design turns the graceful letterforms of Adobe Trajan into a dramatic, eye-catching graphic statement. Courtesy of Michael Vanderbyl Design.

CURRENCY REDESIGN

Jimmy Moss, Instructor, School of Architecture and Design, Woodbury University, Burbank, California

Objective

To develop facility with typographic hierarchy and initial understanding of typographic systems

Assignment

Redesign a set of United States paper currency. There are two stages to this project. In the first stage, you will design a single bill, utilizing one typeface, one color, and only two type sizes. In the second stage, you will design a set of three bills, utilizing one typeface, two colors, and three type sizes.

Process

Step 1: Do an analysis of the kinds of typographic information and the relative importance of that information on a one- or five-dollar bill (hierarchy). Take into consideration all of the text on the front of the bill. Next, sketch a variety of layouts that visually emphasize the information you believe to be most important, of secondary importance, of lesser importance, etc.

Pay attention to meaning and clarity in your sketches. Look for opportunities to simplify or to magnify essential elements of your renderings to create a striking currency. Remember, you are only able to use two sizes of one typeface for the first part of the project, so be sure that your sketches reflect this limitation. Your initial sketches may be in colored pencil; however, you will create your bill for presentation in digital form and present it as a hi-res (high resolution), full-color proof.

Step 2: Building on what you have learned about how we read visual information from Step 1, develop a set of three bills ($1, $5, $10). Each bill should have a family resemblance to the other bills in your set, while still easily distinguishable from the others. There should be no confusion as to what is the denomination of each bill. Work toward variety, within a consistent typographic attitude and vernacular.

Specifications

Size: 9.1875 × 3.9375 inches (1.5 times actual)
Color: Step 1: one spot color; step 2: two spot colors
Options: The use of the portraits is optional. Do not use the decorative illustration, as this is a typographic exercise, rather than an illustration exercise.

These two sets of solutions to the Currency Redesign assignment were done by Amanda Cole and Vincent Akuin, respectively. Courtesy of Amanda Cole and Vincent Akuin.

EXPRESSIVE TYPOGRAPHY

Stephanie Nace, Assistant Professor, University of South Carolina, Columbia, South Carolina

Assignment

Using a 4 × 4 inch accordion format, explore the technique of visual story-telling through timing and sequencing of type. Depict a poem or song lyric of your choice using different fonts, sizes, and color to create typographic textures and/or images. The key here is to think about what words sound like and what pauses look like.

Objective
• To understand the use of timing and sequence in visual storytelling
• To explore type forms
• To consider storytelling in a visual context
• To experiment with typefaces, styles, and sizes
• Use expressive and interesting typography

Deliverables
• Weekly sketches and storyboards
• Final accordion-folded book

Process
Step 1: Pick a song lyric or poem that has many expressive, descriptive, and action words in it.

Step 2: Sketch and/or storyboard the sequence of the words and/or letters. It will be key to think about pacing and how your viewer will read your book. Your accordion-panel book may turn 90 degrees at any time, or it may run vertically or horizontally.

Step 3: Once you have finalized your design concept, convert to digital format.

NOTE: Both front and back paper choices are up to the designer.

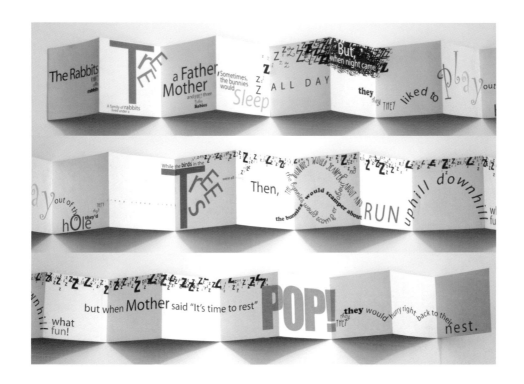

Creative solutions to the Expressive Typography assignment by Kari Taylor, Ferris Ivester Joye, and Daniel Machado.
Courtesy of Kari Taylor, Ferris Ivester Joye, and Daniel Machado.

t is like pre
aring a won
erful recipe
ou can just
hrow in gre
ents togeth
randomly ar
live with w
at you get, o
you can mea

CHAPTER SEVEN

FINE-TUNING AND TWEAKING YOUR TYPE

Becoming type-savvy is like learning to see in a new way. It takes learning, understanding, and digesting the basics, then lots of practice paying close attention to the type that is all around us. Details in the typography of ads, magazines, book covers, movie titles, and credits—even bus and subway posters—will become progressively more apparent to the eye. And details are key. You should never be comfortable with your type until all the details are fine tuned and tweaked to perfection.

Once the actual type is formatted, it is time to make it visually appealing. The typography should look readable, inviting, and not be disrupted by typographic distractions, which, although seemingly insignificant, can make a huge difference in the appearance of your text.

HYPHENATION

Hyphenated words are a necessary evil in much typesetting. They allow for a better looking, tighter rag and help achieve a more natural block of justified type that needs less stretching and squeezing (the spaces, that is!). They also allow you to fit more words in a line.

It is generally considered acceptable to have two lines in a row ending in a hyphenated word—but no more. Be careful not to have too many hyphenated line endings in a paragraph, even if they are not in successive rows, as they affect readability. Most design software allows you to customize the hyphenation preferences to your liking. Familiarize yourself with this function, as it is essential to getting your type to look the way you want.

If tweaking this automatic function does not get the results you want, try manually rebreaking the troublesome lines; or, if possible, edit your copy (or have your editor do this) to achieve a better flow. Additionally, sometimes adjusting the width of the column ever so slightly (especially ragged copy, where it can easily go unnoticed) will result in fewer breaks.

Some people (designers and clients alike) dislike hyphenation and avoid it entirely by turning it off in the preferences. Beware this global point of view and try to be flexible, even if it means making some manual hyphenations. Setting copy with numerous long words (including medical or pharmaceutical copy), as well as text set in foreign languages with very long words (such as German), can result in a rag that is extremely deep and unattractive, and that affects the readability of the text more than the lack of hyphenations.

Here is a man suffering from inner restlessness and cannot abide in his place. He would like to push for-ward under these circum-stances, but repeatedly en-counters insuperable ob-stacles. Therefore his situa-tion entails an inner con-flict. This is due to the obstinacy with which he seeks to enforce his will. If he would desist from this obstinacy, everything would go well.

Here is a man suffering from inner restlessness and cannot abide in his place. He would like to push forward under these cir-cumstances, but repeatedly encounters insuperable obstacles. Therefore his situation entails an inner conflict. This is due to the obstinacy with which he seeks to enforce his will. If he would desist from this obstinacy, everything would go well.

Here is a paragraph with no less than six horrendous hyphenations in a row! It can easily be improved with some manual breaks, as seen on the right. (The I Ching)

Discretionary Hyphens

When manually hyphenating a word within text, always use a discretionary hyphen rather than a standard hyphen. A discretionary hyphen is visible when a word is hyphenated at the end of the line but disappears if the text reflows and the word in which it's placed no longer needs to break, eliminating the need for the hyphenation. This way you will avoid those nasty hyphenated words unexpectedly appearing in the middle of a line.

Discretionary hyphens can be accessed in the following manner:

Adobe InDesign
• Type > Insert Special Character > Hyphens and Dashes > Discretionary Hyphen
Or:
• Command or control + shift + hyphen.

QuarkXPress
• Utilities > Insert Character > Special > Discretionary Hyphen
Or:
• Command or control + hyphen.

HUNG PUNCTUATION AND OPTICAL MARGIN ALIGNMENT

In a block of copy that is aligned flush left or justified, certain punctuation marks, such as an apostrophe or quotation mark, occurring at the beginning of a line can make it appear as if that line is indented slightly, creating a visually uneven alignment. The same is true when these punctuation marks as well as others, such as a period, comma, or asterisk, appear at the end of a line in copy that is justified or flush right. This is because these characters are smaller than most others and have a lot of white space above or below them (or less vertical mass, as I often describe it). To remedy this, many typographers and type-savvy designers extend the punctuated line into the margin a bit to make the line look optically aligned. This is traditionally called hung punctuation.

Today's design software has become very sophisticated; it not only has the ability to hang punctuation but any other characters that impair the alignment, including letters, numerals, and symbols in order to create a visually uniform margin. This sophisticated technique is one of the secrets to creating professional typography.

"We have so asserted our station, both in the old time and in the modern time, also," said the nephew, gloomily, "that I believe our name to be more detested than any name in France."

"Let us hope so," said the uncle. "Detestation of the high is the involuntary homage of the low."

"There is not," pursued the nephew, in his former tone, "a face I can look at, in all this country round about us, which looks at me with any deference on it but the dark deference of fear and slavery."

"We have so asserted our station, both in the old time and in the modern time also," said the nephew, gloomily, "that I believe our name to be more detested than any name in France."

"Let us hope so," said the uncle. "Detestation of the high is the involuntary homage of the low."

"There is not," pursued the nephew, in his former tone, "a face I can look at, in all this country round about us, which looks at me with any deference on it but the dark deference of fear and slavery."

Hanging punctuation is a technique that gives your typography a very professional look. By extending the punctuation beyond the margin, the visual alignment of your margins will improve. Check out both the left and right margins of these "before and after" examples to see the improvement. (A Tale of Two Cities)

Hung Punctuation and Margin Alignment

Hung punctuation is the practice of hanging (or pulling) certain punctuation, such as periods, commas, hyphens, quotes, and asterisks, into the margin of a flush edge of text to create the appearance of a more visually aligned edge. It is considered an advanced technique that was done with regularity by experienced typographers prior to desktop publishing, but it became more challenging, if not impossible, to achieve in the early days of design software.

Today, both InDesign and most recently QuarkXPress have the capability of creating a more optically aligned text margin, and not just with hanging punctuation. They each have differing features and capabilities, but both go a long way toward helping to achieve professional-looking typography.

Adobe InDesign

The Optical Margin Alignment feature of InDesign is controlled by the Story panel. When this is turned on (it is off by default), not only is punctuation "pulled" into the margin (outside the text margin) for a more uniform appearance but so are serifs and as well the edges of certain overhanging characters, such as the cap *A, W,* and the numeral *1.* InDesign gives you control over how much these characters extend into the margin, but the adjustment is for the entire text frame, not each character or paragraph.

To set Optical Margin Alignment:

- Select the text.
- Under Type in the main menu, choose Story.
- Check Optical Margin Alignment.
- Select a point size for the amount of overhang by starting with the point size of the type and going up (or down) from there. Go by what looks good to

your eye, not by the number, which can sometimes be considerably larger than the size of the text.

QuarkXPress

Quark 8's new Hanging Character feature allows you to control the look of your text margin alignment quickly by applying pre-loaded settings for Hanging Punctuation, which hang the full width of the character, and Punctuation Margin Alignment, which can hang characters partially. You can also customize settings to fit the needs of a specific design, client, font, or even character. Settings can be controlled and applied to one or multiple paragraphs, and not an entire text box or story.

To set Hanging Characters:

- Select the text.
- Go to Style > Formats...
- Open the Paragraph Attributes > Formats.
- From the Hanging Character Set drop-down menu, select Hanging Punctuation, or Punctuation Margin Alignment.

To customize the settings, go to:

- Edit > Hanging Characters, then edit as desired.

Note that customizing the hanging character settings is fairly complicated and not for the faint of heart!

Adjusts optical alignment from the Story Palette in InDesign.

Note: (Paragraph Attributes dialog box)

Paragraph Attributes

Formats Tabs Rules

Left Indent: 0"
First Line: 0"
Right Indent: 0"
Leading: auto
Space Before: 0"
Space After: 0"
Alignment: Left
H&J: Standard
Char Align: Baseline
Hanging Character Se...

Drop Caps
Character Count: 1
Line Count: 3

Keep Lines Together
All Lines in ¶
Start: 2 End: 2

Keep with Next ¶
Lock to Grid
Page Grid
Baseline

East Asian Punctuation (Line Fit Priority)
✓ Hanging Punctuation
None
Punctuation Margin Alignment

Apply   Cancel   OK

QuarkXPress's Paragraph Attributes dialog box from which you can select a Hanging Character Set option.

VISUAL ALIGNMENT

Horizontal Alignment

The concept of horizontal alignment takes hung punctuation one step further. Your computer aligns characters (including punctuation, figures, and symbols) by the edge of the character plus its side bearing, which is the blank space assigned to it in a font so it doesn't crash into adjacent characters. When a line of centered type begins or ends with certain characters containing a lot of negative space, such as periods, commas, apostrophes, dashes, asterisks, and quotations marks, that line can appear to be off-center. This problem is magnified in larger type settings, such as centered headlines, subheads, titles, etc.

When this occurs, shift the offending line slightly to the right or left, until it visually or optically aligns. There are several ways to do this. The fastest and easiest way—and the one that gives you the most control—to optically or visually align text is to kern the character in question to an adjacent space (yes, you can kern a character to a space, and vice versa). Add the word space if necessary, then kern until the desired alignment is achieved. Another method is to insert a "thin" space, which is now provided in many design applications, wherever you need a small adjustment.

It is helpful to look at your text from a slight distance when balancing horizontal alignment, since it is difficult to know how much of an adjustment is enough. When in doubt, less is more until you get the hang of it. **NOTE:** When using an italic typestyle, you might notice that it almost never seems to align horizontally. In most cases, this is an optical illusion. Beware

This movie has everything you could possibly want— intrigue, snappy dialogue, and surprises galore.

This movie has everything you could possibly want— intrigue, snappy dialogue, and surprises galore.

Although the upper setting is technically centered, the second line visually appears too far to the left due to the em dash at the end of the line, which doesn't have a lot of vertical mass. The horizontal alignment is improved in the setting below it by shifting the second line a bit to the right. Set in Consul.

of making too many adjustments here (if any at all!), or you will wind up with all of your copy askew!

Vertical Alignment

Visual alignment not only relates to the horizontal positioning of lines of type but to the vertical positioning as well. In settings where all cap lines of type are combined with lines of mostly lowercase, the lines will appear to have varying line spacing while they are all actually the same, due to the fact that the all-cap lines take up more "headroom" than the lowercase lines. The same illusion can happen if one or more lines have many more ascenders and/or descenders than the other lines. To remedy this and to create the appearance of even line spacing, you will need to adjust the spacing between each line as necessary to give the appearance of the lines being equidistant from each other. What matters most is for your type to optically appear to have even line spacing, even if they have varying measurements of space.

At the Seaside

When I was down beside the sea
A wooden spade they gave to me
To dig the sandy shore.

My holes were empty like a cup.
In every hole the sea came up,
Till it could come no more.

In this poem set in italics, some of the lines appear to be too far to the right. This is an illusion! But adjusting them, even just a little, will often result in the whole text block becoming askew. (A Child's Garden of Verse)

Gigantic Tag Sale
EVERYTHING MUST GO
MAKE US AN OFFER!
Every offer considered

Gigantic Tag Sale
EVERYTHING MUST GO
MAKE US AN OFFER!
Every offer considered

Vertical alignment is often overlooked as many assume that consistent leading results in visual balance—not always so! The top example is set 24/28, but due to the lack of descenders in the third line and the few ascenders in the fourth line, these lines appear to be further apart than the rest. When the leading is adjusted for each individual line (the bottom example), the appearance improves, even though the last line is now set with negative leading, 24/23!

YOU'VE probably heard of "Thighs of Steel," "Buns of Steel," and other popular physical fitness titles. But you've probably never heard of an exercise program called "Superior Rectus of Steel"– nor should you. That muscle, along with the inferior rectus and the lateral rectus muscles, controls the movement of the human eyeball. Although I've seen and read many texts that would qualify for the title, our goal, as typesetters, is to avoid giving the reader's eye a workout.

The type that hugs this oversized initial in U&lc has been positioned very carefully to create visual alignment. Notice the open quotes that extend the margin slightly to balance the white space underneath it. Courtesy of International Typeface Corporation.

BAD LINE BREAKS & HYPHENATION POINTS make a reader's eye work harder. What happens? You have to skip *back* in the text — back to the end of the previous line, then ahead to the next line, to try to parse the poorly hyphenated word. When you read a hyphenated word, you do two things: you store the first part of the word in your short-term memory, and you make guesses about what the second part of the word will be. All of this happens very fast, and, for most readers, happens below the conscious level. Poor hyphenation raises this process to the conscious level — and suddenly you're thinking about the mechanism of reading, rather than the content of the text. Your eyes get tired, and you get grumpy.

Damned if you do
Given the risk of producing "read rage," why do we use hyphenation at all? Because, without hyphenation, we face horrible letter- and word-spacing in justified text, or wide variation in line lengths in non-justified copy — both of which are at least as irritating to the reader as bad hyphenation.

Like just about everything else having to do with type, it's a balancing act. You've got to work with the word- and letterspacing of your text (as I've mentioned in previous issues), and you've got to watch every line break. And, yes, this means you have to read and at least partially understand the text. There's just no other way.

The hyphenation controls in your page layout program can help you — provided you understand that they're not (and probably can't be) perfect. You've got to help them out — left to their own devices, today's page layout programs are almost guaranteed to produce hyphenation problems. Namely:

☞ *Bad breaks*. Hyphenation breaks should always fall between syllables, and should never appear inside a syllable — but every desktop publishing program will break inside a syllable in certain conditions.

☞ *Short fragments*. When the part of a word before or after the hyphen is too short, readability suffers. You've probably seen paragraphs ending with a line containing only "ly" or "ed."

☞ *"Ladders" of hyphens*. When you see successive lines ending with a hyphen, you're looking at a "ladder" of hyphens. Ladders of hyphens can cause the reader's eye to skip ahead several lines in the text. This is less of a problem (from the reader's point of view) than badly spaced lines. There are two ways to approach this problem.

16

"I wish I hadn't mentioned Dinah!" she said to herself in a melancholy tone. "Nobody seems to like her, down here, and I'm sure she's the best cat in the world! Oh, my dear Dinah! I wonder if I shall ever see you any more!" And here poor Alice began to cry again, for she felt very lonely and low-spirited."

"I wish I hadn't mentioned Dinah!" she said to herself in a melancholy tone. "Nobody seems to like her, down here, and I'm sure she's the best cat in the world! Oh, my dear Dinah! I wonder if I shall ever see you any more!" And here poor Alice began to cry again, for she felt very lonely and low-spirited.

Aligning initials with punctuation can be tricky. The example on the left is aligned by the quotes; but even though they are set smaller than the initial for better balance, it still creates an unwanted visual indentation. The appearance improves when the initial is aligned by the square serifs, letting the quotes hang into the left margin. There are no rules here–just move things around until it looks right.

RAGS

When setting type with a ragged margin (flush left or flush right), become aware of the shape that the ragged line endings are making. A good rag goes in and out in small increments. A poor rag is one that makes unnatural shapes with the white space or that has deep indents due to lack of hyphenation. When this occurs, it might be necessary to make manual line breaks (making sure a dictionary is on hand to look up proper breaks) or to edit your copy to improve the rag.

Not many days after we heard the church-bell tolling for a long time, and looking over the gate we saw a long, strange black coach that was covered with black cloth and was drawn by black horses; after that came another and another and another, and all were black, while the bell kept tolling, tolling. They were carrying young Gordon to the churchyard to bury him. He would never ride again. What they did with Rob Roy I never knew; but 'twas all for one little hare.

Not many days after we heard the church-bell tolling for a long time, and looking over the gate we saw a long, strange black coach that was covered with black cloth and was drawnby black horses; after that came another and another and another, and all were black, while the bell kept tolling, tolling. They were carrying young Gordon tothe churchyard to bury him. He would never ride again. What they did with Rob Roy I never knew; but 'twas all for one little hare.

When setting type flush left, such as this text set in ITC American Typewriter, be aware of the shape that the ragged line endings are making. A good rag goes in and out in small increments. A poor rag, such as this one, creates unnatural shapes with the white space. (Black Beauty)

The rag in the example at left can be easily corrected by making manual line breaks.

Breaking for Sense

When setting display type that is more than one line, close attention should be paid to the line breaks. In today's digital world, where the designer has become the typesetter, you are responsible for making the text as readable, logical, and attractive as possible, and the line breaks have a major impact on this.

Breaking for sense means breaking a line where one would logically pause when reading it aloud. This can includes keeping adjectives with their nouns, breaking after punctuation, keeping proper names or hyphenated words on one line, etc. In addition, avoid hyphenations totally.

> # The Blues Had A Baby And They Named It Rock 'n' Roll
>
> # The Blues Had A Baby And They Named It Rock 'n' Roll

The upper setting has poor line breaks in terms of context as well as balance. A phrase like Rock 'n' Roll should not be broken, and the very short third line is awkward in any case. The setting below it not only reads better, but it looks better as well. Set in Ed Roman.

Adobe Text Composer

InDesign offers two methods for text composition: Adobe Paragraph Composer (the default setting) and Adobe Single-Line Composer. Either method, or a combination of both, can be used for both justified and ragged copy.

Adobe Paragraph Composer attempts to minimize unattractive hyphenations by evaluating all the lines of text in a paragraph and making breaks accordingly. For justified text, it creates more even spacing with fewer hyphens.

Adobe Single-Line Composer takes the traditional approach, that is, composing text one line at a time.

Paragraph Composer can be a valuable tool for text composition, particularly justified text. But when making manual changes to line breaks or hyphenations, switch to Single-Line Composer for the paragraph in question; this allows you to edit rags and hyphenations manually without affecting the surrounding lines.

Adobe Paragraph and Single-Line Composer can be accessed two ways:
• Go to the Paragraph Palette menu.
• Select Adobe Paragraph Composer (the default) or Adobe Single-Line Composer.
Or:
• Go to the Paragraph Palette or the Control Palette menu.
• Select Justification.
• Select an option from the Composer menu.

TRACKING

Tracking is the global addition or reduction of the overall letter spacing in a selected block of text. In most design software, it can be applied in small increments. This is a very helpful function for fine-tuning the color of your type.

Remember that fonts are spaced and kerned to look their best at certain point-size ranges. If your type size is much smaller than this range, that is, if you're setting a typeface that is intended for display, at small point sizes, you will want to open the tracking to improve the readability, as the letters will probably get too close and tight, and even begin to touch. Conversely, when you set a text typeface at larger sizes, you might need to tighten up the tracking to keep the words from falling apart, so to speak. Some fonts might not be spaced to your liking at any size, and they will need adjusting to give them the balance you are looking for. For example, many older fonts are spaced extremely tightly and often need adjustment.

The term letterspacing can also refer to the style of setting very open type for stylistic and design purposes. This technique is most effectively used with all-cap settings that don't depend on their letter shapes to be recognized. But, unfortunately, it is commonly misused and abused, especially when applied to lowercase. When it is used, it should be limited to a few words or small amounts of copy, as it definitely reduces readability.

Tracking is the addition or reduction of the overall letterspacing in a selected block of text. In most page layout programs, it can be applied in small increments. This is a very helpful function for fine-tuning the color of your type.

Tracking is the addition or reduction of the overall letterspacing in a selected block of text. In most page layout programs, it can be applied in small increments. This is a very helpful function for fine-tuning the color of your type.

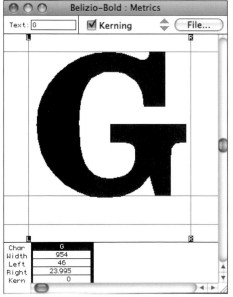

Fonts are spaced and kerned to look their best at certain point-size ranges. If your type is much smaller than this range, especially if it is a very bold typeface—such as ITC Kabel Ultra (as shown here with zero tracking)—you might want to open the tracking to improve the readability, as was done to the bottom example set at +25 tracking. The change might seem subtle, but the readability is improved and it can head off printing problems due to ink spread.

A character's spacing consists of the width of the character plus the right and left side bearings. Think of it as an invisible box around each character. This character has 46 units of space on the left and 24 on the right, as indicated below it.

Adjusting Tracking

Adobe InDesign

There are several ways to adjust the tracking of selected text in InDesign. Begin by highlighting a range of characters. Then choose from these methods:

Character and Control palettes

• Use presets in tracking pull-down menu (increments vary).
• Use the tracking palette arrows (10 unit increments).
• Shift + palette arrows (25 unit increments).

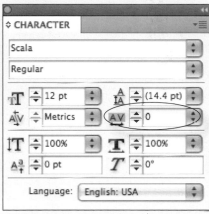

Tracking can be adjusted from the Character palette in Adobe InDesign.

Keyboard commands

• Option + left or right arrow key (20 unit increments)
• Option + command + left or right arrow key (100 unit increments)

Manual

• Enter specific values manually in tracking field.

REMINDER: Don't forget to highlight or select desired copy to activate the tracking function. Kerning function will be deactivated when tracking.

QuarkXPress

There are several ways to adjust the tracking in QuarkXPress. Begin by highlighting a range of characters. Then choose from the following methods:

Palettes

• Go to Measurement palette.
• Use the palette arrows to the right of the kerning/tracking field (10 unit increments).
• Option + palette arrows to the right of the kerning/tracking field (1 unit increments).

Keyboard commands

• Command / shift + [or] key (20 unit increments)
• Command / opt / shift + [or] key (1 unit increments)

Manual

• Enter specific values manually in kerning/tracking field.

NOTE: In QuarkXPress 8, both kerning and tracking are controlled by the same field in the Measurements palette; which one is activated is dependent on whether you place a cursor between two characters (kerning) or highlight a range of characters (tracking).

Scaling Logos

When designing a typographic logo that will be used at a range of sizes, such as very small for business cards and very large for a poster or billboard, it will usually need to be tweaked so that it is readable, legible, and visually in proportion at every size. Resizing it will optically change its appearance, so any adjustments you make should be subtle and gradual to give the appearance of the logo being the same at all sizes.

The tweaking can include adjusting the letter, word, and line spacing (making them more open as the logo gets smaller); opening the counters (enclosed negative spaces within a character); and adjusting the weight of the thin strokes or the entire letterforms (heavier as the logo gets smaller, and vice versa). It is not unusual for a company to have three to five versions of the same logo for usage at a range of sizes.

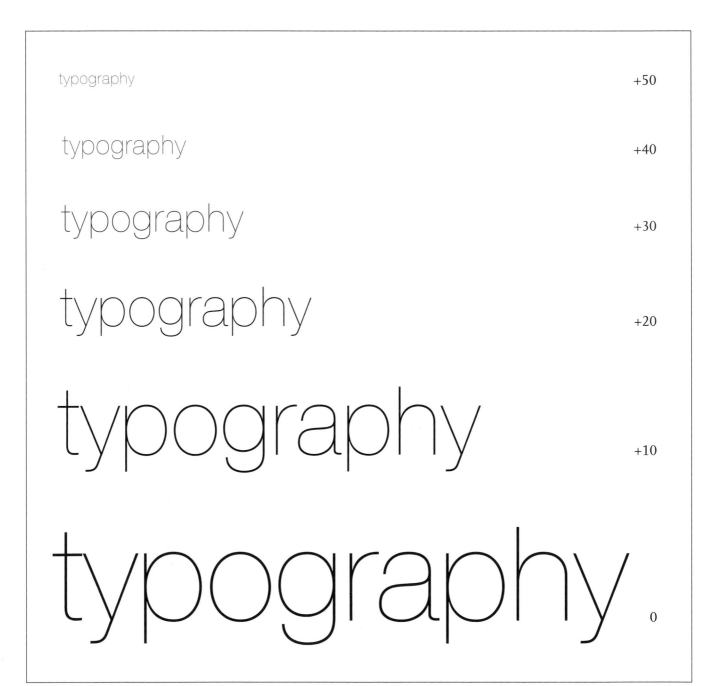

typography   +50

typography   +40

typography   +30

typography   +20

typography   +10

typography   0

In order for Helvetica Neue Ultra Light to look good from 12 point to 100 point, the tracking has been adjusted accordingly.

Glyph Positioning and Baseline Shift

A number of functions built into the software we use every day are often over-looked but are extremely useful. One of those functions is *baseline shift*. This feature shifts a character or group of characters up (positive numbers) or down (negative numbers) relative to the baseline, in tiny increments.

Baseline shift is a great tool for fine-tuning your typography. Try using it to:

- Optically position symbols, such as register, copyright, and trademark (®, ©, and ™).
- Adjust the position of bullets, dashes, ornaments, and other font-based graphics.

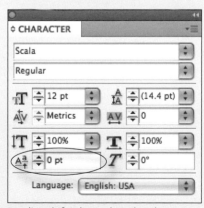

Baseline shift can help fine-tune your type in a variety of ways, as illustrated in these "before and afters."

- Raise the position of hyphens to visually center when used in phone numbers set in lining figures.
- Be expressive with type by raising and lowering individual characters to create a jumpy, jittery effect.
- Tweak the position of parentheses, braces, and brackets relative to the type they enclose.
- Create fractions manually. Use baseline shift to raise the numerator in diagonal fractions.

It is important to note that *baseline shift* does not change the actual line spacing of a character; so when making overall changes in the leading, the baseline-shifted position will be preserved proportionally.

To position glyphs using baseline shift in Adobe InDesign and QuarkXPress, note the following steps:

Baseline shift is located on the Character palette in Adobe InDesign.

Adobe InDesign

- Highlight text.
- Go to Control Panel or Character palette.
- Locate Baseline Shift field.
- Click on the Up or Down arrow key (Shift + click increases the increments).

Or

- Type a numeric value in the Baseline Shift field. Positive values raise the text; negative values lower the text.

QuarkXPress

- Highlight text.
- Select the Text Palette from the pop up menu (click on the A) of the Measurements Tool Bar.
- Click on the up or down arrow to the right of the baseline Shift Field, or enter a value manually.

Or

- Highlight text.
- Use keyboard command shift / opt / com and then + to raise or - to lower in one point increments.

Or

- Highlight text.
- Go to Style > Baseline Shift or Character Attributes Palette (shift / com / D).
- Locate Baseline Shift field.
- Indicate desired value in positive (to raise) or negative (to lower), whole or fractional values.

KERNING

Kerning is the addition or reduction of space between two specific characters. In the days of metal type, it referred only to the reduction of space, but in a digital font, it refers to the addition of space as well. Kern pairs are necessary to balance the white space between certain letter combinations in order to create even color and texture, as well as to optimize readability.

In a quality typeface (or font), each character is spaced to create optimum overall fit with as many characters as possible. The spacing of a character consists of the width of the actual glyph plus the right and left side bearings, which is the space added to keep the characters from crashing into each other when set. (Visualize this as an invisible box around each character.) But due to the quirks of our Latin-based alphabet, there are many combinations that don't naturally fit together well and need adjustments. Therefore, kern pairs are usually built into a font by the type designer or foundry to improve the overall spacing of the typeface.

There are certain commonly known pairs that almost always need to be kerned, such as *a*, *Ye*, and *AV*, etc. Many manufacturers concentrate on a specific set of pairs, primarily consisting of cap and lowercase combos. For this reason, you might find other character pairs that need adjustment, such as letters next to punctuation, symbols, or numerals.

A high-quality font can have over a thousand kern pairs, but this alone doesn't mean it will look good. If a typeface isn't spaced well to begin with, it will need many more kern pairs than a properly spaced font. Kerning, however, ought not to be used as a Band-Aid for a poorly spaced font.

Custom Kerning

There are occasions when the kerning and spacing of a headline, subhead, and other display showings appear uneven and unbalanced, with some pairs too open, and others too tight. While this can happen with any font, it can be particularly noticeable when using a font intended for text settings at display sizes. Fonts are kerned and spaced to look their best at a particular point size range: some are intended for text, others for display–but this doesn't mean you can't "cross the line," so to speak, with some typefaces. When doing this, an important concept to understand is that at larger point sizes, special relationships change, and a well-kerned font might still need tweaking at certain sizes.

If the kerning in a headline or subhead leaves something to be desired, you might need to apply some custom kerning. All current design software has the capability to adjust kerning manually. There are often keyboard shortcuts for these functions that are very helpful when you are making many adjustments. When kerning type, enlarge the screen image as necessary to view the adjustments you are making as accurately as possible. At smaller sizes,

The beauty and elegance of Didot speak for itself in this dramatic one-word poster. Thoughtful and deliberate spacing of the type, including the TY combination, as well as lot of white space, contribute to its effectiveness. Courtesy of Katja Gretzinger.

Fa Pa Ta Ye We rk AV PA AT

F. T. Y. P, ." y. r, f' 7. -7 's

Fa Pa Ta Ye We rk AV PA AT

F. T. Y. P, ." y. r, f' 7. -7 's

Wail Vincent Van Gogh New York

February 7, 1957. (516) 784-1716

Wail Vincent Van Gogh New York

February 7, 1957. (516) 784-1716

There are certain commonly known pairs that almost always need to be kerned, such as Ta, Ye, AV, as well as characters next to punctuation, symbols, or numerals. Here you can see how some of these combinations look before and after kern adjustments.

characters on the screen tend to jump and shift when adjusting the spacing of other characters; this is minimized the larger your screen view. In addition, make sure to proof what you have done on a high-resolution printer. Kerning on the screen is extremely deceptive, as your screen is only 72 dots per inch while the actual printed piece is a much higher resolution. It will become easier to judge how much to kern when you get the hang of it and know what five units actually look like for your application, as unit values can vary from application to application.

Remember that the object of proper letter fit (and the goal of kerning) is to achieve optically even space between all characters, which in turn leads to a consistent overall texture and color. This sounds great theoretically but can be difficult to achieve due to the idiosyncrasies of the individual designs of the characters of the alphabet. One way to look at it is to imagine pouring sand in between each pair of characters; each combination should have roughly the same amount of sand (or negative space, if you will).

Numerals, or figures, have their own special spacing and kerning problems. If you are using a font with only one set of figures, and they happen to have tabular spacing, they might need to be adjusted. (Read more about Figures in Chapter 8, page 177.) Tabular figures all have the same total width, even the numeral one, which is usually a very narrow character.

This is why the "1" in years and dates often appears separated from surrounding numerals. But if you are not creating a chart or a table   (and especially in a headline), tabular figures should be kerned—especially the numeral one. And don't forget punctuation and symbols, the spacing of which might also need to be tweaked to look their best.

It is important to keep a few more things in mind when kerning your work. Any kern changes you make apply only to the pair that you have highlighted and not to the actual font. This means that if you want your document to be consistent (and by all means it should be), you have to search for all same (or similar) combinations and kern them to the same value. This is most important in headlines where variances are most obvious and are extremely undesirable and unprofessional.

Kerning Guidelines
Here are some important guidelines to get you started:
- There are three basic classes of character relationships:
    1. *straight to straight:* the most open of the three
    2. *straight to round* (or, *round to straight*): slightly tighter spacing than straight to straight
    3. *round to round:* slightly tighter spacing than straight to round. Don't jam them together!

Shown above are the three basic classes of character relationships.

- "Like" letterforms should have "like" spacing. A *de* and an *op*, for instance, are both straight to rounds and should look similar.
- Serifs of straight-sided characters should *not* touch.
- Serifs of diagonal strokes (and certain other problematic characters) can overlap a bit, but *if* and *how much* is a question of taste.
- Strive for visually even negative space between all characters. Remember the *sand in an hourglass* principle.
- Consistency is critical! Check your work carefully.

When it comes to custom kerning, don't err on the side of overdoing it—that is, kerning too many pairs too much—especially without a proper understanding of what constitutes good kerning and spacing. In most instances, "less is more," especially until your eye begins to see spatial relationships easily and accurately. Stick with it, and with time and experience, your eye will become highly trained, and fine-tuning type will become second nature to you.

Adjusting Kerning

Adobe InDesign

Automatic kerning

Adobe InDesign offers several options for adjusting automatic kerning, located in both the Character palette and the Control palette.

• The Metrics setting uses a font's built-in kerning pairs. This is the default setting and is usually best when the font has adequate kern pair tables.

• The Optical setting lets InDesign determine the spacing between character pairs. This can be useful when a font has few or no built-in kern pairs, or when the overall spacing seems uneven, particularly in text where manual kerning can be impractical, tedious, and time-consuming. In addition, optical kerning can be used to adjust the spacing when combining different fonts or type sizes of the same font.

Keep in mind that no matter which setting you use, you can always add manual kerns "on top of" them.

Manual or "custom" kerning

There are several ways to adjust individual kern pairs. Remember to begin by placing the cursor between two characters. Then choose from the following methods:

Palettes

• Use presets in kerning pull-down menu (increments vary)
• Use the palette arrows (10 unit increments)
• Shift + palette arrows (25 unit increments)
• Keyboard commands:
    Option + left or right arrow key (20 unit increments)
    Option + command + left or right arrow key (100 unit increments)

Manual

• Enter specific values manually in kerning field.

QuarkXPress

Manual or (custom) kerning

There are several ways to adjust individual kern pairs. Begin by placing the cursor between two characters. Then choose from the following methods:

Palettes

• Go to Measurement palette.
• Use the palette arrows to the right of the kerning/tracking field (10 unit increments).
• Option + palette arrows to the right of the kerning/tracking field (1 unit increments).

Keyboard commands

• Command / shift + [or] key (20 unit increments)
• Command / opt / shift + [or] key (100 unit increments)

Manual

• Enter specific values manually in kerning field.

NOTE: In QuarkXPress 8, both kerning and tracking are controlled by the same field in the Measurements palette; which one is activated is dependent on whether you place a cursor between two characters (kerning) or highlight a range of characters (tracking).

Adobe InDesign's kerning field is located in the Character palette. Kerning values are shown in the same field.

QuarkXPress's kerning field is located in the Measurements palette.

"Work with the best people. Be sure they're fully engaged in the process. Encourage them to disagree with you, and respect their contribution."

Beautiful use of properly kerned italics in this colorful piece designed by VSA Partners, Inc. Notice the closed quotes that are kerned to sit above the period and that also hang slightly into the right margin to appear visually aligned. Courtesy of VSA Partners.

Type on a Curve

Setting type on a curve is a task most designers encounter at one time or another. To achieve professional results and overcome the special challenges presented by this technique, particular attention must be paid to character spacing and positioning.

Placing type on a curved baseline alters the relationship between characters in unpredictable ways, in that it inserts an inverted triangle of space between all of the characters. Depending on the shape of each character and what character it sits next to, the consistency of the overall spacing as well as the spacing between each pair of characters can be affected and disturbed.

Most often, the overall spacing of type becomes too open when placed on a curve. If this happens, reduce the tracking as necessary until the desired spacing and readability are achieved.

Another common problem with curved text is that the spacing between certain letter combinations will become too open in relationship to the rest. If this is the case, adjust the kerning accordingly until the spacing is correct.

Sometimes, even tweaking the tracking and kerning aren't enough to give you the desired result. In these cases, setting the problematic characters separately from the rest of the text will allow for more flexibility in placement.

HAPPY MOTHER'S DAY
❶

HAPPY MOTHER'S DAY
❷

HAPPY MOTHER'S DAY
❸

HAPPY MOTHER'S DAY
❹

1. This type is nicely spaced as long as it stays on a horizontal baseline.
2. When the same type is placed on a curve, the spacing becomes too open and uneven.
3. Reducing the tracking improves the overall spacing, but there are still some uneven letter combinations.
4. Consistent spacing is finally achieved by adjusting the kerning between problematic letter pairs, most noticeably around the Ys.

WORD SPACING

The amount of space between words is called word spacing, naturally. The word spacing should not be so little that the words start to run into each other and not so much that your eye has trouble reading groups of words, because it is interrupted by large white blocks. A good preliminary guideline for word spacing in text is that it should approximate the width of the lowercase *n* or *o*. This is because word spacing should be in proportion to the overall width of the type design, that is, the word spacing of a condensed face should be narrower and an expanded design wider. The word spacing for display type should be slightly narrower than for text.

The word spacing of a typeface is predetermined by your font (and differs from font to font), but it can be modified by changing the "optimum space" value in the justification preferences in your page-layout program.

For example, some commercial fonts have too much word spacing, which can lead to visual hesitations, which reduce readability. In some of these instances, the spacing can be improved by setting the word space to around 80 to 85 percent, but be sure to look over the type and make any necessary adjustments to this value until the desired color is achieved.

MASSAGE THE RAPIST

MASSAGE THERAPIST

Look how an improperly placed word space can totally change the meaning, as is cleverly demonstrated in this promotional piece designed by Stephen Banham of The Letterbox.

The amount of space between words is called word spacing, naturally. The word spacing should not be so little that the words start to run into each other, and not so much that your eye has trouble reading groups of words because it is being interrupted by large white blocks.

The amount of space between words is called word spacing, naturally. The word spacing should not be so little that the words start to run into each other, and not so much that your eye has trouble reading groups of words because it is being interrupted by large white blocks.

The amount of space between words is called word spacing, naturally. The word spacing should not be so little that the words start to run into each other, and not so much that your eye has trouble reading groups of words because it is being interrupted by large white blocks.

Word spacing should not be so little that the words start to run into each other, as in the first example, and not so much that your eye has trouble reading groups of words, because it is interrupted by large white blocks, as in the second text block. The third example is the most balanced and the most readable.

Adjusting Word Spacing

The ability to adjust the word spacing of any selected text is a somewhat obscure but important feature. Although this method is most often used to adjust word spacing in justified type, the same feature can be used to adjust the word spacing of text with any alignment. Here's how it is done:

Adobe InDesign
To change the default or create new word spacing settings:
• Highlight the text.
• Open the Paragraph palette.
• Select Justification from the flyout menu.
• Enter a value in Word Spacing row in the middle field labeled Desired. The value will be a percentage of the normal, or built-in value of the selected font.

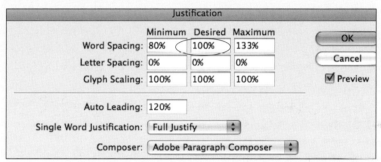

Word spacing can be adjusted in the Justification dialog box of InDesign by adjusting the "desired" word-space value. This works for any text alignment, not only justified text.

QuarkXPress
To change the default or create new word spacing settings:
• Open Hyphenation & Justification (H&J) dialog box via Edit > H&J or keyboard command opt / com / J.
• Edit *Standard* to alter the default or click on *New* to create a custom setting.
• Under Justification method, enter the desired value in the Space row in the middle field labeled Opt. The value will be a percentage of the normal, or built-in value of the selected font.
• Name the setting if it is new.

To access the setting:
• Highlight text.
• Go to Style > Formats, which opens the Paragraph Attributes dialog box, or use keyboard command Shift / com / F, which opens the Paragraph Attributes dialog box.
• Select setting from H&J pull-down menu.

NOTE: The Desired/Opt value must be in between the Minimum and Maximum values, so adjust these as necessary even though it will have no effect on nonjustified text.

IMPORTANT: If you change the font or use a document as a template, note that the previous kerning, tracking, and word spacing settings will still be in effect unless you change them.

INFORMATION HIERARCHY BOOK
David Kadavy, Instructor, Metropolitan Community College, Omaha, Nebraska

Objective
This project will teach the student how to express the difference in importance and semantic meaning of information using basic typographic techniques.

Assignment
Using restricted methods of differentiating information (proximity, size, weight, ornament, and color) develop a layout for each of the projects below using the supplied text.

Examine the information in the text, which is from the cover of *The Elements of Typographic Style* by Robert Bringhurst. Determine a hierarchy for the information.

After you have read and understood the text to be arranged, create an appropriate visual hierarchy, using only the factors indicated in each of the elements below. Develop three options apiece for each of the following:

Project 1: use only position to establish hierarchy
Project 2: use only position and weight
Project 3: use only position and size
Project 4: use only position, size, and weight

Specification
• Final "canvas" size must be 8 ½ × 8 ½ inch.
• All type must be black (no color or shades of gray).
• The canvas must be white.
• The font Helvetica Neue must be used (or any font family selected by instructor).
• Only the normal width font may be used (no condensed or extended versions).
• No "factors" may be used other than those indicated for the appropriate project (again, no color, also no rule lines, boxes, bullet points, or other ornament).
• The exact text supplied must be used. No text is to be repeated or layered into a "texture."
• For Projects 1 and 2, all text must be set at 9 point.
• No italics.
• All type must be set horizontally.

Text

The text used for this assignment is *The Elements of Typographic Style* by Robert Bringhurst. The five elements of the text are numbered (which are to be removed for the assignment).

1. *The Elements of Typographic Style*
2. Robert Bringhurst
3. "All desktop typographers should study this book. It is not just one more publication on typography, like so many others on the market. It is, instead, a must for everybody in the graphic arts, and especially for our new friends entering the field. Written by a noted expert, Robert Bringhurst's book is particularly welcome in an age where typographic design is sometimes misconstrued as a form of private self-expression for designers. As Bringhurst puts it: 'Good typography is like bread: ready to be admired, appraised and dissected before it is consumed.' I wish to see this book become the Typographer's Bible."–Herman Zapf
4. Second edition, revised & enlarged
5. Hartley & Marks
   ISBN 0-88179-132-6
   $24.95 in the USA / $34.95 in Canada

SPACING, KERNING, AND VISUAL ALIGNMENT EXPLORATION
Ilene Strizver, Faculty, School of Visual Arts, New York, New York

Objective
To develop a sensitivity and awareness of the spacing between the characters, words, and lines. Doing the spacing manually with marker and paper first forces one to slowly and methodically explore the shapes of each letter, word, and line of type and the relationships between them.

Assignment
Step 1: Set the following text in a serif text face from a major foundry. Set in five centered lines at 60/72 point (72 point leading).

New grilled wooden key's
"To Be DAVID WALDEN
UNITED STATES 10011."
Van Gogh New York in Awe
May 7, 1957. (511) 784-1710

Turn off kerning (turn off in the application preferences if using Quark, or set kerning to zero for that text if using InDesign); set tracking very open so the text is completely letterspaced. The concept is to eliminate all visual spacing and kerning cues. Set the text twice, one underneath the other.

Step 2: Using tracing paper and a pencil or fine black marker, trace and space each character in the text, tightening and adjusting the spacing between the letters and the words. Pay particular attention to "difficult" or troublesome letter combinations. Redraw as many times as necessary until even color and balance is achieved. One you have spaced each line to your satisfaction, redraw and adjust the vertical and horizontal alignment as necessary.

Step 3: Go back to the first text on your computer and adjust the spacing as follows: using *only* the kerning function (do not use tracking) and leading, manually space the text until it looks like your tracing. (Keyboard commands for kerning work great here.) Continue to adjust and fine-tune until it looks the best it can.

Step 4: Go to the second text, set tracking back to zero, and turn on kerning. Compare the two texts. Evaluate the differences, if any, and tweak your first version if necessary. If you "disagree" with any of the built-in spacing in the second version, be ready to explain and justify your opinion.

REMEMBER: Not all fonts come with perfect spacing and kerning.

New grilled wooden key's
"To Be DAVID WALDEN
UNITED STATES 10011."
Van Gogh New York in Awe
May 7, 1957. (511) 784-1710

New grilled wooden key's
"To Be DAVID WALDEN
UNITED STATES 10011."
Van Gogh New York in Awe
May 7, 1957. (511) 784-1710

The upper showing is set in Adobe Minion Pro with kerning turned off and with +30 tracking in Adobe InDesign units. The lower showing has kerning turned on, zero tracking, and additional custom kerning.

hyphenated words are a necessary evil in typesetting. they allow for a better looking, tighter rag or a more natural block of justified type which needs less stretching, as well as more words

CHAPTER EIGHT

FINESSING YOUR TYPE

Some designs call for a particular typographic style or treatment to make a point effectively and to drive that point home. This can be something as seemingly subtle as selecting the right style of numeral to improve the aesthetics and increase readability or as powerful and dramatic as using a highly designed initial letter treatment to pull it all together. No matter what typographic elements you incorporate into your design, the key to their success is in the details.

Here are some guidelines for finessing some of the often overlooked typographic details that can make all the difference in a well-designed and well-executed piece.

FIGURES

Figures, or numerals as they are often referred to, are a very common element in design. They are used to indicate quantities, prices, dates and years, measurments, and a lot more. Figures come in several flavors, all of which are more commonly available in OpenType fonts.

There are two styles of figures: *lining,* also called aligning, ranging, or cap figures; and *oldstyle,* also called lowercase figures. Lining figures are all the same height and align (thus the name, aligning) on the baseline and cap height. Oldstyle figures are a style of numeral that approximates lowercase letterforms by having an x-height as well as fixed-arrangement ascenders and descenders.

There are also two kinds of spacing for figures: *tabular* and *proportional.* Tabular figures are those where each numeral has the same total character width (that's the width of the numeral itself plus the white space on both sides). Tabular spacing allows

1234567890
1234567890

Lining (or aligning) figures imitate caps in that they all align on the baseline and the cap height. The oldstyle figures below them approximate lowercase letterforms by having an x-height, as well as varying ascenders and descenders.

AT seven, he gave a concert in Warsaw. At 17 he made his Paris debut. And in 1906, at 19 he made his first appearance in Philadelphia.

AT seven, he gave a concert in Warsaw. At 17 he made his Paris debut. And in 1906, at 19 he made his first appearance in Philadelphia.

Oldstyle figures work well in text as they blend in beautifully by not disturbing the color of the body copy as much as lining figures do.

numerals to align vertically in tables (thus the term, *tabular*), financial statements, price lists, invoices, and other columns of figures. Have you ever noticed that the numeral 1 in many fonts has extra space around it? That is because it is a tabular figure.

Proportionally spaced figures, on the other hand, have varying (or proportional) widths so that they look evenly spaced, giving them a more even color and texture, especially around the numeral 1. Proportional figures are not intended for use in charts and tables, since they won't align in vertical columns.

While tabular lining figures are the most commonly available and usually the default in fonts that have more than one style, consider all available figures in the font you are using (especially if it is an OpenType font): proportional oldstyle figures look great in text where they blend in smoothly, while not disturbing the color of the body copy as lining figures do. Proportional lining figures blend better with all-cap settings, and make numeric data stand out from surrounding body text. Tabular lining and oldstyle figures are intended for use in tables, price lists, or anywhere that numerals must align vertically (although tabular oldstyle figures are too irregular to look good set vertically).

When making your font selection, consider how you will be using numerals in your work, and make sure the font you choose offers the style of figures you need. While it is fairly simple to kern one or two tabular ones to improve the spacing for nontabular use, it is nearly impossible to convert the spacing of proportional numerals to tabular spacing so that they align vertically in tables and financial statements.

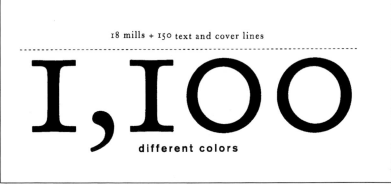

A small amount of information is made visually interesting and eye-catching with the use of oldstyle figures and a simple, yet bold, design in this promotion piece designed by VSA Partners, Inc. Courtesy of VSA Partners.

Accessing Figures in OpenType Fonts

The default figure style in many (but not all) OpenType fonts is tabular lining figures. If that is not what you want, use the OpenType palette in your design application to see if others are available. Here's how:

Adobe InDesign
• Highlight text or select text box.
• Go to Character palette.
• Select OpenType palette.
• If the figure styles at the bottom of the palette are unbracketed (and thus available in that font), select desired style.

NOTE: When both lining and oldstyle figures are available for a font, both tabular and proportional spacing will remain unbracketed, even if only one spacing option is available for that figure style, so let the user beware!

QuarkXPress
• Highlight text.
• Go to Measurements toolbar.
• Select OpenType palette.
• Select desired figure and spacing styles from unbracketed options in the middle of the palette.

InDesign	Quark
Discretionary Ligatures Fractions Ordinal [Swash] [Titling Alternates] [Contextual Alternates] All Small Caps [Slashed Zero] Stylistic Sets ▶ Positional Forms ▶ Superscript/Superior [Subscript/Inferior] [Numerator] [Denominator] Tabular Lining ✓ Proportional Oldstyle Proportional Lining Tabular Oldstyle Default Figure Style	✓ Standard Ligatures Discretionary Ligatures [Small Caps] [All Small Caps] Tabular Figures ✓ Proportional Figures Lining Figures ✓ Oldstyle Figures Fractions [Swashes] Ordinals [Titling Alternates] ✓ [Contextual Alternates] ✓ [Localized Forms] Position ▶

InDesign's figure options are at the bottom of the OpenType palette.

Quark's figure options are located in the middle of the OpenType palette.

SMALL CAPS

Small caps are capital letterforms that are shorter than cap height. When created for a text face, they are usually the height of the lowercase (or a tiny bit taller). Small caps created for a display face have more flexibility in their design and are often taller than the x-height. True-drawn small caps are superior to computer-generated small caps (which are created by using a Small Caps option in your page-layout program or manually reducing the full caps), as they are drawn to match the weight, color, and proportion of the caps, as well as to optically match the height of the lowercase. Computer-generated small caps are just reduced caps and therefore look too light, too tightly spaced, and often too narrow.

Prior to OpenType, true-drawn small caps were only available for a select few typefaces—sometimes available with the primary font at no extra cost, sometimes as a stand-alone font, or sometimes as part of an expert set. But these days, many OpenType fonts come with true-drawn small caps built into the font. They are very easy to access and do not require loading or selecting a separate font.

True-drawn small caps (left) are superior to computer-generated small caps (right) in that they are drawn to match the weight, color, and proportion of the caps. Computer-generated small caps are just reduced caps and therefore look too light and often too narrow and too tightly spaced, as you can see in this comparison.

Small caps are very useful when the look of all caps is desirable but with a more refined appearance. They are often used in publishing for title pages and page headings, but they are also used in headlines, subheads, column headings, and very often as lead-ins for an opening paragraph, usually after an initial cap. Try them instead of all caps for two- or three-letter abbreviations, such as states, times (a.m. and p.m.), acronyms, etc. They stand out nicely without disturbing the color of lowercase text as much as all-cap settings do, and they take up less space.

The management team from IBM left their office in NY at 11:30 A.M. and arrived at the meeting in NJ at 1 P.M.

The management team from IBM left their office in NY at 11:30 A.M. and arrived at the meeting in NJ at 1 P.M.

Small caps can be substituted for caps when a more subtle look is desired, such as for two- or three-letter abbreviations, states, times (a.m. and p.m.), companies, etc. They stand out nicely without disturbing the color of lowercase text as much as all-cap settings do, and they take up less space. They look particularly good when used with oldstyle figures.

THE AMERICAN LAWYER

The even color and texture of this logo designed by Gerard Huerta is the result of perfectly balanced caps and small caps as well as precise kerning. Courtesy of Gerard Huerta.

peterson ARCHitects

This logo by MendeDesign was created in Mrs. Eaves roman and small caps. ARCH is rendered in small caps to emphasize the structural components of the letterforms and architecture itself. Courtesy of MendeDesign.

How to Access True-Drawn Small Caps

Many OpenType fonts have true-drawn small caps, but accessing them (and avoiding the computer-generated, fake variety) can be a bit confusing.

Adobe InDesign

InDesign has two options for converting text to small caps, but they each behave differently. To begin with, select the text, then:
• From the Character palette's flyout menu, select Small Caps. This will convert only the lowercase in selected text to small caps—either the true-drawn ones that are available with some OpenType fonts, or fake, scaled-down ones for fonts that don't have the real thing. It will leave the caps unconverted.
Or:
• Click the Character palette's flyout menu and select OpenType > All Small Caps. This command is accessible only for OpenType fonts that contain true-drawn small caps, making it impossible to wind up with the fake variety. However, it does convert all characters in selected text to small caps, including the full caps.

If you want to stick to the true-drawn variety (as you should) but want a cap/small cap setting, first make sure the font contains real small caps, then convert the selected characters using the

first bulleted point above. But first check whether the font has real small caps by seeing if the phrase "All Small Caps" under the Character palette's OpenType option is unbracketed, or by checking for them in the glyph palette (Window > Type & Tables > Glyphs).

QuarkXPress

QuarkXPress has two options for converting text to small caps, but only one accesses the true-drawn small caps available in some OpenType fonts. The other creates fake, scaled-down small caps (even if the font contains the true-drawn variety), which are typographically undesirable and considered a type crime.
• Select the text you want to be set in small caps.
• Click the OpenType icon on the Measurements palette and select either Small Caps (the caps remain full sized) or All Small Caps. Either way, you will get true-drawn small caps. This feature is bracketed when true-drawn small caps are not available for the selected font.

NOTE: Some Type 1 and TrueType fonts have true-drawn small caps that are located in separate fonts, such as in expert sets, or weights within the family designated with SC; these must be accessed directly from your font menu.

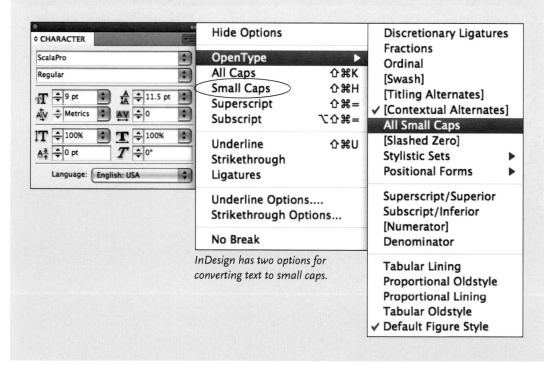

InDesign has two options for converting text to small caps.

INITIAL LETTERS

An initial letter is an enlarged character, usually the beginning letter of the first sentence of a paragraph, that is set in a decorative or graphic way. It can liven up a page and add typographic interest to an otherwise dull and boring page or section. Initial letters can be a different weight or style of the typeface in use, or they may be from a completely different font. Highly contrasting weights and styles, as well as elaborate, decorative, calligraphic, or ornate type styles in contrasting colors and tints are often used and can work well.

Proper alignment on all sides is key to using initials tastefully and professionally. If the initial letter is meant to appear flush left, align it optically rather than mechanically. Certain characters, such as rounds and diagonals, as well as characters with serifs that get proportionally larger with size, will need to be pulled out a bit to appear visually aligned and balanced. **NOTE:** You will have more flexibility if you put the initial in a separate text box from the rest of the word so that you can manipulate it independently. The Initial Cap option in most programs won't allow you to make fine adjustments.

Message *from* ITC

N OCTOBER, ITC WENT TO England & France. In London, we hosted a launch party at the St. Bride Printing Library for an ambitious new type family, ITC Founder's Caslon a direct revival by Justin Howes of William Caslon's type designs from the 18th century. In Lyon, we participated in the 1998 conference of the Association Typographique Internationale (ATypI), typography's premier international gathering of professional practitioners.

In England we were celebrating the first typeface family to bring the quirks & subtleties of Caslon's distinct & various type sizes into the digital realm. In France we were celebrating the myriad ways in which typography can be approached, in distinct languages and cultures, in a variety of unpredictable technologies, and in the quirks & subtleties of the people who make up the typographic world.

– *Mark Batty, President*

Mark van Bronkhorst goes to exciting extremes with this colorful drop cap (dropped capital), which creates a strong vertical element in a very horizontal message in U&lc. Notice the small caps leading into the body of the text. Courtesy of Mark van Bronkhorst.

The following are some of the more common styles of initial caps:

Drop Cap

When a character begins at (or aligns with) and drops below the first line of text, it is referred to as a drop cap. Drop caps usually visually align (different from mechanical alignment) with the cap height of the first line, and they should base-align with a line of type below. Dropping into an odd number of lines is most tasteful and pleasing; go at least three lines deep.

Body copy can be wrapped around the initial if the character is large and uncomplicated enough to keep it visually clean. To help the initial read as part of the first word, you can tuck in the remaining characters of the word closer to the initial, even if that line extends beyond the alignment of the lines below it.

Once more she found herself in the long hall, and close to the little glass table. 'Now, I'll manage better this time,' she said to herself, and began by taking the little golden key, and unlocking the door that led into the garden.

To help a drop-cap initial read as part of the first word, tuck in the remaining characters of the word closer to the initial even if it extends out of the text indent's left margin. (Alice in Wonderland)

First came ten soldiers carrying clubs; these were all shaped like the three gardeners, oblong and flat, with their hands and feet at the corners: next the ten courtiers; these were ornamented all over with diamonds, and walked two and two, as the soldiers did.

This drop cap aligns with the cap height of the first line and base aligns with the third line of type. The serifs overhang the left margin so the stem of the character aligns with the text below. (Alice in Wonderland)

First came ten soldiers carrying clubs; these were all shaped like the three gardeners, oblong and flat, with their hands and feet at the corners: next the ten courtiers; these were ornamented all over with diamonds, and walked two and two, as the soldiers did.

This raised cap base aligns with the first line of type and rises above the body copy. If the initial is the first letter of a word as opposed to a single-letter word, tuck in the remaining letters close enough so that it reads as a word.

Raised Cap (also called *stick-up* cap)

A raised cap is one that base-aligns with the first line of type and rises above the body copy. It is much less complicated to do tastefully and correctly than a drop cap. If the raised cap is the first letter of a word (as opposed to a single letter word such as *A* or *I*), make sure you space the rest of the word close enough to the initial to read as a word. When the rest of the word seems to be floating away from the cap, the word might be hard to read, as well as make the general treatment appear amateurish.

aLICE was beginning to get very tired of sitting by her sister on the bank, and of having nothing to do: once or twice she had peeped into the book her sister was reading, but it had no pictures or conversations in it, 'and what is the use of a book,' thought Alice 'without pictures or conversation?'

A lowercase letter can be used as an initial as well as a cap. Using small caps can be a very effective way to lead into the rest of the text (Alice in Wonderland)

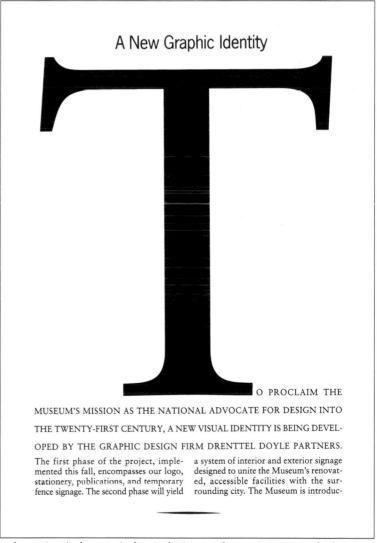

A New Graphic Identity

TO PROCLAIM THE MUSEUM'S MISSION AS THE NATIONAL ADVOCATE FOR DESIGN INTO THE TWENTY-FIRST CENTURY, A NEW VISUAL IDENTITY IS BEING DEVEL-OPED BY THE GRAPHIC DESIGN FIRM DRENTTEL DOYLE PARTNERS.

The first phase of the project, implemented this fall, encompasses our logo, stationery, publications, and temporary fence signage. The second phase will yield a system of interior and exterior signage designed to unite the Museum's renovated, accessible facilities with the surrounding city. The Museum is introduc-

A dramatic raised cap (raised capital) sits atop the opening paragraph, denoting an important announcement in this piece designed by Doyle Partners. Courtesy of Doyle Partners.

Decorative Initials

Sometimes a very unusual, elaborate, or ornate initial is appropriate and can do a lot to enhance a design, especially if color is an option as well. Some fonts contain decorative initials in addition to the standard character compliment, while others consist exclusively of decorative initials and are designed primarily for this purpose. In addition, some very interesting and unusual initials are available not as fonts but as .eps (Encapsulated PostScript) picture files. They are worth looking into, especially if your job is text-based, with few or no illustrations or photos, and needs livening up. A typeface with elaborate swashes or calligraphic forms can also add grace and visual interest to an otherwise dull design, as long as the chosen letterform is appropriate to the content.

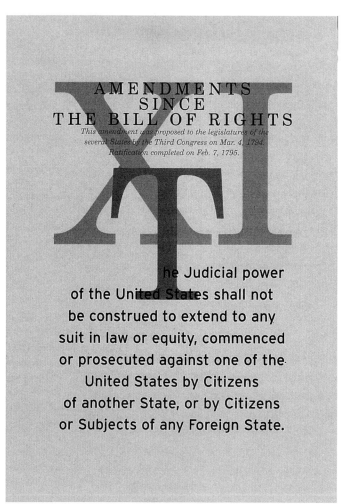

ought to have been specially careful on a Friday," she used to say afterwards to her husband, while perhaps Nana was on the other side of her, holding her hand.

A graceful and elaborate script initial such as this one set in ITC Edwardian Script makes a very dramatic statement. The opening quotes are set smaller than the initial and are kerned and positioned so they don't float in the margin. (Alice in Wonderland)

even flung down his brush, and had just begun 'Well, of all the unjust things—' when his eye chanced to fall upon Alice, as she stood watching them, and he checked himself suddenly: the others looked round also, and all of them bowed low.

This stately initial is layered between the text and other colorful typographic elements to bring a restrained excitement to a U.S. Amendment in this piece designed by Doyle Partners. Courtesy of Doyle Partners.

This decorative initial is part of an initial font that comes with ITC Kendo. (Alice in Wonderland)

Boxed, Reverse, Oversized, and Overlapped Initials

There are other techniques to add visual interest and originality to initial characters. The initial can be contained within an outlined box, and tints or colors can be added if desired. Or you can set the initial in reverse, dropping it out of a box of black or any solid color. Another approach is to make a rather large initial a light tint of black, or a color, and insert it partially behind the body copy. Just remember that whatever you do, readability should never be sacrificed. Your imagination is the limit to what you can do with initial characters; just remember to keep them tasteful and appropriate to the content and the rest of the design.

She had not gone much farther before she came in sight of the house of the March Hare: she thought it must be the right house, because the chimneys were shaped like ears and the roof was thatched with fur.

Initials can be placed in outlined, tinted boxes...
(Alice in Wonderland)

She had not gone much farther before she came in sight of the house of the March Hare: she thought it must be the right house, because the chimneys were shaped like ears and the roof was thatched with fur.

...or tinted and positioned behind text. Your imagination is the limit as long as the initials are tasteful and don't impair readability.

It was late summer when everything is full of fire and rounding to fruition.

— Mary Oliver

We're committed to generating per-ton returns for our members that exceed market rates over time and providing a stable outlet for member processing-grade fruit by adding value and developing markets for that fruit.

Tree Top, Inc. is an agricultural cooperative owned by 2,500 apple and pear growers in Washington State, Oregon, and Idaho.

— Tree Top Mission

This layered initial adds color, dimension, and graphic interest to this annual report designed by Hornall Anderson Design Works, Inc. Courtesy of Hornall Anderson Design Works, Inc.

She had not gone much farther before she came in sight of the house of the March Hare: she thought it must be the right house, because the chimneys were shaped like ears and the roof was thatched with fur. It was so large a house, that she did not like to go nearer till she had nibbled some more of the lefthand bit of mushroom, and raised herself to about two feet high: even then she walked up towards it rather timidly, saying to herself. 'Suppose it should be raving mad after all! I almost wish I'd gone to see the Hatter instead!'

*Body copy can be contoured or wrapped around an initial if the character is large and uncomplicated enough to keep it visually clean.
(Alice in Wonderland)*

Things to keep in mind when using initial letters:

- A lowercase character can be used as an initial letter as well as a cap (artistic license allowed here!).
- Small caps can be very effective when used for the first few words or an entire line after an initial letter, and they add additional emphasis and visual appeal.
- Never repeat the enlarged initial in the text unless its size, style, and position make it difficult for the eye to connect with the rest of the word.

66

MEAT

dishes do not play as important a role on the Italian table as they do in other cuisines, particularly the American and British. They appear as the *secondo,* "second course," of the Italian meal, preceded by the *antipasto,* if there is one, then by the *primo,* or "first course" of pasta, rice, or soup. Meat is used imaginatively with other ingredients in various courses, or it is served in small portions after a sizable carbohydrate-centered first course. ❁ Most important in the category of meat *antipasti* are *salumi,* air- and salt-cured or spiced and precooked hams, *salame,* and such. *Salumi* are prepared differently in the various regions. For example, a *prosciutto* produced in Friuli has a different flavor, texture, and look than one from Emilia or Tuscany; a *capocollo* from Calabria differs also from one produced, for example, in Apulia. Once sliced, *salumi* are called *affettati,* which essentially means "cold cuts," and they are by far the most common form of *antipasto* on the Italian table. Some sausages are eaten fresh and others are dried, which intensifies their flavor. A more thorough discussion of the various *affettati* is included in chapter 1. ❁ Probably the most prized of the *affettati* is *prosciutto crudo,* which is becoming increasingly popular in America. With its popularity, however, has come a great deal of misunderstanding about the best ways to serve and to eat it. It's a shame to do anything more to the finest *prosciutto* than to eat it raw, sliced paper-thin (although not so thin that it falls apart), accompanied perhaps only by *grissini,* Italian breadsticks (see chapter 7 for Palio's Rosemary and Sage Breadsticks). Despite the practice that persists of serving *prosciutto crudo* with figs or melon, it is best eaten on its own without sweet distractions. The tradition of eating *prosciutto* with fruit and confections came about in past times when hams were salted excessively in order to preserve them, and sweet tastes were necessary to foil the saltiness. ❁ The bone is seldom removed in Italian *prosciutti,* because it keeps the ham moist and gives it flavor. In contrast, *prosciutti* that are exported to America are boned for the convenience of being able to slice them by machine. But skillful cutting with a knife results in slices that Italian culinary expert Massimo Alberini describes as more "aggressive" and "compact" in flavor. The thickness of the slice affects the taste. Cooking this fine ham destroys

57
INSALATA DI PETTO DI POLLO
ALLA GRIGLIA
grilled chicken breast salad
59
INVOLTINI DI POLLO
stuffed chicken breasts
60
CIMA ALLA GENOVESE
stuffed breast of veal,
Genoese style
63
VITELLO TONNATO
poached veal with tuna sauce

64
SPIEDINI DI AGNELLO
CON LIMONE
skewered grilled lamb with
lemon zest
66
INSALATA DI MANZO
beef salad
67
CROSTINI DI FEGATO
ALLA TOSCANA
toasts with chicken liver spread

Not just an initial cap but an initial word is used to set off chapter title pages in this exquisite cookbook, entitled Antipasti, *designed by Aufuldish & Warinner. The rustic caps, which were designed by George Deaver based on Charlemagne, relate to the authentic nature of the recipes. Decorative borders and ornamental paragraph separators break up the dense, justified text. Courtesy of Aufuldish & Warinner.*

SWASH CHARACTERS

These are extremely decorative characters that have a flourish or extended stroke at the beginning or the end of the character. They are often available in addition to the standard characters, most often in an OpenType font but also as a secondary font or buried within your primary font. The use of swash characters is an effective way to draw attention to type, especially a title, headline, logo, or product branding. When used this way, a swash can add an air of elegance or importance. They are also wonderful when used as initial letters. Keep in mind that when used in text, they should be used sparingly and thoughtfully so they don't overwhelm and overpower.

There is one thing to avoid like the plague–that is using swash characters in all-cap settings. They are almost impossible to read when set one next to the other, as they were never intended to be used this way. Unfortunately, many a type novice will think they are pretty and set an invitation, menu, or flyer this way. Just don't do it–it is the surest sign of an amateur.

Rain

The rain is falling all around,
It falls on field and tree,
It rains on the umbrellas here,
And on the ships at sea.

These graceful swash characters enhance the appearance of this poem set in ITC Bodoni Seventy-Two.

Avoid using swash characters in all-cap settings. They are very difficult to read when set one next to the other, and they are not intended for this kind of setting.

ALTERNATE CHARACTERS

An alternate character is a separate and distinct version of the character in the regular position. Alternates are most commonly found within OpenType fonts (Read more about OpenType Features in Chapter 2 on page 40), which have room for thousands of characters; but they can also be found as part of an expert set or a supplementary font. The difference between regular and alternate characters can be as subtle as a slightly longer descender or a slightly raised crossbar, or as obvious as a one-story *a* or *g* to compliment a two-storied "regular" character.

Bickham

Bickham

Adobe Bickham Script Pro looks great without the use of any alternates (upper); but when contextual alternates are turned on in an application supporting this font's OpenType features, the result is a more dramatic and lyrical version of the same word (lower).

Alice was not a bit hurt, and she jumped up on to her feet in a moment: she looked up, but it was all dark; before her was another long passage, and the White Rabbit was still in sight, hurrying down it.

There was not a moment to be lost: away went Alice like the wind, and was just in time to hear it say, as it turned a corner, 'Oh my ears and whiskers, how late it's getting!' She was close behind when she turned the corner, but the Rabbit was no longer to be seen: she found herself in a long, low hall, which was lit up by a row of lamps hanging from the roof.

ITC Highlander Pro contains many alternate characters, including tall ascenders and descenders as well as swash and initial letters.

TAWNY

TAWNY

PAWN

PAWN

House Industries went to town creating dozens of contextual alternates for Ed Interlock, a typeface based on an original Ed Benguiat design. These two words look fine without contextual alternates, but turning that feature on (below in both cases) automatically converts the wide crossbar A to one with a better fit, which happens to be a different design in each case.

TYPE AND COLOR

Color and typography work together in many ways. Color can help attract attention to an element, emphasize, contrast and organize content, reinforce impact and recognition, create a mood, strengthen an identity, and even assist readability. Color and type interact dynamically in logos, packaging and product design, movie titles and credits, motion graphics, greeting cards, book covers, compact discs (CDs), and posters. Color can be critical in establishing powerful corporate identities and product branding.

Think of color as an accessory to a basic wardrobe, something to enhance an already strong foundation. Many designers actually design in black and white first, then add color as a separate step.

Readability should be your primary consideration when combining type and color. Contrast is the key: maintaining a high degree of contrast between type and background colors helps keep type readable, while reducing contrast reduces ease of reading.

This assignment includes aspects of the Introduction to Type Design: Symphony exercise by James Montalbano in Chapter 12.

Concert Poster Design
Frank Armstrong, Lecturer, California State University, Chico, California

Objective
This assignment will introduce the fundamentals of typographic information design: form, space, and structure. Its goals are to:
• Develop an awareness of typographic attributes and their interaction.
• Develop an awareness of negative space.
• Develop an awareness of typographic hierarchies and visual structure.

Assignment
Using the text provided, create a 10 × 10 inch square, two-color concert poster. Investigating various typographic attributes and formats, develop a concept, several preliminary studies, and a final composition. Clarity of communication and functionality are the primary criteria for a well-designed piece.

Requirements
• All fonts (except for the headline: Symphony) must be selected from the Frutiger type family, including the Frutiger Condensed series. The headline can be set in the typeface of your choice or the custom typeface designed for the Introduction to Type Design: Symphony exercise in Chapter 12.
• Do not select a solid black fill color for the background (100%).

Process
Step 1: Define the design problem and objectives by considering the requirements and interests of the producer (client) and consumer (audience). Draw several conceptual sketches. Fine-tune and revise until you decide on a workable and appropriate concept or two.

Step 2: Transfer your concepts into digital form. Create a modular typographic grid to help organize and structure information within the square-format image area.

Step 3: Gradually and methodically, modifying one variable at a time, alter the visual structure of the composition by specifying various character attributes and paragraph formats. At each stage, evaluate and analyze the visual effectiveness of your composition.

The final composition should demonstrate typographic hierarchies and a visual structure by using at least one example from each of the following categories:

Font: use a maximum of three fonts within the Frutiger type family.

Size: use a maximum of three different type sizes within a proportional scale.

Color: use two colors (black plus a spot color).

Shade: use a maximum of three black shade values (including 100%).

Indent: consider different indent styles.

Rules: use maximum of three different rule weights.

Required Text

San Francisco Symphony
Michael Tilson Thomas, conductor

Ludwig van Beethoven
Symphony No. 5, in C minor (1808)

Aaron Copland
Inscape (1967)

Felix Mendelssohn
Violin Concerto, in E minor (1845)

Chee-Yun, violin

Friday, 10 March 2000
7:30 pm

California State University, Chico
Laxson Auditorium

Concert Poster Design solutions by Holly McGarr and Shawna Kirby. Courtesy of Holly McGarr and Shawna Kirby.

When most of u
quirmed throu
rammar lesson
grade school
ve assumed tha
ve were taugh
verything abou
reading and w
ting the Engli
language tha
ver need to kn

CHAPTER NINE

TYPOGRAPHIC TYPOS (AND HOW TO AVOID THEM)

When most of us squirmed through grammar lessons in grade school, we assumed that we were taught everything about reading and writing the English language that we would ever need to know. But if you use a computer for typesetting (as most of us do in this digital age), this is no longer true. You need to know a number of seemingly small but very important things if you want your work to be professional looking and grammatically correct.

In some cases, there are several variations of punctuation that we were taught came in only one style, such as dashes, quotation marks, and apostrophes. While this might be true for handwriting, it isn't so for typesetting. Prior to desktop typography, typographers were responsible for knowing the differences between similar characters, where they were located on the keyboard, and what was grammatically and typographically correct. Once designers, administrative assistants, and the rest of us started setting type, a lot of this information fell through the cracks unless one was particularly knowledgeable about typography.

This problem was compounded by the fact that many of these characters are hard to locate on the keyboard and (prior to glyph palettes) required depressing combinations of keys to access them. This, to some degree, can be attributed to the engineers who designed the standard keyboard layout that we all use today. Since there are a limited number of keys (and keyboard combinations) in the standard computer keyboard, decisions had to be made with regard to which characters (including punctuation, as well as accented, foreign, and mathematical characters) to include and where to put them. Engineers tend to think mathematically and scientifically rather than grammatically and typographically, which resulted in some commonly used characters, such as quotation marks and fractions, being hidden or nonexistent. They basically followed the keyboard of the typewriter, which was never intended to be a typesetting device.

In other cases, typographic typos relate to styles and conventions that are not considered typographically tasteful or professional. Design software has gotten so sophisticated that it gives the user enough "rope to hang themselves," typographically speaking, with features that can easily be misunderstood or even misused. In today's digital world, it is up to the designer to learn right from wrong and how to achieve professional-looking typography that meets the highest standards.

WORD SPACES

There is never a need for double spaces between sentences when setting type on your computer, as was done in typewriter days. In fact, it is a serious type crime in professional typography. Curious how this practice came about? Typewriter fonts (such as Courier) were basically monospaced and designed so that all letters had a similar width (even the narrow letters such as the *i* and wide letters such as the *m*), allowing them to fit and/or fill up the width of the hammers on the typewriter. This made for very open-looking spacing, and the practice of using two word spaces was established to help achieve a noticeable separation between sentences.

These days, just about all fonts on a computer (except Courier) have proportional spacing, and a single space is all that is necessary to create the subtle yet noticeable visual separation between sentences, while maintaining good readability.

Many people still use double word spacing on a computer and don't know it is incorrect in proper typesetting. Why? Because typing is often still taught based on those old typewriter conventions, not typesetting ones. Be particularly aware of this practice in copy that is created by those who still use typewriter conventions. An easy way to fix these double spaces is to use the search-and-replace feature of your word processing or design program so you can catch them all. If you fix them manually, it is easy to miss some; but if you choose to do it this way, proof the printed piece rather than on screen, where it is difficult to spot double spaces (unless you turn on the invisible formatting).

```
Alas!  It was too late to wish
that!  She went on growing and
growing and very soon she had
to kneel down on the floor.
Still she went on growing, and,
as a last resource, she put one
arm out of the window and one
foot up the chimney, and said
to herself, "Now I can do no
more, whatever happens.  What
will become of me?"
```

Alas! It was too late to wish that! She went on growing and growing and very soon she had to kneel down on the floor. Still she went on growing, and, as a last resource, she put one arm out of the window and one foot up the chimney, and said to herself, "Now I can do no more, whatever happens. What will become of me?"

Alas! It was too late to wish that! She went on growing and growing and very soon she had to kneel down on the floor. Still she went on growing, and, as a last resource, she put one arm out of the window and one foot up the chimney, and said to herself, "Now I can do no more, whatever happens. What will become of me?"

The use of two spaces to separate sentences was the accepted style for typewriter faces such as Courier, shown in the top example. It is incorrect in fine typography. The example on the lower left, set in Goudy Oldstyle, shows the typographically incorrect practice of adding two word spaces between sentences. It creates lots of holes throughout your text. The example on the lower right has been corrected to one space, and the color and texture of the text is improved as well as being typographically correct. (Alice in Wonderland)

QUOTATION MARKS

One of the most misused typographic elements in desktop typography is the use of straight typewriter quotation marks, or "dumb" quotes, instead of true typographic quotation marks, also called "smart" quotes, "curly" quotes, or typographer's quotes. Smart quotes have an opening and a closing version, and they are design sensitive, usually being designed differently for each typeface. "Dumb" quotes are usually simple straight or tapered marks. They are often referred to as "primes" or inch and foot marks, which is a function they can be used for unless the typeface has true primes.

Misuse of "dumb" quotes is one of the most common typographic faux pas, which is repeatedly found in high-end print, multimedia advertising, movie credits, as well as nonprofessional work. Once again, the standard Mac layout—which was designed by engineers, not graphic designers or typographers—has old-fashioned straight quotes in place of real quotes in the keyboard layout, and we are left to straighten out the mess, so to speak.

"smart" quotes "smart" quotes
"dumb" quotes "dumb" quotes

"smart" quotes "smart" quotes
"dumb" quotes "dumb" quotes

"smart" quotes **"smart" quotes**
"dumb" quotes **"dumb" quotes**

"smart" quotes "smart" quotes
"dumb" quotes "dumb" quotes

The design of both "smart" and "dumb" quotes varies from face to face.

There are several things you can do to avoid dumb quotes sneaking into your work. One is to import copy properly at the onset, which can convert dumb quotes to smart quotes automatically (Read more about Importing Copy in Chapter 5 on page 122.) Another is to turn on "smart" quotes, or "typographer's" quotes, in the preferences of your software, which works for any newly keyboarded copy only. And finally, if you receive changes or corrections from an e-mail, a PDF, or the Web, make sure the punctuation is corrected either before you copy and paste it (there are utilities that can help with this), by typing it directly in the document with preferences adjusted as indicated above, or doing a "search and replace" for any offending dumb quotes. In today's world of designer as typesetter, it is your responsibility to proof your work carefully for any type crimes.

TECHTIP

Unwanted Smart Quotes

Both Adobe InDesign and QuarkXPress can automatically convert "dumb quotes" into "smart" (or typographer's) quotes for an entire document when a text document is imported as described in Chapter 5 on page 122. In addition, when typing directly into a document, the default settings will usually convert typed quotes to smart quotes automatically.

In both instances (importing and typing), you might wind up with a smart quote you don't want, such as in measurements when you need primes (inch and foot marks), or for certain contractions requiring an apostrophe, not an open single quote. Always proof your work carefully checking for these instances. When this happens, you can easily change them back into inch and foot marks by highlighting the quote, then using the keyboard shortcut Ctrl / quote for single prime (foot mark), Ctrl / shift / quote for double prime (inch mark), Opt / shift /] for apostrophe, or by using the glyph palette.

APOSTROPHES

The glyph for an apostrophe in proper typography is the closed single quote. Therefore, the same rules regarding the use of smart punctuation for quotation marks applies to apostrophes as well. Remember, the default keyboard character is a straight typewriter apostrophe rather than the typographically correct "smart" apostrophe. Replace these as you would dumb quotations marks. **NOTE:** Be on the alert for apostrophes that appear in front of a word or numeral as a contraction (rock 'n' roll instead of rock 'n' roll) as they are often incorrectly being set as a single open quote instead of an apostrophe; change these manually as necessary.

PRIMES

The prime symbol most commonly refers to units of measure, with a single prime representing feet and a double prime representing inches. True primes are tapered, slightly angled marks. Since typewriters did not have smart quotes or true primes, simple, straight marks referred to as typewriter quotes were used for both purposes. While most digital fonts still contain these straight "typewriter" quotes, some of the new OpenType fonts have true primes, either instead of the old-fashioned typewriter quotes, or in addition to them. When available, true primes should be used for measurements, but typewriter quotes (not smart quotes) have become the accepted practice in digital typography.

Never use smart quotes for measurements, as this is a type crime as well, and unequivocally wrong. Unfortunately, when smart quotes are turned on in a word-processing program or design software, they are not smart enough to know not to use them for measurements. So it is up to you, the designer, to proof your document for measurements very carefully, and make the corrections as necessary.

The difference between typewriter quotes, primes, and smart (or typographer's) quotes, is shown above in Arno Pro, which is one of the few fonts which provide all three.

HYPHEN, EN DASH, AND EM DASH

These three similar typographic characters are all horizontal lines of varying lengths. They all have different purposes, but they are often confused and misused, leading to inaccurate and unprofessional typography.

A *hyphen,* which is the shortest in length, is used to hyphenate words that break at the end of a line or to connect elements of a compound word such as go-between, ill-fated, and run-of-the-mill. It is also used for phone numbers. The hyphen is easily found on the keyboard to the right of the zero.

An *en dash* is wider than a hyphen and narrower than an em dash, and is the least commonly used and understood of the three. This dash is used to indicate a continuation of time, years, and dates (similar to using the words "to" and "from") such as 9 am–5 pm, Monday–Friday, May 2–7, or pages 1–5, also described as a range. It is accessed from the Mac keyboard with the (option/hyphen) keys.

An *em dash,* which is the longest of the three, is used to indicate a break in thought–as is illustrated in this sentence. It is also occasionally used to separate a thought within a sentence–such as this one–requiring an em dash at the beginning and the end of the thought. It is accessed from the Mac keyboard by pressing the (option/shift/hyphen) keys.

Most of us have seen copy with two hyphens instead of an em dash. This typographically incorrect–and ugly–practice is a holdover from typewriter days when there were no dashes of any kind on the keyboard, just hyphens. It unfortunately still pops up here and there, especially when set by those who used a typewriter before a computer or were taught to type with typewriter conventions, as many still are.

The lengths of these characters are not standard; they vary from typeface to typeface, as do their side bearings (the designated space to the right and left). Some en dashes are the width of the lowercase *n,* and em dashes the width of the *m,* keeping them in proportion to the rest of the typeface; others have no relationship to the overall width of the type design at all and are 500 and 1,000 units (a measurement relative to the point size), respectively. There are different philosophies behind these differences, but the principles of their usage remain the same.

As you can see here, the length and style of hyphens, en dashes and em dashes vary tremendously from typeface to typeface.

An en dash is wider than a hyphen and narrower than an em dash. It is used to indicate a continuation of time, years, and dates.

Some room for artistic license is allowed in the use of dashes when their design or spacing seems inconsistent or out of proportion. For instance, where the em dash seems too wide for the typeface, it is the practice of some designers to replace it with an en dash. Another stylistic preference is to add extra space before and after either dash if it appears too close to neighboring characters. The recommended method to resolve such problems with dashes is to open the kerning between the dashes and their surrounding letters; this way you have total control over the space. Another solution is to add a word space on both ends, but this practice is more commonly used on the Web, where it is recommended. (Read more about Smart Punctuation on the Web in Chapter 11 on page 227.) Just remember to be consistent throughout or the text will be an unprofessional jumble of varying styles.

His voice and laugh, which per-petually re-echoed through the Custom-House, had nothing of the tremulous quaver and cackle of an old man's utterance; they came strutting out of his lungs, like the crow of a cock, or the blast of a clarion.

A hyphen, which is shorter in length than the en or em dash, is used to hyphenate words that break at the end of a line or to connect elements of a compound word such as those shown in this paragraph. (Scarlet Letter)

This old town of Salem—my native place, though I have dwelt much away from it both in boyhood and maturer years—possesses, or did possess, a hold on my affection, the force of which I have never realized during my seasons of actual residence here.

This old town of Salem–my native place, though I have dwelt much away from it both in boyhood and maturer years–possesses, or did possess, a hold on my affection, the force of which I have never realized during my seasons of actual residence here.

This old town of Salem -- my native place, though I have dwelt much away from it both in boyhood and maturer years -- possesses, or did possess, a hold on my affection, the force of which I have never realized during my seasons of actual residence here.

An em dash, which is longer than both the hyphen and en dash, is used to indicate a break in thought as illustrated in the first paragraph. It can be replaced with an en dash when the em dash is extremely wide (second paragraph). The last paragraph illustrates what never to do! Using two hyphens to indicate an em dash is a holdover from typewriter days, and it is incorrect in fine typography. (Scarlet Letter)

WIDOWS AND ORPHANS

A widow is a very short line of type at the end of a paragraph, usually consisting of one or two short words or of a hyphenated word. A widow is typographically undesirable, as its short length results in a visual interruption, creating the appearance of too much white space between paragraphs or at the bottom of a page. It is considered poor typography, so adjust it by manually rebreaking the rag, altering the column width a smidge, or editing the copy. There is no formula for the number of characters that constitute a widow, as it depends on the length of the line, numbers of characters in a line, and other factors; it is purely a visual determination requiring you to use, and constantly improve, your visual skills.

An orphan is related to a widow (no pun intended!) in that it is a single word or a very short line appearing at the top of a column or a page. This terminology is not as commonly used and understood as widow, but the concept is the same, and so is the solution: fix it!

The next unpleasant business was putting on the iron shoes; that too was very hard at first. My master went with me to the smith's forge, to see that I was not hurt or got any fright. The blacksmith took my feet in his hand, one after the other, and cut away some of the hoof.

to it.
The next unpleasant business was putting on the iron shoes; that too was very hard at first. My master went with me to the smith's forge, to see that I was not hurt or got any fright. The blacksmith took my feet in his hand, one after the other, and cut away some of the hoof.

An example of a horrible widow on the bottom line... (Black Beauty)

...and an equally unsightly orphan at the top of this paragraph.

COMPUTER-GENERATED STYLING

One of today's most widespread type crimes is the use of computer-generated styling, that is, the stretching, squeezing, and slanting of type–all of which are a major typographic offense. Why? The design of a typeface is a very time-consuming, detail-oriented endeavor; it requires a great deal of skill, with particular attention paid to every detail of each letterform's shape, proportion, and spacing. When computer-generated styling is applied to a well-designed typeface, the letterforms become progressively distorted and degraded, akin to what happens when one looks into a funhouse mirror. Unfortunately, this type crime is a byproduct of the digital age, because, as I have said before, most design software gives you enough typographic rope to hang yourself. The solution is simple–DON'T DO IT! A good designer will solve type and design challenges using other means.

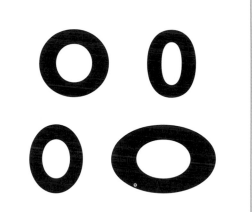

The letter O belonging to ITC Avant Garde Gothic and its true-drawn condensed version are perfectly proportioned (upper). When the regular O is squeezed or stretched by computer software, the proportions are distorted and degraded into egg shapes, akin to a fun-house mirror (lower).

POORLY JUSTIFIED TYPE

When the spaces between the words and characters in lines of type are stretched and squeezed beyond a minimal amount in the process of aligning both margins, the color, texture, and readability of the type can be degraded tremendously. In some cases (dependent on your software and the settings in your preferences), the actual characters are compressed or expanded electronically as well. All of this can lead to poorly justified text, which is considered a typographic travesty. (Read more about Alignment in Chapter 5, page 108.)

FAKE SMALL CAPS

Avoid using computer-generated, or fake, small caps which are often created by using the Small Caps option in your design application or by manually reducing the full caps. They are just reduced caps and therefore look too light, too tight, and often too narrow. True-drawn small caps are superior to computer-generated small caps, as they are drawn to match the weight, color, and proportion of the caps, as well as to optically match the height of the lowercase. (Read more about Small Caps in Chapter 8, page 180.)

LETTERSPACING LOWERCASE

The practice of letterspacing, or tracking out lowercase characters to achieve an intentionally open look, is considered to be a type crime by type traditionalists and connoisseurs, as it greatly reduces readability. We read words by their shapes, which are created by the pattern of ascenders and descenders, and not letter by letter, as children learning to read do. For this reason, when type is tracked out, it loses its characteristic shape, and becomes hard to read. Don't be a type criminal, and don't letterspace lowercase characters!

There were six young colts in the meadow besides me; they were older than I was; some were nearly as large as grown-up horses. I used to run with them, and had great fun; we used to gallop all together round and round the field as hard as we could go.

When justifying type, avoid rivers of white space and lines with too much letter spacing or word spacing. Try to maintain an even color and texture, even if it means editing the copy, changing the point size of the type, or altering the line length.

EDITORIAL DESIGN

Ilene Strizver, Faculty, School of Visual Arts, New York, New York

Objective

Design an editorial spread, paying as much attention to the typographic details and refinements as to the overall layout and design.

Instructor Preparation

Select three headlines (with subheads) of varying content and presentation requirements. They can be fictional or from real magazines. Headlines should suggest visual images capable of being translated typographically. Suggested categories are: (1) food magazine spread, include at least one recipe and optional sidebar; (2) music magazine interview, include introduction, then question-and-answer section; and (3) news or psychology magazine, include at least one sidebar.

Assignment

Select one of the three chosen editorial (magazine) topics; design a spread (two adjoining pages) for an 8 ½ × 11 inch magazine. Include images, illustrations, or photos. Use dummy text, not "greeking." Try to make the first sentence and/or paragraph relate to the headline. Add a byline for all. Add folios, footers, pull quotes, and other elements (captions, credits, etc.) to make it appear authentic.

Process

Step 1: Do your research by studying three well-designed magazines. Select two or three feature spreads; analyze the layout, design, and typography. Write a brief summary of each discussing which elements contribute to, and which elements detract from, the success of the spread.

Step 2: Design your chosen spread, taking into consideration everything you have learned about type and typographic design, including appropriate headline and text font, point size and leading, information hierarchy, emphasis, indents, alignment, hyphenation, justification (if used), initial caps, widows and orphans, and overall letter spacing (tracking and kerning). Pay close attention to column width, inner and outer margins, and overall white space.

Editorial Design solution by Michael Pallozzi.

CHAPTER TEN

FRACTIONS, SIGNS, SYMBOLS, AND DINGBATS

There are a number of other typographic elements not previously mentioned that you will need from time to time. Not surprisingly, they are often misunderstood, as well as improperly or tastelessly used.

FRACTIONS

Fractions are a fairly common element in typeset copy. Sometimes they appear with great regularity, such as in recipes and cookbooks, manuals, and other documentation; sometimes they appear sporadically, as in the occasional measurement, dimension, and quantity. But in either case, good typography calls for professional-looking fractions, which in most cases are diagonal fractions.

Prior to OpenType, setting good-looking diagonal fractions was a challenge, especially if you needed more than the standard ¼, ½, and ¾, which are available in some (but not all) Type 1 and TrueType fonts. But today's OpenType fonts not only contain a wider assortment of prebuilt fractions but often can create any fraction on-the-fly. Unfortunately, not every OpenType font is capable of this, as they vary greatly in their fraction-making capability.

Diagonal fractions (½, not 1/2) can be either prebuilt and part of the font or created on-the-fly by your software. The best way to view which prebuilt fractions are part of a font is to search for them via the glyph palette. Fractions built on-the-fly vary in appearance: they can look as good as the prebuilt variety–or not so good and with bad spacing, heavy fractions bars, and/or light numerals. Both Adobe InDesign and QuarkXPress have a feature that can turn fractions on and off easily, but not all fonts have the ability to either substitute or create on-the-fly.

¼ ½ ¾ ⅓ ⅔
⅛ ⅜ ⅝ ⅞

A wide variety of prebuilt diagonal fractions are available in many OpenType fonts, such as these set in Expo San.

Creating Fractions in OpenType Fonts

Many of today's OpenType fonts contain a wide assortment of pre-built diagonal fractions, including the standard 1/4, 1/2, and 3/4, as well as 1/8, 3/8, 5/8, 7/8, and sometimes 1/3 and 2/3. In addition, many–but not all–have the capability of creating any fraction (such as 18/256) on-the-fly. Here's how:

Adobe InDesign and QuarkXPress
• Type the fraction manually (regular numerals and a forward slash).
• Highlight the fraction.
• From the Character panel or the Control panel menu select OpenType > Fractions. Note that if Fractions is bracketed,

this feature is not supported in this font.

OpenType fonts vary greatly in their fraction-making capability, which is then activated by your software. If the font you are using has full fraction-making capability, not only will the proper diagonal fraction appear with true-drawn numerators and denominators but the forward slash will be replaced with a fraction bar, the typographically correct glyph for diagonal fractions.

If the Fractions feature isn't available for the font in question, you can make fractions manually if the font has a full set of numerators and denominators, which can be viewed in the glyph palette under Numbers. Just remember to use the fraction bar, not the forward slash.

Fractions can be created on-the-fly in many (but not all) OpenType fonts, as shown above using Expo Sans and InDesign.

Fractions in QuarkXPress

For non-OpenType fonts or any fonts that do not have the above fraction capability, Quark can make diagonal fractions in these two ways:
• Type in the numerator, slash, and denominator.
• Highlight the fraction.

• Go to Script (under the little icon on the far right) > Typography > Make Fractions, Or
• Go to Style > Type Style > Make Fraction.

Note that neither of these look as good as OpenType fractions.

BULLETS

A bullet is a large dot used to draw attention to a list of items that either have been extracted from your text or are independent of the text. The bullet that is part of your font might need to be altered in size or position, as many are too large or small, or too high or low for your usage. Don't make the mistake of assuming that if it is in the font, it is the right size.

Bullets shouldn't be too large or too small.

Bullets should be centered on either the cap height or x-height, depending on the nature of your listing. If all of your items begin with a cap, center the bullet on the cap, or a bit lower, so it balances with the negative spaces created by the lowercase. If your items all begin with lowercase, center the bullets on the x-height (if they are not already). Either insert a space after the bullet or set a tab for the following text to avoid crowding.

Bulleted points are usually aligned with the left margin, but they can also overhang the left margin with the actual text aligning with the margin, or they can be indented underneath the text above–it is a matter of personal taste. Continuing text, if there is more than one line, can be aligning with the text above it. This creates an indent that draws attention to each new bullet. If you prefer, you can align the continuing text with the bullet, creating a flush left alignment for all elements.

Things to have in your case at all times:
- A tuner
- New set of strings
- A few cords
- Tools for adjusting your guitar
- Metronome

Things to have in your case at all times:
- a tuner
- new set of strings
- a few cords
- tools for adjusting your guitar
- metronome

- a tuner
- new set of strings
- a few cords
- metronome
- tools for adjusting your guitar
- Phillips screwdriver

If you want to be a bit more creative, you can substitute other symbols for the actual bullets, such as squares, triangles, or check marks–just not all at once as shown here!

Bullets should be centered on either the cap height or x-height, depending on the nature of your listing.

If you want to be a bit more creative, you can substitute other symbols and dingbats for bullets. Simple shapes, such as squares, triangles, and check marks, work well, as well as more decorative graphics, such as those found in ITC Zapf Dingbats or other ornamental fonts. You can even use color to enhance and direct attention to them. Just make sure to keep them clean and simple, and make sure they are sized, vertically positioned, and horizontally spaced to look tasteful and appropriate.

TECHTIP

Indenting Bulleted Lists

When setting bulleted text and you want to create a hanging bullet—that is, multiple lines of text aligning with the first line of text and not the bullet—an easy way to achieve this is to use the "indent to here" command.

To use this feature, place your curser in front of the character you want all other lines to align to, then press Command / Control + backslash. To undo, delete the space before the character.

• Parentheses are primarily used to enclose interjected, explanatory, or qualifying remarks.

• Brackets are usually used to enclose copy within a parenthetical phrase, or more simply put, copy already enclosed within parentheses.

• Braces are a more decorative form of bracket, and are traditionally used for certain mathematical expressions.

• Parentheses are primarily used to enclose interjected, explanatory, or qualifying remarks.

• Brackets are usually used to enclose copy within a parenthetical phrase, or more simply put, copy already enclosed within parentheses.

• Braces are a more decorative form of bracket, and are traditionally used for certain mathematical expressions.

The default flush left alignment of bulleted copy (upper) can easily be converted into hanging bullets (lower) using the Command / Control + backslash command. Set in Expo Serif Pro.

REGISTERED, TRADEMARK, AND COPYRIGHT SYMBOLS

At some point, every designer needs to use one or more of these three symbols: registered, trademark, and copyright. There are a few essential things to know about them—nothing is worse than seeing a tiny, unreadable registered mark in text or a huge, annoying trademark in a headline.

The registered, trademark, and copyright symbols vary in design from font to font. Sometimes they are design sensitive, and other times they are not. If the design appears inappropriate, illegible, or unclear, you can substitute a symbol from another font. Although many people prefer to use serif symbols with serif fonts and sans with sans, I personally prefer to use a nice, clean sans symbol for text usage (such as those from Helvetica, Arial, or Franklin Gothic), as they tend to be very readable and print cleanly and clearly at small sizes. When setting a headline, more latitude is given with the design, as readability is less of a problem.

Now let's talk about size, especially since this element varies so much from font to font. When using a ® or a ™ after a word, the point size should be adjusted as necessary, independently from the rest of the text, to look clear and legible yet unobtrusive. A general guideline for text is to make these symbols a little smaller than half the x-height; as your text gets larger, they can become proportionately smaller, especially in headlines. These symbols are legal designations, not exciting graphic elements, and making them too large can detract from the design. Once they are

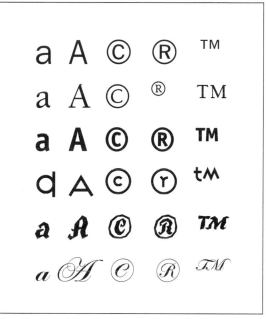

These three symbols, shown next to other characters in the font, vary in design in every font. Sometimes they are design sensitive, and other times they are not.

© 1957 Slowcraft Inc.

© 1957 Slowcraft Inc.

© 1957 SLOWCRAFT INC.

© 1957 SLOWCRAFT INC.

Placed before a year, the copyright symbol should be somewhere between the x-height and cap height of the other type. When using oldstyle figures, match the size of the numeral one, not the other, taller numerals.

sized correctly, you might have to adjust their vertical and horizontal position, using baseline shift and kerning.

The copyright symbol (©) is used in two manners: it is sometimes treated the same sizewise as the ® and the ™, but more frequently it is used in a much larger size. When it appears before a year, as in ©1998, or the name of a company, the size should be somewhere between the x-height and cap height. If using oldstyle figures for a year beginning with a figure one, be sure to match the size of the one, and not some of the other, taller numerals in the year.

Circle P

If you look closely at compact disc (CD) or digital video disc (DVD) packaging, you will probably see a tiny circle P in the fine print. This is a sound recording copyright symbol, and it is an internationally recognized symbol of protection of a recording, similar to the copyright or registered symbol.

Typefaces with their own circle Ps are far and few between. The most common are Microsoft's Webdings (a font included with many browsers), Lucida Grande (a Mac OS X system font), and Lucida Sans Unicode (preinstalled on Microsoft Windows versions since Windows 98). Some other foundries do include it, so you have to check them individually to find out. The best way to locate circle Ps is via the glyph palette, as their location varies from font to font.

Both Webdings and Lucida Grande contain circle P symbols, as shown above.

If the font you are using does not have a circle P, you can create your own circle P as a graphic and insert it in your design (a particularly useful solution for the Web). There are also some symbol fonts you can find on the web that contain it.

Macintosh®
MACINTOSH®
Slowcraft™
SLOWCRAFT™

Macintosh®

MACINTOSH®

Slowcraft™

SLOWCRAFT™

LAB®

A general guideline for text is to make these symbols a little smaller than half the x-height; as your text gets larger, they should become proportionately smaller, especially when used in headlines.

ACCENTS AND ACCENTED CHARACTERS

Most well-made fonts by reputable manufacturers include a selection of accents, accented characters, and other diacritical marks needed to set foreign words and names. Some are composite characters that combine characters with accents or marks to create a separate character; others are accents and marks by themselves, called floating accents. These floating accents can be used to create many more accented characters than are available within the font.

OpenType fonts often contain a greater selection of accents and accented characters than Type1 and TrueType fonts, as they have the "room" for them. Some OpenType fonts, many of which contain the designation *Pro,* contain expanded foreign language support, including a full range of Central European glyphs. Some Pro fonts contain other languages as well, such as Greek or Cyrillic; it varies from font to font.

The easiest way to locate accented characters as well as floating accents in a particular font is to use the glyph palette. You can then easily copy and paste the character(s) you need.

áàâäãå ÁÀÂÄÃÅ çÇ
éèêë ÉÈÊË ñîï ÍÌÎÏ
ñÑ óòôöõ ÓÒÔÖÕ
úùûü ÚÙÛÜ ÿŸ

These are standard floating accents and accented characters available in many fonts.

PARENTHESES, BRACKETS, BRACES, AND ANGLED BRACKETS

These four symbols are always used in pairs, and all have a similar function, which is to enclose text not directly related to the context of the sentence.

Parentheses are the most common of the four, and they are primarily used to enclose interjected, explanatory, or qualifying remarks. They also are of particular use for area codes and mathematical formulas, usually algebra.

Brackets, also called *square brackets*, are usually used to enclose copy within a parenthetical phrase, or more simply put, copy already enclosed within parentheses. Brackets are also used to enclose explanations or comments by the author, as well as for mathematical expressions and specific scientific compounds.

Braces, also called *curly brackets*, are a more decorative form of bracket, and are traditionally used for certain mathematical expressions. They are occasionally used (with creative license) to replace parentheses in certain instances, such as to enclose a Web site or e-mail address.

Angled brackets used to enclose text has become the accepted style in e-mail and on the Internet, particularly when copying part or all of an e-mail as part of a reply. There does not seem to be a definitive style, as it varies from browser to browser in the direction the brackets face, as well as whether they are used in single or double form: anything goes on the Internet, it seems.

( )	parentheses
[ ]	brackets
{ }	braces (or curly brackets)
〈 〉 《 》	angled brackets

The design differences between parentheses, brackets, braces, and angled brackets are clearly seen here.

Following a quasi–high school science book feel, each spread in this technology company brochure by A N D uses a variety of fake equations (including parentheses) to spell out the main topic—in this case, INFO. The layout, type treatment, and color scheme were all chosen to suggest the look of textbooks from the 1950s and 1960s.

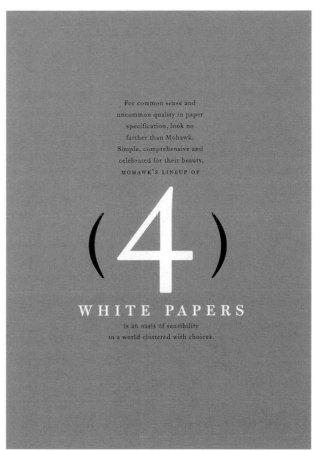

For common sense and
uncommon quality in paper
specification, look no
farther than Mohawk.
Simple, comprehensive and
celebrated for their beauty,
MOHAWK'S LINEUP OF

(4)

WHITE PAPERS

is an oasis of sensibility
in a world cluttered with choices.

The use of parentheses to accentuate an important typographic element in this piece designed by VSA Partners, Inc. Courtesy of VSA Partners, Inc.

Be[com]ing digital.

[rocket science]

Brackets are sometimes used as design elements, as seen in this promotional piece (left) by Rigsby Design and in this business card (right) by Michael Vanderbyl Design. Courtesy of Rigsby Design and Michael Vanderbyl Design.

EURO

Since 2002, the euro has been the exclusive currency of twelve European countries: Austria, Belgium, Finland, France (except Pacific territories using the CFP franc), Germany, Greece, Ireland, Italy, Luxembourg, Netherlands, Portugal, and Spain. The euro symbol looks like a capital C with a double crossbar (¤).

Three examples of the Euro.

Both Apple and Microsoft have included euro symbols in fonts distributed with their operating systems and applications since 1998, and most fonts released since then contain the euro symbol (it replaces the little-used international currency symbol). The euro symbol can be accessed on a Mac by pressing shift / option / 2, but it is most easily located and inserted using the glyph palette.

Many foundries have remanufactured their font libraries to include the euro mark and have included the symbol in all new releases. Others have offered freely available fonts that contain euro glyphs in various weights and styles, designed to blend in with a wide range of typestyles. It is a good idea to download several of these for when you need euros and are using an older, pre-euro font.

ELLIPSES

The ellipsis (…) is a character consisting of three evenly spaced dots (usually, but not always, periods) and is used to indicate missing type or words or a continuation of a thought or phrase. The ellipsis exists in a font as a totally separate character that is usually spaced the same as or more open than three periods.

If the spacing in the ellipsis is too tight or too open for your liking, try using three periods instead of the actual ellipsis character, and track out as desired.

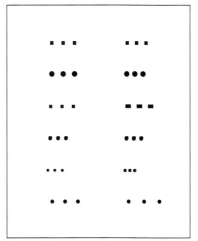

The size, design, and spacing of ellipses vary from typeface to typeface (left) compared to periods in the same font (right).

END MARKS

An end mark (as opposed to an end note) is symbol or ornament placed at the end of an article as a reader's cue to signify the ending. It is most often used in long articles in magazines, newsletters, and journals where articles jump to another page and where the location of the ending can be confusing; but it can also be used in books, shorter articles, or even on the Web–anywhere a decorative or graphic element is desired.

End marks can be as simple as a circle or square, as decorative as a fili-gree flourish, or as customized as a logo. Some publications set their name in type in a way that can be reduced successfully and used in this manner. End marks can be shapes, symbols, ornaments, dingbats, icons, or images; your imagination is the limit.

A good source for end mark graphics is one of the dingbat fonts that are available with most operating systems. Other sources are ornament, image and design fonts, clip art, and even the occasional ornament and dingbat "hidden" in some fonts. You can also design your own end mark, then create an .eps (Encapsulated PostScript) file or make into a font: just keep it simple and uncomplicated, and be sure it retains its clarity when reduced. Just make sure it is sized, spaced, and aligned properly for maximum effectiveness.

> A good source for end mark graphics is one of the dingbat fonts that are available with most operating systems. Other sources are ornament, image and design fonts, clip art, and even the occasional ornament and dingbat 'hidden' in some fonts. You can also design your own, create an .eps file or make into a font: just keep it simple and uncomplicated, and be sure it retains its clarity when reduced. Just make sure it is sized, spaced, and aligned properly for maximum effectiveness. ♣

The ending of this text is punctuated by an end mark in the shape of a cloverleaf. Be sure to adjust the size and vertical alignment of the end mark as necessary. Set in Tangent and Adobe Wood Type Ornaments.

DINGBATS

There are a number of nontypographic dingbat fonts available on most computers that contain many useful elements not found in other fonts. ITC Zapf Dingbats, Webdings, and Wingdings have dozens of signs, symbols, and dingbats that can be used for print, the Web, and motion graphics.

Some of the most commonly used elements are solid circles, squares (and other geometric shapes), arrows, check boxes, hearts, and leaf flourishes. Dingbats can be used for many things, such as calling attention to items in a list, separating paragraphs, and indicating the end of an article as end marks. It is worth the time to check them out and become familiar with them.

TYPOGRAPHIC PRINCIPLES CARD SET *(Class Project)*
Regina Rowland, Professor, City College of San Francisco, San Francisco, California

Objectives
• Apply typographic theory by exploring issues of legibility.
• Use type for function and form, syntactically and semantically.
• Demonstrate fully refined design process.
• Refine capacity to collaborate as a team.

Assignment
• Each student chooses a particular typographic rule (or principle) from Chapters 4 through 10, designing front and back of cards that belong to a set.
• Each student to follow these layout specifics: 1/1 with bleeds, document size of 3 ½ × 5 ½ inches. Front of card to be used as needed, back of card to follow established grid and structure for listing name of designer, stating the rule, and describing selected typographic rule or principle.
• For each chosen rule, demonstrate the rule itself woven into a concept that refers to an issue of interest in a major city (the city closest to the location of the class is suggested).
• Design and produce, deliver as (1) a comp on bristol board and (2) a final design converted to an electronic file, then printed, and trimmed on a heavy or thick stock.

The success of this set as a whole depends on the quality and consistency each card demonstrates in design and content.

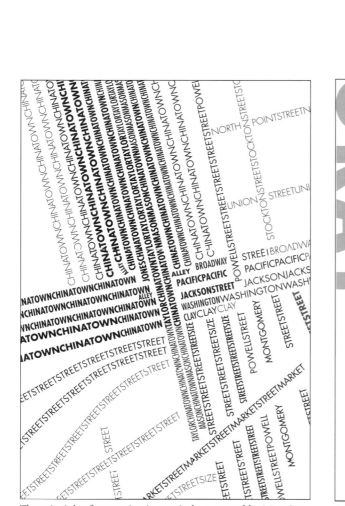

The principle of proportion is creatively expressed by May Gee by using type of different widths and weights to represent the streets and neighborhoods of San Francisco. The denser, blacker type represents the busier areas. Courtesy of May Gee and Églantine Granier-Gwinner.

Antonio Rusevski and Églantine Granier-Gwinner express typographic texture by cleverly overlapping different text and display type in varying tints and alignments. The result is an illustration created completely with type. Courtesy of Antonio Rusevski and Églantine Grunier-Gwinner.

The typographic theory of proximity, or type grouping, is effectively expressed using the word WEALTH in all caps, stretched to drop out of the entire background, while the lowercase word poverty is set multiple times in a distressed face, crowding the feet of the word WEALTH. Designed by Thomas Jason Carpio. Courtesy of Thomas Jason Carpio.

Spa Brochure
Ilene Strizver, Faculty, School of Visual Arts, New York, New York

Objective
Design projects with lots of text containing numerous hierarchies of information as well as price lists can be intimidating to any designer. This assignment focuses on confronting, analyzing, and solving this kind of text-intensive design problem. It also requires a mastery of text composition in the chosen software.

Instructor Preparation
Select a spa name, address, and tag line. Research spa brochures and web sites to harvest content. Text should include numerous categories of service, detailed descriptions, and several pricing tiers for each with decimal points. Supplement content with text for new treatments, special services, price breaks, and a 20 percent off coupon. Supply the assignment content in print form as well as a text file for download.

Assignment
Design an brochure for a day spa. Suggested (but not mandatory) format is 8 ½ x 11 inch, trifold. Use color, image, illustration, and photographs as desired, as well as colored stock.

Process
Step 1: Read the text carefully and use your imagination to identify a client base. Then imagine the look and architecture of this imaginary spa. The design and layout of the brochure should reflect your audience as well as the personality of the spa. You are encouraged to research other spa brochures to see what works and what does not in terms of organizing complex textual content.

Step 2: The brochure consists of two separate elements: the spa logo or logotype and the body text. Each should be well thought-out. Solve each of them individually, but design them to blend together. Pay acute attention to all type and design details, including appropriate type style, size and leading, folds and margins, accurate informational hierarchy, clear and organized price lists, proper price alignment, and overall consistency. **HINT:** Start off with an accurate template trifold to avoid major changes and adjustments later.

Deliverable
Completed assignment shall consist of one folded dummy of the brochure (front and back), as well as a separate proof of both the front and back, with folds indicated in ½ point perforated or dotted lines.

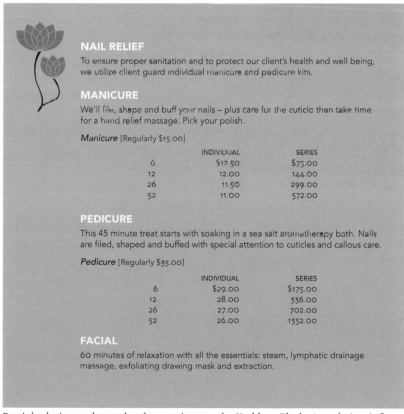

NAIL RELIEF

To ensure proper sanitation and to protect our client's health and well being, we utilize client guard individual manicure and pedicure kits.

MANICURE

We'll file, shape and buff your nails – plus care for the cuticle then take time for a hand relief massage. Pick your polish.

Manicure [Regularly $15.00]

	INDIVIDUAL	SERIES
6	$12.50	$75.00
12	12.00	144.00
26	11.50	299.00
52	11.00	572.00

PEDICURE

This 45 minute treat starts with soaking in a sea salt aromatherapy bath. Nails are filed, shaped and buffed with special attention to cuticles and callous care.

Pedicure [Regularly $35.00]

	INDIVIDUAL	SERIES
6	$29.00	$175.00
12	28.00	336.00
26	27.00	702.00
52	26.00	1352.00

FACIAL

60 minutes of relaxation with all the essentials: steam, lymphatic drainage massage, exfoliating drawing mask and extraction.

Partial solution to the spa brochure assignment by Kathleen Black. Actual piece is four pages and in color.

CHAPTER ELEVEN

NONPRINT TYPOGRAPHY

In today's digital age, typography no longer solely refers to black ink on white paper, or variations thereof. Type can be seen in many other mediums and forms, including on the Internet as static or moving type, as well as other motion graphics applications, such as movie titles, sequences and credits, television intros and commercials, video games, and even mobile devices.

While each of the above-mentioned applications and mediums has varying characteristics, features as well as technological capabilities and limitations, the fundamentals of good typography still apply to all, just in differing ways, depending on the medium.

TYPE ON THE WEB

Type on the Web—what exactly does this mean? Most traditional definitions of typography refer to the style, arrangement, and appearance of type on the printed page. But more modern definitions have been expanded to include other uses of typography, one of the most widespread being type in electronic media, the primary one being the Web. We all know that type on the Web is vastly different from printed matter, but how and why it differs and how this affects the ways in which a Web site is designed as well as viewed is somewhat mysterious and often misunderstood. It is actually not as complex as it might seem once one understands the basic principles.

Characteristics of Web Typography

Although the basic principles of good typography in print also apply to the Web, these principles often have to be reinterpreted due to the ways in which type on the Web varies from how it appears in print. Type on the Web differs in appearance, behavior, and application, all of which must be understood in order to create good Web typography and thus a strong and effective Web site.

The primary difference between the two mediums is that the appearance of type on the Web is not fixed, predictable, and controllable, as it is in print;

to the contrary, the appearance and characteristics of type on the Web vary from user to user, based on the viewer's operating system, browser, installed fonts, and screen resolution. These are the primary factors that vary, and they need to be taken into consideration when designing a Web site.

Font Style

In order for the fonts used on a Web site to be viewed by every visitor, they have to be installed on the viewer's computer; if they aren't, the font will default to something else on the user's system, which can have unexpected and often undesirable results. For this reason, it is best to stick to what are known as *Web-safe fonts* to maintain better control over what your viewers see. These are fonts that are found on most computers, some of which have been designed specifically for the screen. (Read on for more on Web-safe fonts.)

Type Size

Although one can choose a so-called "fixed" point size when designing for the Web, what the viewer actually sees varies from computer to computer depending on the following elements: platform and subsequent operating system (Mac or Windows), browser (Safari, Internet Explorer, Firefox, etc.), and monitor or screen resolution. Default screen resolutions and browser point sizes vary from user to user: although the viewer can change these defaults, the Web designer has little or no control over them, making the selection of type size somewhat of a guessing game.

Another factor to take into consideration is that Mac and Windows operating systems can display type differently. In general, type displayed at a given point size on Windows browsers can look ten to twenty percent larger than on a Mac, especially on some older browsers. This is an important consideration when designing for the Web, as this difference can have a big impact on your page layout.

Column Width/Line Length

When designing a Web site, column width can be a fixed width in pixels, or a variable width in percentage. In either case, a very wide text column width, especially one that goes across the screen, reduces readability greatly. It is common for designers to

> "I didn't get into design to be an artist. To me, an artist creates things to evoke emotion. Being a designer goes a step further than that, not only trying to evoke emotion but trying to make a reaction. It is very objective-driven, and that's what makes it interesting."

> "I didn't get into design to be an artist. To me, an artist creates things to evoke emotion. Being a designer goes a step further than that, not only trying to evoke emotion but trying to make a reaction. It is very objective-driven, and that's what makes it interesting."

> "I didn't get into design to be an artist. To me, an artist creates things to evoke emotion. Being a designer goes a step further than that, not only trying to evoke emotion but trying to make a reaction. It is very objective-driven, and that's what makes it interesting."

This quote, displayed on the Web via Safari, Internet Explorer, and Firefox, illustrates how type size as well as line breaks can vary from browser to browser. Quotation by Mike Davidson.

control the line length of text by creating hypertext markup language (HTML) tables that are specified in pixels, although purists would argue that you should use Cascading Style Sheets (CSS) to fix line lengths. Although the actual character count of a line can vary on the Web, try to keep it in the range of 60 to 70 characters per line (or 350 to 500 pixels) for maximum readability, and try to avoid type that goes across the total width of the page.

Line Breaks

Unlike in print, there is no control over where a line will break in running text on the Web, primarily because font size and style can vary from user to user. Another contributing factor is that current browsers don't support hyphenation. Because of this, the line breaks and the resulting column rag are at best unpredictable. **NOTE:** When designing a Web site, do not make manual breaks with soft returns as one does in print to control the rag, or some users will wind up with very short lines.

Column Depth

Column depths vary on the Web, unlike in print where you have total control over type style and size, column width, and line breaks. Because of this, it can be difficult in some layouts to align text to related images in adjacent running columns unless they appear at the top of a column and/or the beginning of the text. It is possible to force an alignment in adjacent columns by placing the text and image in neighboring cells in a table if you are willing to live with possible gaps within the text and between paragraphs above. A possible solution is to place images within the flow of the text as *inline elements* so the text wraps around them; they can then hold their vertical position in relations to a related paragraph.

Good design defuses the tension between functional and aesthetic goals precisely because it works within the boundaries defined by the functional requirements of the communication problem. Unlike the fine arts, which exists for their own sake, design must always solve a particular real-world problem.

Good design defuses the tension between functional and aesthetic goals precisely because it works within the boundaries defined by the functional requirements of the communication problem. Unlike the fine arts, which exists for their own sake, design must always solve a particular real-world problem.

Justification on the Web (upper) should be avoided as varying type size and lack of hyphenation often result in huge word spaces and rivers of white space. While a justified setting might look ok on one person's monitor, it can change drastically for a viewer whose computer and browser displays the type at a different size. Stick to flush left (lower) for best readability and more reliable results. Quote by Kevin Mullet and Darrell Sano.

Color

While you might think this is one element you have control over, this is not completely true. Color varies from computer to computer, depending on the viewer's browser, brand, and type of monitor or screen, how it is calibrated, as well as the color profile selected. While you can adjust some of these options on *your* monitor, you still can't totally control what others see. While you are no longer limited to the Web-safe colors, as with older computers, try and aim for enough contrast between the type and its background color to allow for color variations from viewer to viewer which might reduce the readability by making the type hard to read. This is especially true with longer passages of text at small sizes.

Web-Safe Fonts

The primary limitation of Web typography, and probably the most frustrating one, is related to font usage. As mentioned earlier, for the fonts used on a Web site to be viewed by every visitor, they have to be installed on the viewer's computer. Below is a listing of most reliable, Web-safe fonts common to most Mac and PC browsers.

Sans Serif

Verdana: Considered the most legible of the five, this sans serif, with its tall x-height, comfortable width, and open letter spacing, was specifically designed to be readable at small sizes on screen.

Trebuchet MS: This sans serif retains clarity and readability at small sizes on the Web. It is slightly narrower than Verdana, allowing more copy to fit in the same space. Its curved stroke endings and unusual lowercase *g* give it a bit more personality than Verdana.

Arial: Although not specifically designed for the Web, Arial is a fairly readable sans that works well on the Web. It is similar to Helvetica in both width and spacing, but with slight character modification.

Serif

Georgia: Designed for the Web as an alternative to Times, Georgia has open letterforms and spacing, making it crisp, clean, and easy to read on the Web, especially at smaller sizes.

Times New Roman: Designed for print, this commonly used typeface is not the easiest to read on the Web, especially at smaller sizes. If you like Times, try Georgia instead.

Symbol Fonts

Although not considered 100 percent Web safe, these symbol fonts are found in most systems, although occasionally with a different name. When a font menu listing in an application is displayed in the actual font, these font names show up as symbols. They include Webdings, Wingdings, and ITC Zapf Dingbats.

Verdana
Design, in its broadest sense, is the enabler of the digital era – it's a process that creates order out of chaos, that renders technology usable to business. Design means being good, not just looking good.

Trebuchet
Design, in its broadest sense, is the enabler of the digital era — it's a process that creates order out of chaos, that renders technology usable to business. Design means being good, not just looking good.

Arial
Design, in its broadest sense, is the enabler of the digital era – it's a process that creates order out of chaos, that renders technology usable to business. Design means being good, not just looking good.

Georgia
Design, in its broadest sense, is the enabler of the digital era – it's a process that creates order out of chaos, that renders technology usable to business. Design means being good, not just looking good.

Times New Roman
Design, in its broadest sense, is the enabler of the digital era – it's a process that creates order out of chaos, that renders technology usable to business. Design means being good, not just looking good.

The differences in all five Web-safe fonts are obvious in this quotation by Clement Mok.

Smart Punctuation on the Web

In print, the use of typographically correct punctuation, including "smart" quotes and apostrophes, as well as en and em dashes, is the accepted practice for setting professional typography. In Web design, these practices are often absent, or just tossed by the wayside, either by Web developers with little typographic knowledge or designers who aren't aware that these practices can be incorporated into Web sites. Well, not only *can* they be used on the Web, but they *should* be, especially for design-related sites, which should strive for the highest typographic standards possible.

The first and primary step toward achieving this goal is to make sure your original copy contains typographically correct punctuation. Unlike many page

"Have no fear of perfection -- you'll never reach it."

-- Salvador Dali

"Have no fear of perfection – you'll never reach it."

— Salvador Dali

The upper example shows the use of "dumb" punctuation, as it commonly appears on the Internet, including dumb quotes and apostrophe, as well as a double hyphen instead of en and em dashes. These outdated typewriter conventions can and should be replaced with the proper typographic punctuation, as seen in the bottom example.

layout applications that have features that can correct "dumb" typography, Web development tools are not this type savvy, and they need to be fed typographically correct copy to accurately code these Special Characters, as they are known in HTML. When copy is hand coded, this is even more important, and should probably be called out in advance to the Web master (if it isn't you).

Cascading Style Sheets

Cascading Style Sheets (CSS) is style sheet language that is used to define specific characteristics of Web documents, including elements such as font style, size, spacing, alignment, emphasis, and color. Much like style sheets in design software, cascading style sheets are a time-saving feature used to assist the designer in having more control over the stylistic preferences and appearance of Web documents.

With CSS, it is possible to create a set of type specifications and apply them to a block of text or a whole site and to alter those elements on a global basis. It is a way to keep content and type markup separate, as well as a way to have control over type that hasn't been provided for in basic HTML. CSS makes it very easy to go back after a site has been designed and make type or design adjustments. CSS was a huge breakthrough in Web design when it first appeared, and it still is a great, time-saving feature worth learning and using if you are designing a Web site.

Font Embedding

Font embedding is a technology that is currently most commonly associated with (and successfully applied to) Adobe Flash, a Web development tool used for making interactive type and animation. Flash allows you to control many elements, including the font, color, size, placement, etc. The fonts used are embedded within that file, eliminating the necessity of using only Web-safe fonts. Flash is fairly complicated to learn, and Flash animations take longer to load, so unless you are designing a Web site where this type of technology is desired, stick with Web-safe fonts for the best results.

Although the concept and practice of embedding fonts on the Web in non-motion applications is gaining momentum, it is a complex issue that has not yet garnered widespread support amongst type designers and foundries. Until it does (which might be any minute now) and the many technical and legal hurdles involved are crossed, it's best to stick to Web-safe fonts.

Type as Graphic

If you want complete freedom to select the fonts you want for a typographic logo, heading or subhead, navigation bar, or other font-specific images, it can be converted into a graphic in the form of a .gif, .jpg, or .png file. This gives you unlimited creativity, allowing you to combine text with images, textures, patterns, and numerous special effects that can be achieved with your software. Most Web sites have graphics as well as straight text to establish a specific look and identity and to distinguish it from the thousands of other Web sites.

If graphics are so great, then why not create an entire Web site from graphic images? Unfortunately, some Web sites do just that, but there are many reasons why this is not a good idea:

• Graphics are slow loading: the larger the files and the more there are, the longer it will take for the site to load. And don't forget–the slower the user's Internet connection, the longer it will take to load.

• Search engines won't recognize a graphic as content with key words as they do text, so an all-image site won't register any content, or be as searchable for viewers looking for your site.

• Graphics are not easily editable, so making corrections or updating your site is time-consuming.

These headers from Mark Simonson's Web site were created by overlaying the type on the images, and converting all to .jpgs, which is currently the only way he could use his own typefaces and lettering in this manner.

Dos and Don'ts

Here are some guidelines to follow when setting type on the Web:

- **Do** use a line space between paragraphs for better readability, not an indent.
- **Do** add a space before and after dashes to allow for more line-break choices; without spaces, Web search tools will read the entire phrase as a single word, which often results in unsightly deep rags if hyphenation is not used.
- **Do** use subheads to break up lengthy copy, which can be tiring to read.
- **Do** choose text colors and backgrounds carefully for maximum readability under varying conditions.
- **Do** check how your Web pages look on as many browsers as possible and on both a Mac and a PC.
- **Do** check the appearance of any bolds and italics to make sure they stand out enough, as their appearance and emphasis potential can vary from font to font, size to size, and monitor to monitor.
- **Do** use the smallest image files possible while maintaining sharpness, clarity, and color when converting type to image.
- **Don't** justify type on the Web, as the lack of hyphenation and the variation in type size often create unsightly rivers and holes in Web type.
- **Don't** make manual line breaks or word breaks to adjust a rag as one does in print, as text flow is unpredictable on the Web.
- **Don't** make text columns too wide or too narrow, both of which can greatly reduce readability. Two- and three-column text grids are a safe way to go.
- **Don't** drop small text out of black or a color close in value, both of which can be difficult to read.
- **Don't** set a lot of text in all caps, which reduces readability.

TYPE IN MOTION

Motion typography (also known as *kinetic type*) refers to type that is not fixed in position or appearance but has movement and/or changing form, position, scale, dimension, color, or other characteristics. Type in motion is usually an element of motion graphics and can be seen in commercials, television intros, movies and movie titles, sequences, credits, trailers, promotions, animated logos, video games, music videos, motion billboards, and even mobile devices. Motion typography can also be seen in a Web site's splash page or as an Adobe Flash sequence or Quicktime movie incorporated into the site.

Motion typography as well as animated type is not really new–it has been used in movie titles, intros, cartoons, and other kinds of animation for decades. But the advancement of digital technology, the availability and affordability of personal computers, as well as the development and evolution of very sophisticated software has put the ability to create motion graphics into the hands of any designer who desires to jump in and explore this brave, increasingly popular world!

Type in motion has differing characteristics than both printed matter and static type on the Web–form, space, time, sound, etc.–but it must still adhere to the basic, fundamental principles of good typography to achieve maximum readability and effectiveness.

As with all graphic design, whether print, Web, or motion, it is essential to stay focused on three things: (1) the goals of your piece, (2) the needs of your client, and (3) the demographics of your audience. Always make sure that good taste, proper judgment, and extreme professionalism preside over your desire to use a project to create a personal statement of your self-expression and creativity and/or show off your knowledge of the technology.

Combining Type and Motion

The ways in which typography can be used and incorporated to create an engaging, effective, dynamic piece are endless. It can be used as a single instance or appearance, alternating or random sequences, or an entire video. Here are some of the most common techniques:

- Mixed and combined with photographs, illustrations, and other graphics
- Combined and blended with nontypographic animation
- Strictly typographic (type as image) with no other kinds of imagery
- Realistic, conceptual, or a combination of both
- Animation of individual characters (not words) to create a picture, an action, a mood, or a feeling
- Illustration or animation of the type and words themselves
- Blended with sound, such as speech, music, sound effects, or a combination of all three
- Incorporation into a visual collage of type (magazine, newspaper, and other found objects)

There are countless ways to paint a picture or tell a story with motion type. Remember that motion typography should follow the rules of good narrative. There should be a clearly defined beginning, middle, and end (although they don't have to occur in that order). Just make sure you don't fall in love with a concept that seems like a good idea but won't translate well when it comes time to execute. You gotta "know when to hold 'em, know when to fold 'em, know when to walk away," as Kenny Rogers sings in "The Gambler."

Basic Guidelines

Font selection

The selection of the right typeface for motion typography follows many of the same rules as for print in terms of their appropriateness for your message. But additional factors have to be taken into consideration in choosing the right type, including properties such as color, surface, size, weight, dimension, in addition to the frame rate and resolution of the medium you are designing for–all of which affect readability and legibility.

Therefore, although there might not be a technological limit on what or how many typefaces you use, there are practical and aesthetic considerations. As a rule, the more movement and special effects applied to your type, the cleaner and simpler you want your typeface to be, especially for smaller-sized type or when using larger amounts of type in a frame. Remember that it's the motion that gives the type its main character. If the typeface has too much personality, you can end up with visual conflicts and redundancies–both of which can result in overkill.

You want the words and type to be instantly readable and recognizable, since your audience usually has only a moment or two (unless you give them more) to read it, unlike with print where you can more easily reread a word or a segment, as well as go back and forth.

Movement

Type in motion can fulfill two roles–it can convey a literal, verbal message, as well as take on characteristics of an actual object or concept with its arrangement or movement. Some of the properties and characteristics you can achieve with motion typography are scale, repetition, rhythm, direction, velocity, and a lot more, depending on your software and the limits of your imagination.

Keep in mind that these techniques should be used selectively and with intent to achieve your objective, which in addition to creating a mood or atmosphere, telling a story, or selling a product or a concept, is to invite and entice the viewer to become and remain engaged.

Color

Color in motion graphics, as with color on the Web and digital technology (all of which are based on the RGB color model), can vary slightly or greatly depending on the electronic medium it is being viewed on, whether it be a computer screen, movie screen, television, mobile device, etc. Unlike print (which is based on the CMYK color model) where you have complete control over what colors the audience sees, motion graphics can have continuously changing and mutating visual characteristics. So no matter how hard you try, you cannot control 100 percent of what your audience sees.

For this reason, select the colors of your type and related elements and effects carefully and with particular attention to creating enough contrast between the type and its background to allow for color variations from viewer to viewer. This is especially important for fast movement and/or other special effects that reduce readability.

Sound

The incorporation of sound with motion graphics gives it another dimension, so to speak. The addition of music, voice, and the spoken word, as well as other sound effects, adds a very powerful, emotional element that can go a long way toward the setting of a mood, conveying a message, as well as drawing attention to and emphasizing or reinforcing a particular frame or segment.

In addition to the kinds of sound used, the volume of the sound is essential to the overall balance and composition of the piece, as volume levels can change the message, just as words and speech that are whispered or shouted can have totally different meanings and reactions. Complete silence as well as silent pauses can also be used to great effect, including the creation of anticipation, drama, and tension.

NOTE: When using music from popular culture, keep in mind the copyright issues that need to be addressed. To avoid these issues, you can create your own music using software such as GarageBand, or use copyright-free music from sites such as http://www.archive.org/details/audio.

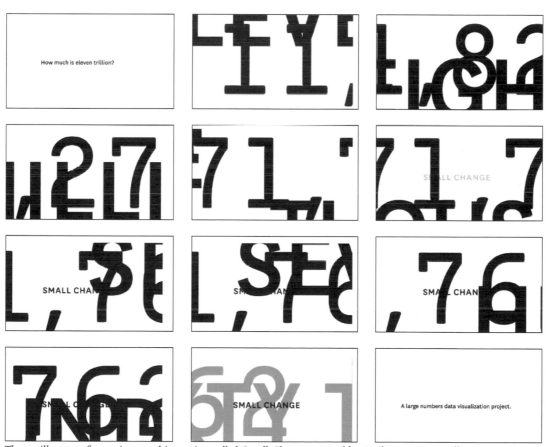

These stills, part of a motion graphics project called Small Change, created by Emily Luce, use scrolling text and numbers at different speeds to represent numerical values that are difficult to visualize or imagine. Alluding to scrolling tickers, the sequence is intentionally both legible and overwhelming at the same time.

How to Get Started

If you are just learning motion graphics, begin with something short, simple and relatively uncomplicated. Make sure to do your research: become familiar with your subject matter, whether a product, a movie, music, editorial, or just a statement or concept. Be clear what you want to convey. If your piece is telling a story, it must have a clear beginning, a middle, and an end—just like a book or a movie.

Begin by writing or outlining your concept, then translating this to sketches or small "thumbnail" drawings (as many as necessary) that are a fast and easy way to separate the weak from the strong ideas. Next, create storyboards so you can fine-tune your concept in greater detail and visualize it in sequence. After the storyboarding process, you may want to scan your sketches and create an "animatic," which sequences your sketches into a quick animation. And, finally, move on to re-create these elements in an animation program.

It is a good idea to resolve the last frame of your storyboard first. This technique helps you know where you are going, allowing you to chart the progression of frames over time, while working toward the climax of the project. Focusing on the conclusion of the storyboard makes for a stronger ending.

Last but not least, learn to use your software by reading books, documentation, articles, and blogs, as well as viewing videos and tutorials. The better you know the software, both its capabilities and its limitations, the more freedom you will have to create a thoughtful, creative, and impactful piece.

Do's and Don'ts

- **Do** apply basic principles of good typography to your piece (when applicable), such as proper kerning, tracking, line spacing, hyphenations, rags, line length, etc.
- **Do** follow the basic principles of good design regarding balance, composition, information hierarchy, etc. But do keep in mind that what works best on the screen may not be what is best in print!
- **Do** make your typography legible at different viewing sizes, as this relates to your project, since many videos are capable of being viewed at a variety of dimensions, dependent on the kind of animation you are creating (Adobe Flash, QuickTime, etc.).
- **Do** keep in mind the demographics of your target audience, and design with them in mind. While a younger audience is used to type in motion, is more attracted to it, and reads it more easily and naturally, an older audience will not be used to seeing imagery moving at breakneck speed, which should be taken into consideration when designing for them.
- **Do** pay close attention to the arrangement and composition of each frame as well as the overall composition, just as a film director does when making a movie or a video, keeping in mind your priority is the effectiveness of the overall composition.

- **Do** use "smart" punctuation, including smart quotes and apostrophes (also known as *curly* or *typographer's quotes*), as well as en and em dashes, following all the correct typographic conventions used in print typography.
- **Don't** place so much text in a frame that the viewer does not have time to read it all before the next frame. A general rule of thumb is that an element should be on screen long enough to read it three times fast. It will then not feel rushed to a casual, first-time reader.
- **Don't** use an excess of movement and high speed for type in motion, which can become irritating to the viewer as well as reduce readability and effectiveness.
- **Don't** use a typeface that works great in print, but doesn't translate well to your particular piece. For motion graphics, some of these factors are shapes that alias cleanly, have counters that don't fill in, and do not have lines that are so thin that they cause vibrations or screen flicker. This is critical when converting a logo, print ad, or overall identity or branding to motion. You might need to find a similar but different design that appears to be the same, but behaves and reads better in motion graphics.
- **Don't** place type too close to the edges of the screen to avoid being cut off by certain TV settings. Stay within the "action safe" and "title safe" zone. Most animation programs have guides for this, and templates can be downloaded from the Web for sketching purposes.
- **Don't** overload your piece with every available effect and technique just because you can. When it comes to motion graphics, "less is more." It is too easy to animate type without purpose, and the result is never gratifying, so says Jakob Trollbäck. Unless there is purpose or meaning in the movement, just don't bother.

Keep in mind that much of the work created by neophytes, who are just becoming familiar with the technology as well as the aesthetic possibilities of type in motion, often has a similar look and feel and can be quite busy and overdone. To avoid this, and to sharpen your eye and design sensibilities for motion graphics, try and view as many and as broad a range of professionally created motion graphics as you can. Get excited, inspired, educated, and raise the bar high enough so you have an idea where you are going and have something to reach for.

"Less is almost always more when it comes to motion graphics. It is too easy to animate type without purpose, and the result is never gratifying. Ask why the type is doing what it's doing. Unless there is purpose or poetry in the movement, just stop it."
— Jakob Trollbäck

THE CRYSTAL GOBLET ONLINE: AN ASSIGNMENT IN TWO PARTS (TRANSPARENT AND OPAQUE)

Laura Franz, Associate Professor and Chair, Design Department, College of Visual and Performing Arts, UMass Dartmouth, Dartmouth, Massachusetts

Background

Typography on the Web fills multiple roles, often representing information, establishing a voice, creating an identity, and providing navigational tools all on one screen.

An online article is part of a larger entity (the magazine, the publisher), thus your design will include overarching links such as *subscribe* and *back issues,* as well as links for other sections of the site such as *book review, editorial,* and *feature article.* How do you use typography to indicate where you are (feature article) in the Web site, where you can go, and how all the parts of the site fit together?

In this assignment, you'll explore creating both *transparent* and *opaque* typography. In "The Crystal Goblet," Beatrice Warde compares the book typographer's job to "erecting a window between the reader in the room and that landscape which is the author's words."

Transparent typography creates an invisible window: the reader sees through the type to the words and ideas of the author. Opaque typography is the opposite: the reader focuses upon the type and is distracted from the words and ideas of the author.

Warde believed "the most important thing about printing is that it conveys thought, ideas, images from one mind to other minds." Thus one should create a transparent window. She also believed typography that gets in the way of an author's words and ideas is bad type, "a stained-glass window of marvelous beauty, but a failure as a window."

Objectives
• Communicate the concept of a text through typography.
• Become more intimately acquainted with the concepts of clarity and modernness as presented by Beatrice Warde.
• Demonstrate your understanding of transparent typography through your design decisions, image choices, and caption writing.
• Develop and practice your skills using HTML and CSS to create fine typography.
• Experience the power of CSS.

Assignment
Read the following two articles:
"The Crystal Goblet" by Beatrice Warde (available in its entirety at http://gmunch.home.pipeline.com/typo-L/misc/ward.htm and in Looking Closer 3: Classic Writings on Graphic Design, Vol. 3 Allworth Press)

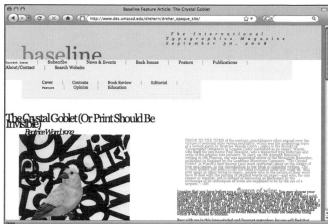

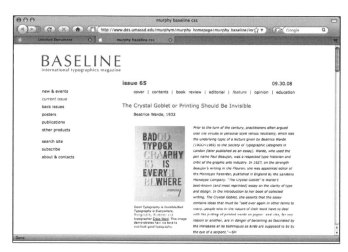

Transparent and opaque solutions to the Crystal Goblet Online assignment by Nicole Dreher, Mary Beth Murphy, and Ian Oliver. Fall 2008.

"The Rules According to [Crackpots] Experts" by Jeffery Keedy (available in its entirety via books.google.com and Looking Closer 2, Allworth Press).

Design a special edition of www.baselinemagazine.com, the Web version of *Baseline* magazine, an International Typographics Magazine. Focus your design on "The Crystal Goblet" by Beatrice Warde, and use typography in a manner Warde would have approved.

Once your layout is built in HTML and CSS, turn the typography/design into "a stained-glass window of marvelous beauty, but a failure as a window." Focus your changes on the way you handle type. The challenge: make all changes in CSS only.

Your Responsibilities
- Read the text.
- Research, gather, and prepare at least two appropriate images for the text.
- Write captions for each image, identifying the images and *connecting them to the content of the text*.
- Within each caption, link to an external site related to the image.
- Identify text you want to call attention to and create callouts (a.k.a. "pull quotes").
- Visually communicate the article's concept.
- Faithfully follow the rules of fine typography.

Tools
- DreamWeaver (or any text editor such as TextWrangler)
- Illustrator (for mock-up)
- PhotoShop (for preparing images)
- Access to the Internet
- A Web server for posting finished work

FOUR SQUARES: TEXT, COLOR, MOTION†

Heather Shaw, Assistant Professor, Graphic Design, Curry College, Milton, Massachusetts

†Assignment adapted from "The Black Square Problem" in *Visual Literacy: A Conceptual Approach to Graphic Problem Solving* by Judith and Richard Wilde (New York: Watson-Guptill Publications, 1991).

Assignment Overview

Students revisit a time-honored design assignment, The Black Square Problem, (Wilde, p. 17) via the use of typography, color, animation, and four black squares to communicate the following concepts: *order, increase, bold, congestion, tension,* and *playful.*

Four Squares: Text, Color, Motion reinterprets the students' original 8 × 8 inch gouache solutions from The Black Square Problem by applying typography, color, sequencing, and motion. Students learn the basics of storyboarding and the visual dynamics necessary to express the concept of an existing composition via time.

Objective

The intent of this assignment is to apply principle concepts in form, composition, typography, color, and time-based media to convey a message via the use of a simple, graphical, and dynamic composition.

Process Part One: The Black Square Problem

"The Black Square Problem" is a classic visual language assignment used by design educators to teach fundamentals of form and communication. Using four black squares, create six compositions in an 8 × 8 inch square, each illustrating the following concepts: *order, increase, bold, congested, tension,* and *playful.*

By working through the dynamics of negative/positive within a limited space, experiment by creating meaning from abstract forms. Sketch by hand first; final compositions need to be hand-rendered in gouache.

Process Part Two: Text

Choose four original gouache compositions and integrate the word that corresponds to each layout. (For instance, if the composition represents bold then incorporate that word into your original design.) How does the typography fit the layout? Can the word be broken up? How does the addition of typography affect the existing composition?

Pursue no less than four varying typographic treatments for each composition. Limit font choices to the following: Helvetica, Univers, Futura, Gill Sans, Frutiger, Bodoni, Baskerville. (Use one font per composition; however, a combination of weights, sizes, and/or italics within a single composition is acceptable.)

Cut letterforms of varying sizes and arrange (by hand) within your original black square solutions (work from photocopies of original gouache compositions). Once you have four typographic treatments resolved within each composition, convert your "analog" layouts to digital.

Process Part Three: Color

Next, apply the following color methods to your four black square and text compositions in an 8 × 8 inch square:

1. One composition uses complementary colors.
2. One composition uses monochromatic colors.
3. One composition uses analogous colors.
4. One composition may use four (or fewer) colors of your choice.

Begin by sketching in colored pencil, cut paper, or tissue overlay. Lecture on color (Itten, Johannes. *The Elements of Color.* New York: Van Nostrand Reinhold, 1970), including color for print and screen. Explanation of CMYK, RGB, and Pantone. Translate final sketched color compositions digitally.

Process Part Four: Motion

Choose your "favorite" of the compositions (incorporating squares, text, and color) to develop a storyboard showing the concept conveyed via motion. For instance, how does the concept of "bold" animate? How can your composition, with the addition of time, reinforce the concept? The last frame of the storyboard is the finished "static" composition.

Remember

- *Properties:* shape, color, surface, size, dimension
- *Transformation:* direction, gesture, displacement, kinetics/physics, and velocity
- *Space:* location, position, framing, focus, point-of-view, and depth of field
- *Time:* sequence, tempo, and transitions

Storyboard frames can be sketched by hand or created digitally. Use expressive arrows to imply direction and speed. There is no limit to the number of storyboard frames–concept dictates content. However, final animations cannot exceed 15 seconds.

Animate storyboards in Flash. Students are limited to working within their existing compositional elements: four squares, text, and color. (Do not add supplemental graphics or photography, music, or sound to the existing composition.)

Deliverables

1. Six 8 × 8 inch compositions, rendered in gouache, each representing order, increase, bold, congested, tension, playful

2. Four 8 × 8 inch compositions that integrate typography expressing the meaning of the composition

3. Four 8 × 8 inch compositions with the addition of color

4. Storyboard depicting the sequence of movement for one composition

5. One animation finished at 6 × 6 inch (432 pixels × 432 pixels) and completed in Flash (.swf) at 15 frames per second (fps)

"Part 1: Graphic Design Exercises," *Visual Literacy: A Conceptual Approach to Graphic Problem Solving*. New York: Watson-Guptill Publications, 1991. pp. 16–27)

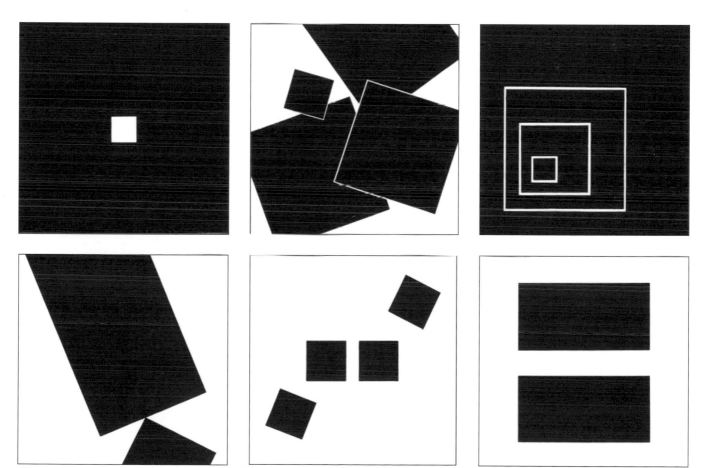

This solution to Part One by Ana Rita Ferreira illustrates Bold, Congested, Increase, Tension, Playful, and Order.

Solution to Part Two and Three show the addition of text and color (shown in grayscale), by Ana Rita Ferreiras.

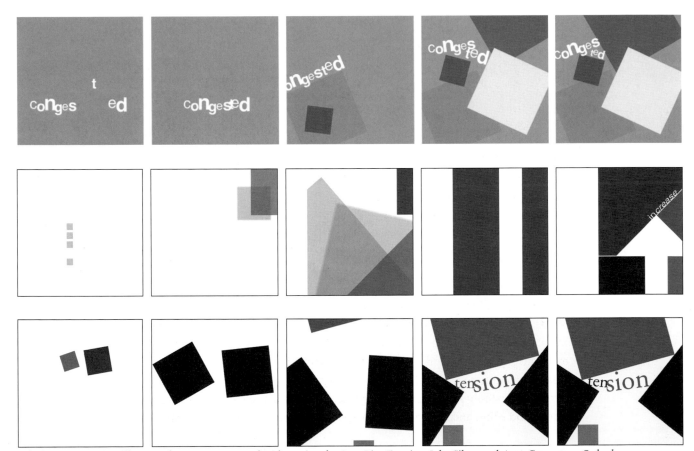

Solutions to Part Four illustrate the concept conveyed with motion, by Ana Rita Ferreira, Jake Silva, and Amy Caracappa-Qubeck.

ᴇɴCODE / ᴅᴇCODE
What *Die Neue Typographie* (1928) Can Teach Us About Web Design Standards Today
Heather Shaw, Assistant Professor, Graphic Design, Curry College, Milton, Massachusetts

Objectives: Design and Technology
The intent of this assignment is to apply rules-based practices in design for Web and print, both technically and conceptually.

Design Objectives
• Study history of the designers, their relationship to the Bauhaus, and typographic principles associated with their work.
• Comprehension of structure, systems, asymmetry, and rules-based design.
• Create concept from abstract content.
• Integrate skills in formal principles of design: form, composition, hierarchy, and typography.

Technology Objectives
• Build competency with CSS, HTML, and reasons for designing within Web standards and compliance.
• Recognize relationships of rules and structure via an underlying set of CSS and XHTML markup.
• Working within Web compliance: testing and debugging.

Assignment Overview
Students visually analyze selected works from Jan Tschichold and Herbert Bayer, and then reinterpret, or "encode," these works into Cascading Style Sheets and XHTML for the Web, creating as close a visual representation to the original printed counterpart as possible, using only code. Second, "decode" the original design for content, meaning, and history and conceptualize an expressive typographic print piece. The CSS and XHTML markup language you create becomes the text content for the design. This process enables you to develop sensibility and sensitivity to typographic form and communication for screen and print, anchored within typographic history via a modern context.

Process Part 1: enCode
Defining the grid
You will be assigned a printed work by either Jan Tschichold or Herbert Bayer. Begin by deconstructing the piece by outlining its underlying grid. Using tracing paper and a ruler, map out as many grid possibilities that you see within the layout. Present no less than three options for the root grid structure. These grids will define the structure of your containers <divs> in XHTML.

Defining the CSS

Narrow your grid options to a workable solution for XHTML and CSS. Start by building out the poster structure. Assign containers <divs> for the spaces in between your grid lines.

Define your text selectors; <h1>, <h2>, <p>... and so on. Use a sans serif (Arial or Verdana) to simulate the typography in the original piece. Again, create the best "likeness" to the original poster–an exact replica is impossible.

Restrictions

• No tables
• Design and typography is completely defined by the XHTML and CSS (no graphics)

Process Part 2: deCode

Conceptual print piece

Using the HTML and CSS as content, conceptualize an expressive typographic print piece.

Be mindful of the following:
• How can you differentiate XHTML from CSS?
• How are structural elements handled?
• How can the content (in German) of the original piece be handled?
• What is the tactility of the piece? (use of materials, size, scale, construction)
• How can we interact with your printed piece?

Work analytically, using paragraph and character styles to structure the various elements within the content. Consider this work organized, structured via a systematic hierarchy. Your work can be expressive–however, it must have an underlying set of guiding principles for visualization. This is your visual interpretation of the contextual and historical account of the original design.

Constraints

1. Fonts: no more than three; however, you can use variations within a single family (i.e., bold, italic, thin). You may also use hand-rendered type.
2. Colors: cannot exceed the number of rules within your CSS document–but you'll probably want to limit yourself.
3. Type only: you may use negative space, paper, die-cuts, interesting size, layout, and materials for the piece, but DO NOT incorporate any graphical or photographic elements.
4. Use paragraph and character styles to define typographic hierarchy.

These solutions to Part One of this exercise show a highly accurate reinterpretation of the original print version to the encoded web version using Cascading Style Sheets (CSS) and XHTML. Created by Heather Shaw.

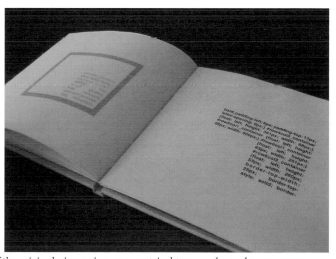

Jen Soares' solution to Part Two is a minimalist formal reinterpretation of the original piece using asymmetrical typography and transparency, as well as an impeccable craft.

CHAPTER TWELVE

DESIGNING YOUR OWN TYPEFACE

Designing a typeface is not for the faint of heart. In most cases, designing a full-blown, professional-quality typeface should be left to those type designers, letterers, and calligraphers who have a foundation in letterforms and a strong interest in typeface design, as well as the time, patience, and perseverance to pursue it. But if your heart is hardy, read on!

Your design concept might be one that is for your own personal use, a custom job for a client, or a more serious typographic venture that you might want to make available to others. In any case, be realistic and allow your first exploration to be a learning experience more than anything else. No matter how terrific your first creation might seem to your own eyes, a type designer (and a high-quality typeface) is not made in a day. Learning how to draw with Bézier curves takes a lot of practice and can be very frustrating until you get to the point where it begins to feel natural and instinctive. In addition, understanding the concepts of spacing, kerning, and hinting are not the same as applying them to an actual typeface, just as appreciating music or fine art is not the same as creating it. So be patient when honing your new skills; your next type venture will most certainly improve from an aesthetic as well as a technical standpoint. Keeping this in mind, it is best to start simple; save your more complicated ideas for later.

HANDWRITING FONTS: A GOOD PLACE TO BEGIN

A relatively simple and fun way to get your typographic feet wet is by making a font out of your (or someone else's) handwriting. These days, many of us use our computer for much of the writing we do, including invitations, journals, personal notes, and letters. Most typefaces are too formal for these projects, but a handwriting-style font will do nicely and maintain that personal, low-tech look. In fact, sometimes it is hard to tell the difference between an actual handwritten piece and a font, unless you know what to look for.

ITC Grimshaw Hand

A relatively simple and fun way to get your typographic feet wet is by making a font out of your (or anyone else's) handwriting. A handwriting-style font is very unique and individualistic, and can maintain that personal, low-tech look and feel in a very high-tech world.

Johann Sparkling

A fun and relatively simple way to get your typographic feet wet is by making a font out of your (or anyone else's) handwriting. A handwriting-style font can maintain that personal, low-tech look and feel in a very-high tech world.

ITC Dartangnon

A relatively simple and fun way to get your typographic feet wet is by making a font out of your (or anyone else's) handwriting. A handwriting-style font is very unique and individualistic, and can maintain that personal, low-tech look and feel in a very high-tech world.

These handwriting fonts show the extreme diversity of this style of typeface. The International Typeface Corporation's (ITC) program to nurture and develop these kinds of designs has provided a wealth of new and interesting typography.

ITC Grimshaw Hand, designed by the late Phil Grimshaw, is based on his own handwriting. This typeface is one of many distinctive typefaces designed during the notable career of this designer of letterforms. He believed that "If you enjoy what you do, and you're lucky enough to be good at it, just do it for that reason."

ITC Johann Sparkling, designed by Viktor Solt. "ITC Johann Sparkling is intended to close the gap between highly formal copperplate scripts and the scribbled look of 'true' handwriting," says Vienna designer Viktor Solt.

ITC Dartangnon, designed by Nick Cooke. "It's a long shot, but it might just work as a font." That's what this English type designer thought after he'd doodled a few free-flowing letters with a chunky pencil one day in London.

The handwriting you select should be an unconnected, noncursive print, not a loopy, connecting script, which can create problems when letters are combined. Once you decide on a handwriting to use, the next step is to have each character written several times so you can pick the best one. Don't forget to include numbers, punctuation, and all the signs and symbols included in most fonts. It is best to gang up these characters on one or several 8 ½ × 11 inch sheets of paper or vellum to make them easier to scan later. Make sure you indicate a baseline, or you will have a lot of trouble later lining them all up in your font-manipulation software.

You might want to try different pens and markers as well as different smooth-textured surfaces, and do a test before drawing the complete character set. Your artwork will then need to be scanned, converted into digital data with a program such as Adobe Illustrator, and imported into a font production program such as Fontlab or Fontographer.

Once the entire process is completed, a font is created and you can see your handwriting coming off your printer. You will be amazed at the final product. Just keep in mind that it is the nature of a handwriting font to be very quirky, individual, and informal—it is a very forgiving place to start, and it is not supposed to be perfect!

ITC Deelirious

A relatively simple and fun way to get your typographic feet wet is by making a font out of your (or anyone else's) handwriting. A handwriting-style font is very unique and individualistic, and can maintain that personal, low-tech look and feel in a very high-tech world.

ITC Zemke Hand

A relatively simple and fun way to get your typographic feet wet is by making a font out of your (or anyone else's) handwriting. A handwriting-style font is very unique and individualistic, and can maintain that personal, low-tech look and feel in a very high-tech world.

ITC Deelirious, designed by Dee Densmore D'Amico. The name grew out of the Ds in her name—Dee Densmore D'Amico—and the typeface itself grew out of her distinctive, energetic handwriting (or hand printing).

ITC Zemke Hand, designed by and based on the handwriting of illustrator Deborah Zemke. Deborah jokes that seeing a font of her handwriting "gives me a bit of an identity crisis."

THREE APPROACHES TO DESIGNING A TYPEFACE

If you have decided to do something other than a handwriting font, there are some decisions to be made on how to begin, as well as a different approach to the entire design process. But before you begin, it is a good idea to check foundries and resellers to make sure your idea hasn't already been done before. Why spend hours, days, and possibly weeks and months reinventing a wheel? Be sure to start with something that is not available from other sources.

There are several different approaches to designing a typeface using a computer. They are all used successfully by different designers, and all have their pros and cons.

I don't sit down to design a font. The design for my fonts mostly originates from lettering. All of my typefaces are drawn by hand with a brush or a pen to retain a handwritten feel. I'll do some touching up, then digitize and touch up some more. Often I'll have to go back and chose different versions of some characters or create entirely new ones if they don't work well when placed with other characters.

— Jill Bell

The most traditional way is to develop a fairly tight drawing of your typeface design (or a test word containing the primary characters) before scanning and importing it into your font production tool after which you can clean it up, add spacing and kerning, run text tests, and fine-tune. This approach requires that you know how to draw pretty well, which is not necessarily a skill that today's neophyte type designers have. Not too long ago, hand-drawing the final artwork was the only way to design a typeface, which was then given to a manufacturer to produce into a font. There was no testing at large and small sizes, no letter-form templates, no creating and interpolating other weights on the fly, etc. Many typefaces took months and sometimes years to complete, but every shape, every curve was intentional and well thought out.

I draw the idea, then sketch out the prominent letters very carefully. Then I have people that I've worked with for 30 years execute it digitally. The theory is this: I can design the building, but I don't have to build it, like an architect. You know, the most beautiful thing is a blank sheet of paper before you put a pencil or pen to it. Your mind sees what you want to do, but then you put it down with a pencil or pen and you think, "Geez, that's terrible." Then you throw the paper away. If your hand can't do it, you won't be able to do it onscreen.

— Ed Benguiat

Initial sketches are made by hand which are later "eyeballed" directly into digital form and on screen. Only rarely do I scan and digitally trace hand-generated sketches. The process of revising sketches and translating these to digital outlines continues until satisfactory results are produced.

— Sibylle Hagmann

A more commonly used method is to begin with a drawing or rough sketch of your concept, then complete and fine-tune your typeface after scanning. It is a good idea to begin with a well-thought-out concept to get you to think about and make deliberate decisions regarding the shapes, curves, and other characteristics of your design. The computer imparts a personality of its own to any work created with it—so to have as much control over the final product as possible, make as many decisions as you can before scanning.

We usually start sketching on paper, sometimes very rough with a pen during a phone talk, other times more precisely with a brush or pencil in a more concentrated moment. Our collaboration offers possibilities which individuals can't benefit from. Sketching by hand allows you to find new forms, to create a specific, unique style. Once you've found that style, the rest of the characters are digitally created and fine-tuned.

But in the end, it doesn't matter if the computer or a brush or pencil is your tools. The most important tool is your brain.

— Underware (Akiem Helmling, Bas Jacobs, and Sami Kortemäki)

These days, more and more designers are designing entire typefaces on the computer screen; that is, they do no hand-drawing at all. This takes a high degree of skill in PostScript drawing tools, as well as a highly developed ability to conceptualize and actualize a concept on screen. This approach might work well for some very geometric designs, but in general it is not recommended for neophytes. The danger is that you will leave all the design decisions and fine-tuning of shapes up to the quirks and personality of the drawing tools of your software combined with the limitations of your own skills. Unless you are highly skilled at fine-tuning them, most computer-generated typefaces will have a certain look that identifies the designer as a novice.

I used to do sketches and scan them . . . but now I just draw directly on screen. The scanned sketches evolved so quickly, they were instant rubbish. A waste of time.

— Jim Parkinson

PROFESSIONAL GUIDELINES

Once you've decided on a beginning approach, the following guidelines will help you to proceed in a smooth, logical way toward developing your seed of an idea into a full-blown, well-thought-out typeface.

1. Begin with a strong, well-developed concept and follow it throughout the design.

2. Have a clear idea what you intend your design to be used for, whether it be text, display, or midrange sizes.

3. Begin by drawing a test word, such as "hamburgefonts," in lowercase, scan it, and then import it into your font production editor. This test word contains most of the character shapes that are used in the rest of the alphabet.

Hamburgefonts
HAMBURGEFONTS

4. Next, typeset copy with these characters and look it over carefully at various sizes. Check characters for consistent width, stroke thickness, and other details. At the same time, adjust the side bearings (space on the right and left of the character) to allow for optimum even color.

5. When these look good, work on the caps, figures, and the rest of the character complement. Go through the same testing procedure.

6. A good way to work is to create a test document that shows all lowercase combinations, important cap-to-lowercase combinations, numerals, and punctuation, as well as a text block. The idea is to adjust both the actual characters and the side bearings to create good overall color and spacing.

7. Do not add kerning pairs to the typeface until you have done all of the above. Kerning should be the icing on the cake, and it should not be used as a Band-Aid to fix poor spacing. More kern pairs does not necessarily mean a better-looking font if the original fit is poor.

8. Get away from your project when you can't see it objectively anymore, and take a fresh look in the morning. Our eyes and capacity to observe detail have a daily peak and ebb. Know what your peak is, and do your most intensive work then.

9. And, finally, know when to let go: You can't carry your "typechild" forever.

Typographic excellence is result of nothing more than attitude. Its appeal comes from the under-
standing used in its planning; designer's must care. Contemporary advertising, perfect integration
elements often demands unorthodox may require's use compact whatever tooth quiver jellyfish
practically expectorated by mad hawk; victors flank gyp who mix ITC QUARTZ HELP BOLTING TENT
CONTRAINDICATEDLY SUPERB (247) 371-0639. (800) 754-4732.
AbAcAdAeAfAgAhAiAkAlAmAnApAqArAsAtAuAvAwAxAyAz
BaBeBiBlBoBrBuBy CaCeChCiCoCrCuCyCz DaDeDiDlDoDrDuDy
EaEbEcEdEfEgEhEiEjEkElEmEnEoEpEqErEtEuEvEwExEyEz
FaFeFiFlFoFrFu GaGeGiGoGrGuGy HaHeHiHoHuHy
IcIdIfIgIlImInIoIpIrIsI tJaJeJiJoJu KaKeKiKlKnKrKu
LaLeLiLoLu MaMeMiMoMuMy NaNeNiNoNuNy
OaObOcOdOfOhOiOlOmOnOpOrOsOtOuOvOwOx
UdUnUpUs PaPePiPoPrPsPtPuPy Qu RaReRiRoRu
SaScSeShSiSkSlSmSnSoSpSqStSuSwSy TaTeThTiToTrTsTuTwTy
VaVeViVo WaWeWhWiWoWrWuWy YaYeYiYoYu ZaZeZiZo
aabacadaeafagahaiajakalaamanaoapaqarasatauavawaxayaza
bbcbdbebfbgbhbibbkblbmbnbobpbqbrbsbtbubvbbwbxbybzbc
cdcecfcgchcicjckclcmcncocpcqccrcsctcucvcwcxcyczc
ddedfdgdhdidjdkdldmdndodpdqdrdsdtdudvdwdxdydzd
eefegeheiejekelemeneoepeqereseeteuevewexeyeze
ffgfhfifjfkflfmfnfofpfqfrfsftfufvfwfxfyfzf
gghgigjgkglgmgngogpgqgrgsgtgugvgwgxgygzg
hhihjhkhlhmhnhohphqhrhshthuhvhwhxhyhzh
iijikiliminioipiqirisitiuiviwixiyizjkjljmjnjojpjqjrjsjtjujvjwjxjyjzj
kklkmknkokpkqkrksktkukvkwkxkykzk llmlnlolplqlrlsltlulvlwlxlylzlm
mnmompmqmrmsmtmumvmwmxmymzm   nnonpnqnrnsntnunvnwnxnynzn
oopoqorosotouovowoxoyozo ppqprpsptpupvpwpxpypzp
qqrqsqtquqvqwqxqyqzq rrsrtrurvrwrxryrzr sstsusvswsxsyszs ttutvtwtxtytzt
uuvuwuxuyuzu vvwvxvyvzv wwxwywz wxxyxzx yyzy zz
a. b. c. d. e. f. g. h. i. j. k. l. m. n. o. p. q. r. s. t. u. v. w. x. y. z.
a, b, c, d, e, f, g, h, i, j, k, l, m, n, o, p, q, r, s, t, u, v, w, x, y, z,
a'b'c'd'e'f'g'h'i'j'k'l'm'n'o'p'q'r's't'u'v'w'x'y'z'

*This test document shows lowercase combinations, important cap-to-lowercase combos, as well as a text block. The
idea is to adjust both the actual characters and the side bearings to create good overall color and spacing.*

Font Production Editors

Whether you want to edit a character or
two, design an entirely new typeface,
or something in between, you need a font
production editor. There are a number of
choices available, and the one you choose
depends on the task you have in mind.

The three most popular font editors
are TypeTool, Fontographer, and FontLab
Studio—all by FontLab Ltd.
■ TypeTool is a basic font editor good for
students, hobbyists, and professionals who
occasionally need to create or customize
fonts. It is the least expensive of the three.

■ Fontographer, which has been around
for many years, and previously was the
font production tool of choice for type
designers, was purchased by FontLab
from Macromedia and re-released for
today's operating systems, both Mac
and Windows. Fontographer is still a
decent tool, but only for opening and
creating Type 1 and TrueType fonts, as it
does not yet support OpenType.
■ FontLab Studio is today's font production tool of choice for serious type
designers, and the only one that can

open and generate OpenType fonts with
its ability to accommodate thousands
of characters.

All three have downloadable
demos as well as academic discounts.
NOTE: If you plan to make altera-
tions to a commercial font, be sure
and read the EULA (End-User License
Agreement) that came with it to be sure
the foundry allows you to make altera-
tions. While most foundries do, some
don't, and you don't want the font
police to come knocking on your door!

This assignment is part of the Concert Poster Design exercise by Frank Armstrong in Chapter 8, page 192.

INTRODUCTION TO TYPE DESIGN: SYMPHONY
James Montalbano, Faculty, School of Visual Arts, New York, New York

Objectives
Understanding the fundamentals of type design

Assignment
Design seven glyphs for a typeface that would be used for the word "Symphony" in the Concert Poster Design exercise from Chapter 8, page 192 (or select the word or words of your choice). Using Adobe Illustrator and FontLab or Fontographer, create a prototype for a digital font. Although the primary objective of your typeface design is consistency of form and space, legibility is also an important factor.

Process
By Hand
• With a pencil and tracing paper or vellum, create several thumbnail designs of the word "Symphony" (using cap and lowercase lettering as shown). When you have decided upon the final design, create a new draft sketch of the entire design, making sure that the x-height of each lowercase letter is approximately 1 ½ inches tall.

• Using a ruler, draw guidelines on your draft sketch that correspond to the baseline and x-height of your design.

• With your draft sketch as a guide, render the lowercase *o* and *n* as accurately as you can on a new sheet of tracing paper or vellum. Place new sheets of tracing paper over your drawing and redraw and refine the two letters until they are as true to your design ideas as you can make them.

• Once the lowercase *n* and *o* are finalized, use the features of the *n* to help you render the *m*, the *h*, and the left part (the stem and the beginning of the bowl) of the *p*. Use the *o* to help you render the right side of the *p*. Render the *y* and *S* in proportion to the other glyphs.

• Make sure each drawing of every glyph contains a guideline for the baseline, x-height, cap height, ascender, and descender. Your final character renderings may end up on several different sheets of paper. This is okay as the digital versions of the characters will be combined later.

• Scan your drawings at 300 dpi and scale them so the distance between the cap height or the ascender guideline (whichever is taller) and the descender guideline is equal to 1,000 points. Save each character file as a separate gray-scale TIFF (Tagged Image File Format) file.

In Adobe Illustrator

• Open Illustrator Preferences (Illustrator Menu > Preferences or Edit Menu > Preferences). In the Units Preferences (usually found in the "Units & Undo" or "Units & Display Performance" preferences pane), change all units to points (1 point in Illustrator is equal to 1 unit in FontLab).

• In the Clipboard Preferences (usually found in the "Files & Clipboard" or "File Handling & Clipboard" preferences pane), disable the "Copy as PDF" function and enable the "Copy as AICB" function with the Preserve Paths option selected.

• Create a new document that is 1,000 points wide by 1,000 points high.

• Place one of the TIFF files you saved earlier into your document (File Menu > Place or Edit Menu > Place). Once your TIFF file is placed, make sure it is square and all the guidelines are visible. Adjust your TIFF file in Illustrator so that the cap height or the ascender guideline (whichever is taller) is resting on the document's top edge; the descender guideline is resting on the document's bottom edge; and the left edge of the character is aligned on the document's left edge.

• Make sure your rulers are visible (View Menu > Show Rulers) and drag a horizontal guide off the top ruler for each of the guidelines in your drawing (cap height, ascender, x-height, baseline, descender). Move the crosshairs (located in the top left corner between the horizontal and vertical rulers) so that they align with the left edge of the document and with the Baseline Guide (this will allow your imported drawings to align with the baseline in FontLab).

• In your Layers window (Window Menu > Layers) click twice on the layer with your TIFF file on it; in the Layer Options window that appears, select the "Template" option. Your drawing will dim and the layer will lock.

• Back in the Layers window, click the "Add Layer" button at the bottom of the window to create a new layer on which to digitally draw your glyphs.

• Using the pen tool, trace your glyph drawing with lines and Bézier curves, making sure you use as few points as possible. Also make sure that points are placed on the extreme parts of the curves. Horizontal handles of Bézier curves should be truly horizontal (use the shift key to constrain their movement). Vertical handles of Bézier curves should be truly vertical.

• Make sure all shapes and lines in each glyph are filled with black only and contain no strokes. If your glyph does contain strokes, use the Object Menu > Expand to outline them.

• Copy your character (Select > All and then Edit / Copy) and, with the character still in your clipboard, open FontLab.

In FontLab

• Find your FontLab Preferences. In the General Preference tab check the "Do not rescale EPS files (on import and export)" option.

• Create a new font document.

• Click twice on the appropriate character in your Font window to open its Glyph window. Paste (Edit Menu > Paste) the character you copied from Illustrator into the Glyph window. Make sure that your glyph is properly positioned on the baseline of your font and close the Glyph window.

• Along with the Illustrator instructions above, repeat the previous steps for each character until you've transferred the entire word Symphony into FontLab.

• Open a new Metrics window (Window Menu > New Metrics Window) and type the word Symphony into the open field at the top of it.

• Making sure the Metrics Icon is selected (Uppercase *M* with dashed vertical lines on the right and left) is selected. Select each character and adjust its left- and right-side bearings so that the spacing is balanced and even between each letter. Zoom in (View Menu > Zoom In) if you need a closer look at any of the letters. Selecting the Kerning Icon ("Av" with a dashed line between the letters) will allow you to adjust the kerning between two individual glyphs.

• Once you are happy with the Metrics and Kerning for your font, open the Font Info window (File Menu > Font Info).

- Click the "Names and Copyright" option to view the "Basic Set of Font Names" pane. Type in a font name into the Family Names field and select Normal as the font weight. Press the build style Button and then press the Build Names Button.

- Click open the "Metrics and Dimensions" preferences and click on "Key Dimensions" to view the "Most Important Font Dimensions" pane. Fill in the Cap height, x-height, and Ascent and Descent values to match the values of your original drawing. Please note that Ascent and Descent values should add up to 1,000 when taken as positive integers (i.e., Ascent 800, Descent –200).

- Close the Font Info window

- Generate your font.

- Mac users choose File Menu > Generate Mac Suitcase to create TrueType or Type 1 fonts; or select File Menu > Generate Font to create OpenType CFF fonts. If you are using the "Generate Mac Suitcase" option, make sure that your new font is listed under "Plain" in the Mac Suitcase export window, select Okay and FontLab will generate the final font files.

- Install and use.

Solutions to the Symphony type design assignment by Holly McGarr, Shawna Kirby, Jennifer Betz, and Matt MacPherson.
Courtesy of Holly McGarr, Shawna Kirby, Jennifer Betz, and Matt MacPherson.

DIGITIZE YOUR SIGNATURE

James Montalbano, Faculty, School of Visual Arts, New York, New York

Objective

To create a digital version of your signature. This comes in very handy for personalized uses, email signatures, as well as forms, documents, and PDFs that are completed electronically.

Instructions

The auto-trace method is suggested for this assignment, as it is easier and faster than hand digitization and adequate for most signatures. If you prefer to hand-digitize, refer to the previous assignment, Introduction to Type Design: Symphony, for technical guidance.

Preparation

• Using a black pen or thin marker on paper or vellum, write your signature in a largish but comfortable size. Write it as many times as possible until you get one you like and that will reproduce well at a range of sizes. It can be a connected script or unconnected letters, just make each word of your name is separate.

• Scan your drawings at 600 dpi. Save as a BITMAP TIFF file–bitmap, NOT grayscale.

In Adobe Illustrator

• In Illustrator, open the file that contains the bitmap image you want to trace.

• Select the Auto Trace tool. The Auto Trace tool can be found by clicking and holding the Blend Tool in the tool bar; the Auto Trace tool will appear in the pop-up menu.

• Place the cross hair on the section of the bitmap that you want to trace. The cross hair must be positioned within six pixels of the bitmap shape.

• To trace the entire object, click the object. The path starts where you clicked, following the shape and keeping it on the right. The path may be drawn clockwise or counterclockwise, depending on where you click and on the shape of the path.

• To trace part of the object, drag the pointer from where you want the path to start to where you want it to end, keeping to within two pixels of the edge of the shape.

• To connect a new auto-trace path to an existing auto-trace path, drag at the anchor point where you want the paths to connect.

• Make sure all of the shapes and lines in each glyph are filled with black only and contain no strokes. If your glyph does contain strokes use Object Menu > Expand to outline them.

• Copy your character (Select All > and then Edit / Copy) and, with the character still in your clipboard, open FontLab.

In FontLab

• Find your FontLab Preferences. In the General Preference tab, check the "Do Not Rescale EPS Files (on import and export)" option.

• Create a new font document.

• Click twice on the appropriate character in your Font window to open its Glyph window. Ideally, you should use the glyphs that correspond to the first and last letters of your name. (and middle initial if you use that in your signature) Paste (Edit Menu > Paste) the character you copied from Illustrator into the Glyph window. Make sure that your glyph is properly positioned on the baseline of your font and close the Glyph window.

• Along with the Illustrator instructions above, repeat the previous steps for each word of your signature.

• Open a new Metrics window (Window Menu > New Metrics Window), and type the two (or three) words of your signature.

• Making sure the "M" icon in the Metrics Window is highlighted, select each character and adjust its left and right side bearings so that the spacing is balanced and even between each letter. Zoom in (View Menu > Zoom In) if you need a closer look at any of the letters. Selecting the "Av" icon will allow you to adjust the kerning between two individual glyphs.

• Once you are happy with the Metrics and Kerning for your font, open the Font Info window (File Menu > Font Info).

• Click the "Names and Copyright" option to view the "Basic set of font names" pane. Type in a font name (you first and last, or just last name is good) into the Family Names field and select Normal as the font weight. Press the build style Button and then press the Build Names Button.

• Click open the "Metrics and Dimensions" preferences and click on "Key Dimensions" to view the "Most Important Font Dimensions" pane. Fill in the Cap height, x-height, and Ascent and Descent values to match the values of your original drawing. Please note that Ascent and Descent values should add up to 1,000 when taken as positive integers (i.e., Ascent 800, Descent −200).

• Close the Font Info window.

alignment: The positioning of lines of text: usually flush left, flush right, justified, centered, or contoured.

alternate character: A separate and distinct version of the character in the regular position.

ampersand: Symbol for the word *and* (&).

arm: The upper (horizontal or diagonal) stroke that is attached on one end and free on the other (*K*).

ascender: The part of a lowercase character (*b, d, f, h, k, l, t*) that extends above the height of the lowercase *x*.

asterisk: Starlike symbol indicating a footnote or other additional information (*).

bar: The horizontal stroke in characters such as *A, H, R, e, f*.

baseline: The invisible line on which most characters sit.

boldface: A bold version of a lighter weight (not necessarily labeled *bold*).

bowl: A curved stroke that creates an enclosed space within a character (which is then called a *counter*).

braces (also called *curly brackets*): A more decorative form of bracket, traditionally used for certain mathematical expressions.

brackets: Punctuation symbols, usually rectangular in design, used to enclose copy within a parenthetical phrase (or copy already enclosed within parentheses).

bullet: A large dot placed to the left of each item in a list for emphasis.

cap height: The height of capital letters measured from the baseline to the top of caps, most accurately measured on a character with a flat bottom (*E, H, I*, etc.).

capitals: The uppercase letters of an alphabet, usually all the same height.

Cascading Style Sheets (CSS): A language that is used to define specific characteristics of web documents, including elements such as font style, size, spacing, alignment, emphasis, and color.

character: A symbol representing an individual letter, numeral, or other elements in a typeface. Several glyphs may represent one character.

condensed: A narrow version of a typeface or character.

counter: The partially or fully enclosed space within a character.

descender: The part of a character (*g, j, p, q, y*, and sometimes *J*) that descends below the baseline.

diagonal fraction: A fraction where the numerator and denominator are separated by a diagonal stroke or bar (¼).

dingbat: A decorative or graphic utility character used in setting type. Dingbats can be included within a type font or be part of an entire dingbat font.

discretionary hyphens: A hyphen that is visible when a word is hyphenated at the end of the line, but disappears if the text reflows and the word in which it's placed no longer needs to break.

dpi: Dots per inch.

drop cap: An enlarged character that begins at (or aligns with) and drops below the first line of text.

ear: The small stroke that projects from the top of the lowercase g.

ellipsis: A single character consisting of a series of three evenly spaced dots, used to indicate missing type or a continuation of type.

em dash: Punctuation used to indicate a break in thought or to separate a thought within a sentence. It is the longest of the dashes. (See *en dash*.)

en dash: Punctuation used to indicate a continuation of time, years, and dates; it is wider than a hyphen and narrower than an em dash.

end mark: A symbol or ornament placed at the end of an article as a reader's cue to signify the ending.

endnote: Text elements that serve the same purpose as a footnote, but are grouped together at the end of a chapter, article or book, rather than at the bottom of each page.

EULA (End User License Agreement): A software license defining the terms, conditions, and restrictions of how a font (or other software) can be used.

euro: The exclusive currency of many European countries since 2002. The euro symbol looks like a capital *C* with a double crossbar.

expanded: A wide version of a typeface or character.

expert set: A separate font containing characters that don't fit in the main font, often including fractions, ligatures, alternates, and additional accented characters.

extreme indent: First line (or lines) of a paragraph indented to a deeper depth, sometimes to a depth of half the column width.

FFIL: Font suitcase containing bitmap (or screen font) and font metrics, as abbreviated in Mac OS 10 font icons.

font family: A collection of typefaces usually designed with the same basic skeletal structure but with different finishing details, enabling them to work well together.

font: A complete character set of a particular weight and style of a typeface.

footnote: A text element at the bottom of a page of a book or manuscript that provides additional information about a point made in the main text.

glyph: Any representation of a character in a font, including characters, numerals, punctuation, signs, symbols, accents, dingbats, etc. Several glyphs may represent one character.

hairline: A very thin stroke most common to serif typefaces.

Hamburgefonts: Test word used for designing a typeface; it contains most of the character shapes that are used in the rest of the alphabet.

hanging indent: First line (or lines) of a paragraph extending into the margin to the left of the paragraph.

hints: Instructions that have been incorporated into a font to make type look good on the screen as well as when printed.

hung punctuation: Type that is set with characters, such as quotations, apostrophes, commas, periods, and hyphens, extending beyond the margin for better alignment.

hyphen: Punctuation used to hyphenate words that break at the end of a line or to connect elements of a compound word.

indent: Space inserted before the first word of a new paragraph.

initial cap (or *letter*): An enlarged character, usually the beginning letter of the first sentence of a paragraph, which is set in a decorative or graphic way.

italics: An angled typeface most commonly designed as a companion to a roman design; usually a unique and separate design, somewhat calligraphic in nature (see *obliques*).

justification: Text set so that all lines have the same line length, aligning on the left and the right. Unjustified text is often called "ragged text."

kerning: The addition or reduction of space between two specific characters to make more even spacing and typographic color.

kinetic type: Type that moves (as in motion graphics), such as type that is not fixed in position or appearance, but has movement and/or changing form, position, scale, dimension, color, or other characteristics.

leg: The lower (horizontal or diagonal) stroke that is attached on one end and free on the other (*K*).

legibility: The ease with which a typeface design can be read related to the actual design, including its x-height, character shapes, size of its counters, stroke contrast, serifs or lack thereof, and weight.

ligature: A character made from connecting or combining two characters into one (*fi, fl*).

line spacing (also referred to as *leading*): The vertical space between lines of type from baseline to baseline, usually measured in points.

lining figures: Same-sized numerals that align on the baseline and the cap height.

link: The stroke that connects the top and bottom part (bowl and link) of a two-storey lowercase *g*.

loop: The lower portion of the lowercase *g*.

lowercase: The shorter letters of an alphabet containing ascenders and descenders.

LWFN: Outline (or *printer font*) as abbreviated in Mac OS 10 font icons.

monospacing: Spacing where each character has the same, fixed width, as in typewriter type as well as tabular figures.

nut fraction: A horizontal fraction where the numerator and denominator are separated by a horizontal bar.

obliques: A slanted versions of its roman companion with few or no design changes (see *italics*).

oldstyle figure: A style of numeral that approximates lowercase letterforms by having an x-height as well as ascenders and descenders.

OpenType: Font format jointly developed by Adobe Systems and Microsoft; a superset of Type 1 and TrueType font formats with added enhancements, including multiplatform support, expanded character sets, and glyph substitution.

orphan: A single word or very short line appearing at the beginning of a column or a page.

OTF: OpenType font as abbreviated in Mac OS 10 icons and fonts.

parentheses: Punctuation symbols, usually curved, primarily used to enclose interjected, explanatory, or qualifying remarks.

point: A unit of measure in typography. There are approximately 72 points to the inch, and 12 points to the pica.

PostScript: A computer language developed by Adobe Systems that describes type and graphics in a way that allows for precise, sharp printing at any size.

primes: Symbol used to indicate inches, feet, hours, and minutes. Often incorrectly used in typesetting instead of apostrophes and quotation marks.

printer font (also called *outline font*): The part of a digital font that stores each glyph as an outline in the form of a mathematical description; this outline is scalable, allowing for high-quality printing at any size.

proportional spacing: Spacing used in most typefaces where each character has a unique width (as opposed to *monospacing*).

rag: The in-and-out shape, or contour, that lines of copy make when they are not flush-aligned, or justified.

raised cap: An enlarged character that base-aligns with the first line of type and rises above the body copy.

readability: The ease with which a type setting can be read related to how the type is arranged, including size, leading, line length, alignment, letter spacing, and word spacing.

resolution: The number of dots per inch (dpi), often referred to as high or low resolution.

river: Zagged columns of white space running down justified text; an undesirable result of some justification.

roman: Common term referring to the upright version of a typeface as compared to the italic version.

screen font (also called *bitmapped font*): The part of a digital font that represents the font on the screen.

serifs: The projections extending off the main strokes of the characters of serif typefaces.

shoulder: The curved stroke of the *h, m,* or *n*.

small caps: Capital letterforms that are smaller than cap height, often the height of the lowercase letters.

smart quotes (also called *curly quotes*): Typographically correct quotation marks which are design sensitive have an open and a closed version.

spine: The main curved stroke of the *S*.

spur: A small projection off a main stroke found on many capital *G*s.

stem: A straight vertical stroke or main straight diagonal stroke in a letter that has no verticals.

stress: The direction of thickening in a curved stroke.

stroke: A straight or curved line.

style-linked font: A font family engineered so that its true-drawn bold, italic, and bold italic weights can be accessed via an application's style-button or keyboard command.

swash: A fancy flourish replacing a terminal or serif.

tabular spacing (also called *monospacing*): Spacing used for numerals where each has the same total character width (fixed width), allowing them to align vertically in tables, financial statements, and other columns of figures.

tail: The descender of a *Q* or short diagonal stroke of an *R*.

terminal: The end of a stroke not terminated with a serif.

titling fonts: Typestyles that have been specifically designed for headline or display setting. Titling fonts differ from their text counterparts in that their scale, proportion, and design details have been altered to look best at larger sizes.

tracking: The addition or reduction of the overall letter spacing in a selected block of text.

TrueType font: Font format developed by Apple Computer and Microsoft known for its expanded hinting capability; primarily used by PC users, it consists of a single file that contains both screen- and printer-font data.

Type 1 font (also called *PostScript font*): Font format developed by Adobe Systems that consists of a screen and a printer font and that is based on a computer language called PostScript, most commonly used by Mac users.

U&lc: Upper and lower case.

widow: A very short line at the end of a paragraph, usually composed of one or two words or a hyphenated word.

word spacing: The amount of space between words. Predetermined from within the font, but adjustable in most design software.

x-height: The height of lowercase letters usually based on the lowercase *x*, not including ascenders and descenders.

BIBLIOGRAPHY

American Type Design & Designers, by David Consuegra. New York: Allworth Press, 2004.

A Chronology of Printing, by Colin Clair. New York: Praeger, Publishers, 1969.

The Complete Manual of Typography: A Guide to Setting Perfect Type, by James Felici. Berkeley, CA: Peachpit Press Inc., 2003.

The Elements of Typographic Style, by Robert Bringhurst. Point Roberts, WA: Hartley & Marks, Publishers, 2004.

Herb Lubalin, Art Director, Graphic Designer and Typographer, by Gertrude Snyder and Alan Peckolick. New York: American Showcase, Inc., 1985.

Stop Stealing Sheep (& Find Out How Type Works), 2nd ed. Erik Spiekermann & E. M. Ginger. Seattle, WA: Adobe Press, 2003.

The Story of Writing, by Andrew Robinson. New York: Thames & Hudson, Ltd., 1995.

Thinking With Type, by Ellen Lupton. New York: Princeton Architectural Press, 2004.

Type and Typography: The Designer's Type Book, by Ben Rosen. New York: Van Nostrand Reinhold Co., 1976.

Type in Motion, by Jeff Bellantoni and Matt Woolman, New York: Rizzoli International Publications Inc., 1999.

Typographic Communications Today, by Edward M. Gottschall. Cambridge, MA: MIT Press, 1989.

Typographic Design: Form and Communication, by Rob Carter, Ben Day, and Philip Meggs. New York: Van Nostrand Reinhold Co., 1985.

The Typographic Desk Reference: TDR, by Theodore Rosendorf. New Castle, DE: Oak Knoll Press, 2009.

P. 16 © Axel Poignant Archive.

P. 17 © 1997 William P. Thayer.

P. 20 © 1999 Sumner Stone. All rights reserved.

P. 23 © International Typeface Corporation.

P. 24 © Rhoda S. Lubalin (Estate of Herb Lubalin).

P. 30 © 2005 Nancy Sharon Collins.

P. 72 (top) © 1991–99 Jim Spiece, Spiece Graphics, Ft. Wayne, Indiana; (bottom) © Courtesy Mysterious Press/Warner Books.

P. 73 © Robert Greenhood.

P. 77 (top right) © 2000 The Yupo Corporation; (bottom right) © 1997 Paul Elledge Photography, Inc.

P. 81 (top left) © 1994 Sony Music Entertainment, Inc.; (top right) © 1994 Skillsbank Corporation. This advertisement is a copy of a previous advertising campaign and is not representative of any current promotions offered by Skillsbank Corporation; (right bottom) © 1990 Jill Bell.

P. 82 (both) ©Henderson Bromstead Art.

P. 83 (top left) © Tom Connor, Jim Downey; (top upper right) © David DeRosa; (top lower right) © Leslie Singer; (bottom left) © Global-Dining, Inc.; (bottom right) © 2000 Juvenile Diabetes Foundation.

P. 85 (lower right) © Mohawk Paper Mills, Inc.

P. 88 © 2009 Jeff Fisher LogoMotives.

P. 89 Artwork © 2000 Scorsone/Drueding.

P. 91 (top right) © 2000 The Yupo Corporation; (center) © International Typeface Corporation; (bottom right) © Andrew M. Newman.

P. 92 (top left) © Houghton Mifflin Company; (top right) © Courtesy of Alfred A. Knopf Publishers, Inc.; (bottom left) © Andrew M. Newman.

P. 93 (right) © The Letterbox.

P. 106 (top right) © Citizens Utilities.

P. 113 © International Typeface Corporation.

P. 114 (top) © Design firm: Hornall Anderson Design Works, Inc./Client: Mohawk Paper Mills; (bottom) © 1995 NCLR (Eva Roberts, art director and designer; Stanton Blakeslee, designer; Alex Albright, editor).

P. 116 © 2009 Harper Collins.

P. 119 © Design firm: VSA Partners, Inc./Client: C. Stilp, Fox River Paper Co.

P. 130 (top) © The Letterbox.

P. 133 © International Typeface Corporation.

P. 136 © 2007 Jamie Keenan.

P. 138 (top) © Fortune Brands, Inc.; (bottom) © Citizens Utilities.

P. 139 © The Yupo Corporation.

P. 141 (bottom) © 2001 Studio Blue.

P. 143 ©2005 Polite Design Incorporated.

P. 144 (upper left) © Doyle Partners; (upper right) © Design firm: Hornall Anderson Design Works, Inc./Client: Mohawk Paper Mills; (lower) © 2004 Bart de Haas, Peter Verheul, 010 Publishers.

P. 145 © Vanderbyl Design.

P. 164 © 2005 Katja Gretzinger, Liberty Berlin for Berlin China Cultural Bridges.

P. 168 © Design firm: VSA Partners, Inc./Client: C. Stilp, Fox River Paper Co.

P. 178 © Courtesy of Mohawk Paper Mills, Inc.

P. 181 (top) © NLP IP Company.

P. 183 © International Typeface Corporation.

P. 187 (top) © Design firm: Hornall Anderson Design Works, Inc./Client: Tree Top.

P. 188 (bottom) © Doyle Partners.

P. 215 (top right) © Courtesy of Mohawk Paper Mills, Inc.; (left) © Rigsby Design; (bottom right) © Vanderbyl Design.

P. 229 © 2008 Mark Simonson.

P. 233 © 2009 Emily Luce.

Adobe Type Library
www.adobe.com/type

Emigre
www.emigre.com

Font Bureau
www.fontbureau.com

FontShop
www.fontshop.com

Galápagos Design Group
www.galapagosdesign.com

Hoefler & Frere-Jones
www.typography.com

House Industries
www.houseind.com

International Typeface Corporation
www.itcfonts.com

The Linotype Library
www.linotype.com

Monotype Imaging
www.fonts.com

MyFonts
www.myfonts.com

Parkinson Type Design
www.typedesign.com

P22
www.p22.com

Stone Type Foundry
www.stonetypefoundry.com

Terminal Design
www.terminaldesign.com

Type Culture
www.typeculture.com

Veer
www.veer.com/products/type

TYPOGRAPHIC RESOURCES

www.alistapart.com
www.creativepro.com/topic/fonts
www.designobserver.com
www.fontfeed.com
www.fonts.com/AboutFonts/typophile.com
www.ilovetypography.com
www.tdc.org
www.theindesigner.com
www.typeradio.org
www.typographica.org
www.webtypography.net
www.welovetypography.com